PREPARED TO
WIN

THE 1977-2008 BOYS STATE
TOURNAMENT BASKETBALL COACHES
OF WEST CENTRAL OHIO

BY AMY ZORN

ISBN 10: 0-615-22641-8
ISBN 13: 978-0-615-22641-5

Book layout and design by
Creative Marketing Strategies Inc., Sidney, Ohio

Printed in the United States of America

Contents

PREFACE

T he 1970s were years of great change in the game of high school basketball in Ohio. In those years, boys began to move to more fluid offenses and more aggressive defenses which gave the game an intense, up-tempo rhythm. The most rapid progress occurred as Ohio's girls made the switch from a half-court game to a full-court game and by the middle of the decade were playing in their first state tournament. Basketball has come a long way in thirty years, and each season continues to bring with it new tactics and new strategies. If that progress doesn't slow, the game will look quite different in another thirty years. For those who experienced them, the past several years have been exciting, but for younger enthusiasts, imagination is their only ticket back to those times. I know the people of western Ohio have a fanatical interest in basketball. I also know that very little about this sport has been preserved. Basketball statistics and records are available and consulted with regularity, but other than the newspaper archives in the area, nothing about the people who established them has been recorded. Much has been written about the settlers of this region and the industrialists and the entrepreneurs, but we know very little of the people who made winter Friday nights a regular spectacle. The intent here is to capture a portion of how these changes occurred and the resulting effect they have had on the current game in the words of the men who were either a part of the revolution in this area of western Ohio or the beneficiaries of it. The first state championship trophy came to Shelby County in 1977 so that is where this book begins.

A visit to any high school hosting a basketball game in this region of the state requires a tolerance for noise, heat, and cramped seating. People in cities or other outlying areas don't understand what happens here on Fridays, some Saturdays, and occasional week nights in the counties represented by the coaches in these pages. When I described this project to people in Sidney, for example, they generally gave me only polite encouragement. I grew up in Sidney myself and didn't realize what was going on just a few miles away from my own home. Now that I have taught high school in both Jackson Center and Anna and I've attended many of the big games described in this book, I get it.

Out in the villages, though, I was met with a different reaction. As news of this book began to spread, the first things people said to me were, "How's the book coming?" and, "When is the book going to be finished?" I now know the answer to the second question, but depending on what week or what month it was, my response to the first question varied.

Early in April, I began to lay the groundwork for a project of this magnitude. One of the people I consulted was Bob Wise who had compiled the most comprehensive records of Shelby County basketball into a book containing pages and pages of statistics. He said, "You are going to write a book fans will want to read. They want to know about people." The next problem was determining which coaches I wanted to include. Of course, all groups function by including people and, thereby, excluding others. All state tournament coaches of all sports in Shelby County? All coaches who made it to basketball regional and state competitions? All coaches of both boys and girls basketball teams? How far into the adjoining counties and during what time frame? These questions gave me a number so big that I could not have done justice to them in a book of manageable length. I looked at state tournament history for boys and settled on coaches of Shelby County basketball teams that had made a trip to the state tournament. That gave me seven, including the deceased Fritz Gross of Jackson Center who was the first in 1963 to win a regional championship in Shelby County, and I thought that was too few. I considered teams that are on the schedules of the Shelby County schools and who would be candidates for this list and decided upon the Midwest Athletic Conference schools of Minster, Versailles, Marion Local, New Knoxville, and St. Henry. The only additional coach I added was Bill Elsass who coached the Botkins boys until the year before they went to the state tournament. In his first year out of Botkins, though, Elsass coached Upper Scioto Valley to the state championship. With his former team also appearing there for the first time, Elsass would have coached his Rams against the Trojans in the championship game, had Worthington Christian not stopped Botkins in the semi-finals. Elsass went on to win the state championship that year with USV and was part of the historic record his school set by being the first in Ohio to have both girls and boys as state champions in the same year. Since Elsass spent most of his coaching career in Shelby County and won the state championship his first year away from the area, he had a perspective that needed to be included in this volume.

Having set the criterion for selection as an appearance at the state tournament since 1977, I must acknowledge those coaches – the great coaches, the groundbreaking coaches – whose stories do not appear here. I regret that I could not tell the stories of all the men who gave years, indeed decades, to the game that has enriched the lives of so many players, their families, and their fans. Many of them make fleeting appearances on the pages here, and a few of them will be named repeatedly as the source of knowledge, inspiration, and reassurance to the coaches who rode the bus to Columbus. I have great hope that the fine men who are still encouraging our youth in the gymnasiums of western Ohio, but who have not yet conquered Columbus, will soon make this book obsolete.

The interviews you are about to read were conducted from May to August of 2008. I began with Matt Meyer's interview because Matt and I have been close friends over the years, and I thought he would probably enjoy reliving his recent tournament run. I wanted to experiment before I actually began to start something I, perhaps, couldn't finish, or maybe it wouldn't seem to work with my vision. I drafted a set of fifty-four questions over a period of about three weeks and gave him a copy. The questions were divided into four categories: The Coach, The Game, The Player, and Beyond the Team. We scheduled the interview for a week later in mid-May at his home. When the two-hour-plus session was over, Matt confessed that at first he just wanted to be a good friend and humor me by going through the interview, but by the end of the evening, he had developed an intense curiosity about how the other coaches would answer the very same questions. I returned home, typed up a draft of his chapter, and in a few days, asked him to look it over to see if it was something he thought might be of interest or be useful to the public. His response exceeded my earlier hopes. It was full steam ahead.

All of the coaches I had identified agreed immediately to participate, so I sent out the questions with a cover letter, giving them a couple of weeks to consider the project further. Then I called each coach and set up an interview. These sessions generally lasted a little over two hours, but some ran long because we were interrupted periodically or they had stories to tell or they needed time to think and word their responses exactly the way they wanted. All the coaches were as candid as possible and readily forthcoming, even with follow-up questions, although some coaches were more easily motivated to respond to the questions than others. Several of the photos they provided at the interviews were from their private collections and have not appeared in any other publication. I recorded the interviews and sat at my computer, trying to fit the commentary to a framework, so that there would be a narrative quality to their thoughts. Therefore, the quoted material here is not a journalistic representation of a quotation. I have, in some places, taken part of an answer that fit within another comment and pieced them together. In an interview of this type, people tend to begin sentences, stop and rephrase, or not speak in sentences at all sometimes. I have edited some of their phrasing to make the ideas meaningful to the reader. Preserving the intent as well as the words was the chief target, but some paragraphs were difficult to write because of that very objective. In print, the idea was not the same as that conveyed in our conversation. The goal was not only to maintain the words as much as possible but also to reconfigure a sentence or paragraph to reproduce the meaning more precisely. If a reader finds an explanation or description to be awkward or incongruent, or if there are proofing or editing errors, the fault lies with me. I have attempted to the best of my ability to eliminate those problems, but I know that inevitably some faults slip past even the sharpest reviewer.

My sister, Jenny Zorn, one of the players in the middle of the 1970s revolution in the high school game and later in the college game, provided a trustworthy second eye to some of the pages, and I appreciate, as always, her candid review. The photos that appear in this book have been collected from scrapbooks and personal albums, making their origins difficult to trace. Several are from newspapers and most likely can be credited to the *Sidney Daily News*, the *Celina Daily Standard*, the *Dayton Daily News*, or the *Minster Post*. Other photos have been contributed by friends or family members.

I'm grateful to Creative Marketing Strategies, and I am thankful for John Dunlap who brought a vision of the final product to our very first discussion in June and who guided me through the world of publishing. His talent for giving shape to an idea brought this book to life.

I continue to appreciate Coach Scott Elchert, who has been the source of my growing emotional connection to the game. If not for him, it would have been difficult for me to even begin to understand and convey the degree of preparation, the sacrifice of time, the steadfast perseverance, the commitment to a team, and the shades of joy or despair these coaches have described. He presently has no chapter of his own, but he's on every page.

This book could not have been possible without the coaches who were so generous with their time and their experience. I found each of them to be endowed with common sense and devotion to the game. All their responses centered on their players. Creating optimum experiences for the individuals on their teams so that their lives could be lived more purposefully was paramount to them. The biggest reward for them was seeing their players use their talents to find satisfaction and success later in life. The questions I asked them about their state tournament experiences were often answered by describing, not the perks of being treated as royalty in Columbus, but their focus on the game. Their descriptions of the tournament were generally an observation about how their players, instead of themselves, experienced the moment. In fact, their attempt to explain their personal memory of the state tournament experience was overshadowed by their need for me to understand that they centered their thoughts, rather, on being a good coach, day in and day out. They acknowledged with regret that some of the historically greatest coaches in Ohio never made it to the state tournament and hope that the dedicated coaches in their ranks today will soon have that opportunity.

This book grew out of a single question: Why is basketball so important to this area of Ohio that many of Ohio's greatest teams and traditions have come from this part of the state? It seems that whenever a team from the Midwest Athletic Conference or the Shelby County Athletic League appears at a state basketball tournament, all eyes are upon them. Marion Local, with a high school enrollment of only 311 students, boys and girls, in grades 9-12, continues to hold the attendance record of 17,424 for a state playoff game in Division IV. The coaches all gave me their beliefs about why that is, which were not necessarily surprising, but it was enlightening for me to hear these ideas from a coach's perspective. In the search for the answer to that question, I discovered tendencies and a philosophical alignment that should be instructive to anyone interested in following their example or playing for coaches like these men. I have provided in this introduction a few conclusions based on their views, but I'll allow the fans to follow-up with their own interpretations as well.

In their youth, these coaches grew up playing the game and learning the value of hard work in one way or another. That combination of experiences is what they generally agreed creates a strong foundation for a player's development, as well. Many were influenced later by nationally-known college and professional coaches. The biggest impact on their thinking and how they chose to coach the game, however, came from the people or the coaches they worked with regularly. They spoke of Bobby Knight and John Wooden, but they also gave credit to their own coaches from high school, their rival coaches, or acquaintances from clinics and tournaments. The network each of these men developed is far-reaching, and reasonably so, if a coach is determined to find the right style of play for his team each year. Their mentors were people with a wide range of skills. One could have been a teacher of the game, another maybe an X's and O's fanatic, and another perhaps an observer of the mental aspect of the game. Nevertheless, these coaches recognized that they were coaching alongside – and against – some of the keenest basketball minds in the country, and, instead of relying solely on the national celebrities of the game, they were smart enough and sensible enough to draw wisdom from the gold mine they had in their own backyard.

According to the observations of the men who have been in the game for many years, the big three factors that contribute to the persistent excellence that emerges from this part of Ohio are genetics, the family structure, and the work ethic. Obviously, there are big advantages to being big. With the advent of the three-point shot in the late 1980s, smaller and quicker players could have an impact as well, but the tall Germans continue to dominate the game here, much to the dismay of the Russia fans who in days past would roll cabbages onto the floor to demonstrate their disdain for their Fort Loramie neighbors' heritage. Often, players later marry women from the area and their children are raised in the small towns, continuing the cycle. However, these marriages frequently involve people from rival communities and incubate even stronger rivalries that develop in conjunction with the proximity of these small towns. No family likes to spend the holidays with a cousin or in-law who won the game they lost. Hoarding bragging rights is a vocation. In these family units, both parents raise their children alongside other mostly two-parent families. They attend church regularly and expect their children to work hard at school, at home, or on the farm. These values and lifestyles seem to create an environment that demands excellence in all endeavors and is not replicated to this degree elsewhere.

One of the differences among the men is the era in which they coached. The veteran coaches remember playing nearly every game in tiny gyms. The smaller gyms have given way to the larger capacity gymnasiums with adequate off-court floor space, bright lighting in the locker rooms, and spectator seating positioned farther away from the court. Even those schools that have yet to expand have renovated or restructured their facilities for the modern game of basketball. Surprisingly, many of these coaches reflect on those nights in the "cracker boxes" as producing some of the most memorable basketball games in their careers. They recall fans seated so near the bench that they could lean in toward the huddle to eavesdrop on strategies or motivational techniques and assault the coaches with a slap on the head or a whack with a rolled-up program. They also recall sitting on team benches positioned so close to the lines that players had to sit with their feet tucked under their chairs to avoid being on the court.

The more experienced coaches generally are skeptical of the need for the recent increase in player participation in basketball throughout the year but seem resigned to its continuing presence.

Some current coaches are sensitive to the growing concern about the time spent on the sport in off-season involvement and, although fairly powerless at the state level, are attempting to negotiate dead periods for their athletes at various times of the year at the local level or are implementing blocked-out times the coach establishes at the team level. Scaling back on time spent out-of-season isn't an option for an individual coach if a team wants to compete in-season. Both groups don't see this issue being resolved state-wide anytime soon.

Since the coaches spent an extended amount of time being interviewed for this book, I had the opportunity other sports writers or reporters don't get to follow up and delve into the subjects we covered. Some of the coaches' reflections and conclusions in these pages have not been discussed publicly before so there is some new insight here. This book, though, was not intended to be a trip down memory lane for coaches to relive the fun, the excitement, and the glory that basketball can offer, although there is a fair amount of that.

One of the common bonds among coaches is psychological pain. Generally, that pain doesn't come from the final score of a game. It comes from the limitations of human effort and the failure to overcome life in an imperfect world. These are the times when a game plan collapses, a team doesn't play to its optimum ability, a coaching decision causes hardship for a family member or player, or there is a misjudgment on the part of a coach or official that sends the game spiraling out of reach. Coaches know their job, fundamentally, is to put that pain in context for their players and to use those disappointing moments as lessons for their team to learn how to absorb the bigger tragedies of life that surely await them in the future. The championships and the games when adversity was overcome get a little soft around the edges and melt a little in the warmth of every remembrance, but the pain of the games that slipped away and the despair suffered by teams and players, in particular, never seems to dull.

Some readers may find the absence of statistics to be unusual in a book about a game that is statistics-driven. I have intentionally omitted statistics as much as possible so that the emphasis, even in the look of the text, is on the personal element of the game. If the information provided in each coach's chapter doesn't satisfy the curious fan, I recommend the state tournament program, sold at the state tournament each year, as a source for finding the teams and scores by class or division for each year since the beginning of these competitions.

I expect that readers will want to sample all the chapters and compare and contrast the views of these men. I envision lively discussions in such venues as Fish-Mo's, Bud's or the Inn Between on the topics of shot clocks, positioning during free throws, and the coaches themselves, based on some of the statements in this book. If those subjects are well-worn in certain communities, I'm sure that readers will find within these pages plenty of other grist for the after-game mills.

My hope is that this effort has provided a lasting record of the spirit of the men whose lives have meant so much to their players and their communities. It has been my privilege to spend hours in the presence of these men who represent the legions of coaches all aspiring to give back to the game the honor that coaching it has given them.

Chapter  One

GEORGE HAMLIN

FORT LORAMIE HIGH SCHOOL

1977 STATE CHAMPION

"You play against the game and you have to play hard, no matter what the situation is, or you aren't getting better. If you play a game and don't play your best, you've wasted an opportunity."

The middle of his first season as head coach at Fort Loramie High School was a winter of discontent for George Hamlin with the Redskins owning a 5-6 record, but in the spring of that year his team accomplished what no other team had ever done before. They brought a state championship trophy west from Columbus to Shelby County. The year was 1977 and the excitement flowing out of Fort Loramie that March belied the energy crisis the entire nation was suffering at the time.

Hamlin had come to Fort Loramie to replace longtime coach John Kremer by way of three schools where he came of age as a coach: St. Joseph High School in Wapakoneta, Lincolnview in Van Wert, and Lima Shawnee. Hamlin's first interest was baseball and after college he took his first teaching position in Wapakoneta teaching and coaching basketball and baseball.

"We had a really good basketball team that made it to the regional finals. In those years, I really grew to enjoy the intricacies of the game. Basketball is a very hard sport to coach because the coach actually has very little control. In baseball, you have more time to make decisions and it's more of a plodding type game, whereas, in basketball, it's a lot of decisions on the fly. Those things intrigued me.

"I had many influences, but the biggest were the head coach at Wapak St. Joe and the principal there. What I knew, I learned from them. I became the head coach there for a year until the school closed. I worked as the head coach at Lincolnview one year and then went to Lima Shawnee as an assistant coach. I had kind of taken a step backward, even though Shawnee was a much bigger school, but that was a really good influence. The people on that staff had an entirely different philosophy than what I had learned. That gave me another perspective on the game and changed a lot of the things I believed. I became a lot more of a man-to-man coach.

"When I went to Fort Loramie, I was thirty-one years old and I thought I knew pretty much and I was going to mold that team into my way of thinking and my way of doing things. We got off to a rough start. We struggled. We were 5-6 at one time, but I thought I knew how things were going to be. We were going to play man-to-man defense, and we were going to run and press a little bit, but we just didn't have the personnel to do it. In 1976, during the energy crisis, we were two weeks without a game and when we did practice, we weren't allowed to have the lights on in the gym. We were practicing in the dark. That two-week period allowed us to take a step back and make some changes. We played more zone and played to the strength of our personnel. It was a totally different style than I anticipated when I went there. That is part of coaching. You learn to adapt. We were fortunate that the guys bought into what we were doing.

"When I was at Wapak, we were mostly a zone team. My

first couple of years as a head coach, we played a lot of zone. At Lima, I learned the man-to-man stuff and really thought that was the way to be. I did a lot of Bob Knight stuff. He became the head coach at Indiana and taught the motion offense and the man-to-man defense, so I've always looked at myself as a man-to-man coach and I look at myself as kind of a motion offense coach, but I guess I've been fortunate that my background is such that I can make changes when needed.

You can't be orthodox all the time. A guy like Knight can be because he's going to recruit the players that fit his system. In high school, you can't do that. These kids at Fort Loramie were very talented players, but they didn't

have a lot of experience. That was our big weakness and it hurt us a lot. Many people would say I'm stubborn, and there's a lot of truth to that, but I'm willing to change and adapt."

Two coincidental circumstances besides the fact that his wife was from the area, landed Hamlin, who had not been searching for a varsity coaching position, at Fort Loramie. An acquaintance of his encouraged him to look at the vacant position in Shelby County. After he interviewed, he learned that the Fort Loramie district wanted the head coach at Miller City to fill the position, but the offer had been declined.

"When I interviewed, there was transition occurring. They had just had board elections and the newly-elected members were change agents. I think I was the board's choice for change, even though I was their second choice."

Hamlin credits John Kremer, the coach he replaced, as the man who made Fort Loramie basketball.

"He and Bob Anderson are the two people who made Shelby County basketball. John, though, had been doing it a certain way for twenty-six years. He always emphasized Shelby County League first. It was important to win the county. The game was very plodding. They ran a lot of set offenses and a lot of zone defense. They always had these huge guys, and I think I brought a philosophy in that I would be more demonstrative in the way that I coached. Practices were a lot harder. The kids could relate a little better to me. It seemed that the community was looking for somebody who could challenge others and make Fort Loramie important, having lived in the shadow of Minster and Anna for so long.

"In 1977 Fort Loramie won the state tournament for the first time, and it was the first time for Shelby County, too. Up until that time, Shelby County basketball was not well-respected. We were seen as sort of a Cinderella team at the tournament.

"The first thought that went through my mind [at St. John Arena, playing in the state tournament] was, 'What am I doing here? I don't belong here.' We always talk about the atmosphere in St. John Arena because if you go to Michigan, Kentucky, or West Virginia, there is nothing that compares to Ohio state basketball. I don't know what it's like in Indiana, now that they've gone to classes, but when it was all one class, that was special, too. You have to remember that we have all these divisions and they sell out. We don't have enough people in Fort Loramie to fill St. John, so it is just an incredible atmosphere. As a coach, you think, 'I know what I did as a coach sitting over there.' You're sitting with a couple of hundred other coaches watching this guy coach and thinking, 'Why is he doing that?' So I was thinking, 'There are all these guys who know one hundred percent more than I do. What if I screw up?' It's the crowd and the excitement.

"One thing I remember is walking into Ohio State's locker room. We walked down the hallway and there were all the pictures of Havlicek and Lucas and all these people. There's a lot of history there. And to see your fans so excited, it's just hard to describe. I wish I could re-live it because it went by way too fast. Later on, I was fortunate enough to coach a game in the Schottenstein Center with Columbus Bishop Ready, and the atmosphere there isn't the same. It just isn't the same.

"You can't believe the excitement. When we came back, the whole atmosphere, not just Fort Loramie, was incredible. I think a lot of it was that Fort Loramie had never even won a district [title] before, we had been 5-6 at one time during the season, and we had gone through a lot of things that year. The people were lining the streets. I remember on Route 66, [the brother of one of our players] had a bottle of peppermint schnapps and you couldn't drive through until you took a drink. This was on a major highway.

"The turning point in our year was a game against Minster. The game had been cancelled because of cold. It was supposed to be a Friday night game, but we ended up playing on a Sunday afternoon. The doors of the old Minster gym were frosted over. There were a whole lot of people there. Minster was loaded and they were supposed to kick our pants. We weren't playing very well, but we ended up in double overtime. Charlie Quinter hit the shot that beat them, and at that point we knew that to win a game like that, we could do anything. We went 15-2 from then on."

Surprisingly, Hamlin isn't sure he always wanted to be a coach, but once he started, there was no turning back. He did want to be a teacher, tried administration but didn't like it, and then went back to coaching. A career in the media seemed interesting, but it wasn't something he pursued. Over the course of his tenure in high school coaching, he developed several principles that served as his personal guidelines.

"Players are the most important. Players come first. That doesn't mean you let them do what they want. I believe very strongly that discipline and doing things the right way is the way to approach the game. Bob Knight's definition of discipline is doing what you are supposed to do, when you are supposed to do it, the way it's supposed to be done. Discipline isn't always yelling and punishing. Fundamentals are extremely important to the way I coach. I see myself as a teacher first. A coach is a teacher and the best coaches are the best teachers. Then, playing hard is the foundation of everything. There are a lot of things that go into making a good team, but you must start with that basis of playing hard and doing things the right way.

"Back when I started coaching, clinics were big. Looking back over the years, I learned a lot of good stuff from clinics where there were a lot of coaches. That was the major source of knowledge. I was not necessarily an Ohio State fan, but I always admired Woody Hayes and his book, *You Win with People!*

Although Hamlin believes that all games are big games, two in particular surface as games that changed his team's direction.

"All games are important to me. I want our kids to have a good experience and do the best they can in every game that they play. The Minster game in the middle of our [1976-1977] season, and the regional final against Middletown Fenwick when we beat a good team by twenty points are two games that were very important.

"The Fenwick game was played on a Saturday, after we had both played the semi-finals on Thursday. We played the early Thursday game and they played the late game. We left at half time of their game, and I thought, 'It's going to be one or two o'clock before they get home and get in bed.' I've always thought the second day after interrupted sleep is the worst day. And on Saturday, they did not play successfully or with the enthusiasm or the energy that they had on Thursday. I remember looking at my assistant, Gary Hunter, and I said, 'I can't believe this. We're actually going to play in the state tournament.' We won that game at UD Arena, which is still the best place in the world to play a basketball game because of the atmosphere and the great playing conditions. It's so well organized. They treat you well. You don't have to worry where to go or how to do anything. Dayton and St. John Arena are the best places. I had been coaching for seven years when we went to Columbus, and you look up and all you see is people all the way up to the top. It's like a funnel. It's too bad they didn't keep the tournament there."

To get to the state tournament took a combination of three important factors and Hamlin had all of them.

"Luck is a big part of it. You have to be fortunate enough to stay injury-free, and you have to have kids who believe in themselves. Our motto was, 'If you think you can, or if you think you can't, you're probably right.' Each game further strengthened that belief. The best team doesn't win the NCAA tournament every year. The best team doesn't win the state championship every year. It is teams that are peaking at the right time. That year New Bremen was in the other regional and got beat in the regional finals. They had beaten us by twenty in the regular season, but they leveled off a little bit and we got better. That was the big difference. A lot of people said, 'Well, if you'd played New Bremen, you wouldn't have won the state tournament.' We were a different team when we played New Bremen that year and we'd changed because our kids believed in themselves."

Hamlin not only coached the big games, he learned some lessons along the way to get him there.

"I was a JV coach at Wapak St. Joe and I learned a great lesson. We were up by one and we were shooting a free throw. We missed the free throw and there was maybe one second to go. Our player went over the back of one of their players. It was a foul, so they went down to the other end to shoot two free throws and they made them and won the game. It was something I had never thought of before, but it taught me that there are times when you don't play conventionally. I should have gotten the kids off the free throw lines at that point because we didn't need a rebound. There was no reason for us to be there. In terms of strategy, that was an example to understand situations.

"Another lesson I learned was against Fort Recovery in 1973 in the district finals in Lima. We were both undefeated and ranked one and two in the state. They were a fast-paced team running up and down the floor. Near half-time, we were waiting for a free throw and one of my players on the bench said, 'Coach, man, am I tired, how about you?' I was ready to drop him, but I just looked at him and said, 'Nah doesn't bother me a bit.' The whole idea was not just about conditioning but of never giving in and keeping your eye on where you want to go.

"Then, the year we went to state, we were playing Houston at New Bremen. We were playing there because we rented gyms to play our home games since our gym was too small. We had a five-point lead with twenty-nine seconds to go and we had the ball out of bounds. And we lost the game. It taught me a little about how quickly things can change.

Hamlin can't find one particular game to identify as a time when he wished he'd done something differently, but he made that wish on more than one occasion. He felt that way every time he lost. Of the times he has won, he counts the Sparta Highland game, when he was coaching at Jonathan Alder after his Fort Loramie years, as a time when the plans worked well for his team.

"Sparta Highland had a 7' center and we were playing him with a 6'2" kid, but we beat them because we just wouldn't let him get to the low post. Those are times you feel good about it. I'm not big on game coaching. I'm a believer that preparation is the most important thing. Your job is done in preparing kids to play.

"Teamwork, getting kids to give of themselves, is the hardest thing to teach. Don Goldschmidt at Fort Loramie was a great example of this. Here was a kid who should not have been a point guard but was because of circumstances. He could have been a twelve-to-fifteen-point-a-game scorer in another situation, but that isn't what we needed from him. We had scorers. If you go back and read the articles about our team, everybody was talking about how bad our guards were. So here's a guy who gave up his ability to score. He was willing to give the ball up, handle the ball, and make sure it got in the right spot, and that is so hard to teach kids. You watch on TV and it's all about the 'me' and the dunks and who is the best-dressed coach on the sidelines and who's going to the NBA. A basketball team is an integrated whole and if one part is out of whack, you aren't going to accomplish what you want.

"Lack of talent, too, can be an obstacle to a team's success, but everyone needs to find a role and accept that role, even if it means you won't be the biggest star. Another good example is Doug Brandewie. When I went to Fort Loramie, he was the biggest star. One night, we were winning by twenty. It might have been the beginning of the fourth quarter when I sat him down. A little bit later, he asked, 'Am I going to get back in?' And I said, 'Probably not.' He said, 'Coach, I'm not used to sitting on the bench.' I said, 'Doug, we've got six guys who come to practice every day, bust their butts every day, do what I ask them to do every day, and they don't get to play much. When we get in a situation like this, those guys are going to play.' He said, 'I never thought of it like that.' And that's because no one had ever asked him to. He had to be willing to give up playing thirty or thirty-one minutes every game."

As much as the big moments mean to a coach, Hamlin believes there are times that foreshadow the end of a career.

"It's time to get out when it quits being fun. That's the easiest sign to recognize. The hardest to recognize is when you no longer communicate with the players. They quit listening to you and you quit listening to them. For whatever reason, you lose that connection.

"My biggest peeve is officials that don't take the game as seriously as we do and don't work as hard as we do. They are an integral part of the game and their influence is very important. They have control of the game. I never question the integrity of officials, but they have to be in it for the right reasons, not for their own ego. What irritates me about officials is that they are not in condition and they don't take it seriously. I take it seriously and a game is important to me. They have to work hard. I want officials to be in position to make the call and they have to work as hard as I do for the game to be run efficiently. The best thing an official can do is come to me to tell me he missed a call. I understand that. I make mistakes. I put the wrong kid in or call a time-out at the wrong time. To make a mistake and not be willing to admit it is something I don't have much patience with. If you missed a call, I can accept that, but not if you miss twenty in a game. I don't mind if an official misses a call, but that's probably the biggest peeve I have. That won't surprise anybody.

"The biggest rewards in coaching are the relationships you have with your players and other coaches and getting to meet many good people. I enjoyed, as a JV coach, watching a kid I coached when he was a freshman or sophomore grow up and develop. As the head coach at Fort Loramie, I enjoyed watching the program develop and seeing the kids buy into what we were doing. I think there is still a lot of what Dan Hegemier and I did that's still a big influence in the program there.

"And then, it's such an intricate game. It's always a challenge. One year this works and the next year you can't do the same thing. It's not canned. If you are coaching baseball, there isn't a whole lot of variation. There are certain things in football, but in basketball there are so many ways to do it. Bob Knight is a big influence on my thinking, but he talks about striving to play the perfect game. That's always his goal. You're never going to do it, but it always challenges you just when you think you've got it down. I've been coaching for thirty-seven years and I see things today I haven't seen before.

"Things can change in the game of basketball pretty quickly. In a game we played against Jackson Center, we were down 18-2 at the beginning of the game. I called time-out to tell the kids we were going to win that game. I don't know why I believed it, but I knew we were going to win, and we did. Then there are games that you lead the whole game but you never feel comfortable. Maybe it's because of the way you are playing or some shots go in that shouldn't. I'm a believer that if you take bad shots, it will come back to haunt you.

"There aren't a lot of differences in coaching when you're ahead or when you're behind. Oh, sure, there are strategic things. You may have to foul or you may have to use time-outs differently. You play against the game and you have to play hard, no matter what the situation is, or you aren't getting better. If you play a game and don't play your best, you've wasted an opportunity. You'll never get that opportunity back. We especially talked to seniors about that. You have twenty games to play and if you don't make the most of each situation in every game, you'll never get it back. And you may never play again.

"The pacing of a game is a feel. It comes from experience and knowing your kids. You keep them playing as hard as they can all the time, but sometimes that doesn't happen. I'm not a believer in holding the ball. We tried to do some strategic things and you try to be smart. The pace of the game is probably the hardest thing for a coach in basketball. You don't have much control over the pace. You can use time-outs to try to change the pace and you can try to slow the tempo, but the other team may not let you. Those are all factors.

"New coaches should remember to put players first and be willing to adapt. You can't be wishy-washy, but at the same time if something doesn't work, you have to be willing to learn. That might be another sign of when to give it up, when you don't want to learn. I always tell young coaches that the first thing to look at is to make sure you have administrators that are supportive because too often today as soon as people start complaining you'll need someone to stand behind you. Coaching has become so political and you have to make everybody happy. You know what? You don't go into coaching to make anybody unhappy, but you can't please everyone. Fewer and fewer administrators are willing to stand up for their personnel.

"Make sure your family is on board with what you are doing. There is no bigger obstacle for a coach than a wife or family that isn't willing to go along. I've been fortunate that my wife has made moves and done things and was always willing to let me do my thing. In all honesty, you spend a lot of time with other people's kids that you don't spend with your own. Most successful coaches will tell you that their wives did the majority of the work raising the kids.

"I worry that we aren't getting enough good young people willing to make the commitment to coach. It's hard to be a coach today.

Parents are so much more involved. Even at the college level, parents are involved. With all the criticism coaching gets, you have to love what you are doing.

"The hours of preparation, going in on Sundays, and watching film are all things you are doing by yourself. Most people don't understand how hard it is to make the hard decisions. If you are going to be successful as a coach, you have to be willing to make those decisions. There's nothing harder than cutting a kid or having a kid come to practice every night, bust his butt, and not play a lot, and then you have to look him in the eye and say, 'I love you as much as the others, but this is the way it is.' No one understands how hard that is. Not even your spouse can understand that. You get a lot of criticism for it, but you have to be willing to do that."

The off-season work has multiplied since Hamlin left high school coaching. When he was at Fort Loramie his summer routine involved an emphasis on building his program.

"We didn't have the summer stuff they have now. I was always one who tried to prepare for the tournament. That was a big part of my planning. Early in the year, I was a lot harder on teams. We oftentimes would practice three hours at the beginning of the season. Then, by the time January and February came, we'd be down to maybe an hour or an hour and fifteen or twenty minutes. I think those things are important. You use your camps to build the program. A lot of places have summer youth leagues or associations for little kids. We didn't have that when I was at Fort Loramie, but those are ways you build your program, teach your philosophy, and get kids interested. I think it's really important as a varsity coach. I was always at the camp and teaching at the camp. We used to do a Saturday morning camp with a half-hour of instruction with little kids and then let them play games, and our high-school players would coach them. Those kids would come to our game at night. I can still see little kids sitting behind the bench at night and when I called a time out, it was like God was talking. It's important to use those things to build interest.

"You want kids to like to play, but you also want to build a history. I've always been big on having former players come back to play in the open gyms. That's another thing about the area and

Shelby County. A lot of people stay in the area so we encourage them to come back to play. Also, every year, we tried to honor somebody. One year at Fort Loramie, we honored the first team at Fort Loramie. The coach was still alive. It might have been the 1935 team, and it was great. You want to have people who are forty years old who still have a passion for Fort Loramie basketball. You do those types of things to build your program.

"Depending on the time of year, we would condition, especially early in the year. The off-season is important for strength-training and skill development. That's what I don't like about AAU. Kids play more games, but there is less work on the game. Championships are won from May to October. If you want to have a good team, you have to do it in the off-season. You don't have time once practice starts to develop skills. You can work on those things, but if a kid comes in and hasn't shot all summer, you don't have enough time in practice.

"I'm a firm believer in writing down your practice plans. We always timed everything we did. Another thing I learned from Knight was to keep things short. A forty-minute scrimmage in practice is wasted time. We very seldom did a team thing that lasted more than fifteen minutes or an individual thing that lasted more than five to ten. We did our defensive work early in practice because that was when the kids were fresh and it's what we thought was important. We did our team stuff at the end. We always tried to shoot free throws at the end of practice, but we also interspersed them. If we had done something that was particularly hard, we'd go shoot free throws because they were tired and that's a game situation. Once the season wore on, we did more five-on-five and team stuff, not being on the floor more than forty-five minutes.

"We didn't get a lot of film at Fort Loramie. It wasn't big then. [It was necessary to have] good scouts who knew what you wanted. I've had guys who couldn't commit to coaching, but they would come in and scout for you. Scouting isn't normally a lot of fun. You can go to some games that are real stinkers. If you go to a game as a fan, it's one thing, but if you go as a scout, you might have to sit through a thirty-point game and stay until the end because you never know. They might do something different at the end. Good scouts understand the game. They understand the nuances and they know what we're looking for. The best scouts made suggestions for match-ups. I always tried to do my own scouting and see a team at least once. After I had seen them, we'd send somebody else so that we always tried to see them at least twice.

Hamlin had a routine on game days that involved reviewing his preparations and focusing on the needs of the team.

"I tried to take a nap before the game. I tried to eat something and get to the game early. I went over match-ups, what we were trying to do, what our match-ups were, and I thought it was important to be at the JV game. I didn't like to have anybody around me. I liked to be by myself. I didn't have a varsity assistant, but even when I had volunteers, they knew to stay away.

"Our pre-game was based on the opponent. We reviewed what we were going to do, what our game plan was, and what our match-ups were. You make adjustments at halftime after you review what happened in the first half. That's the thing about high school. In college there aren't many surprises, but in high school, you can see the team two or three times and not see the real team. High school kids are like that. After the game, you can say a lot more in the post-game talk when you win than when you lose. First of all, when you lose, the kids don't want to hear it. Second, when you lose it's easy to say something you'll regret later on and you can never take it back. I tried to say as little as I could if we lost. If we won, there were times when I was a lot more critical than when they lost. One night I called a time-out in a game against Botkins when we were up by thirty. Our second or third group wasn't doing what I thought they should be doing, so I called the time-out. I laid into them and said, 'If you can't go out there and play the way we want, you aren't going to play.' I would tell a young coach to be careful what he says when he loses. I've known coaches who've lost a three-point game come in and go through all the plays and what went wrong. You know what? They are not listening to you at that point."

Hamlin learned that time must be stretched to cover all the responsibilities a coach balances, so when something has to give, it's usually the family.

"A high school coach is almost always a teacher as well. It's not like a college coach whose only responsibility is coaching. You are trying to fit all these things in and after a tough loss or you've had a provocation with a player or a parent, it's easy to take it out on your family. In addition, there are a lot of people over the years that I would have liked to have been friends with, but I wasn't comfortable with it because maybe I was coaching their kids or they were on the school board. Sometimes, coaching affects those things and I wish it wouldn't, but it does. I had some parents who I thought were good friends. When I made a decision that affected their kids, it got uncomfortable. On the other hand, I've met people through coaching who have been lifelong friends.

"I never had a lot of assistant coaches. Eventually we had a freshman coach, but the JV coach was the one on the bench at the varsity games. Once we had a bigger gym, we could practice the varsity and JV together. I always asked the junior high coaches to play strictly man-to-man. We didn't want any zone. I gave them some suggestions for what to do offensively. Once we had a freshman team, they played ninety percent man-to-man. At that point they were doing pretty much what we wanted on offense. Junior high coaches did a lot of scouting. You want junior high coaches who are committed to teaching. They have to be good teachers and they have to buy into your program. At Fort Loramie, Mike Anthony was a great junior high coach because he kept the kids interested and he taught them things. The freshman coaching position is a key position. It's one of the last times you can change a lot about a kid's game. It's the transition from junior high to high school. I believe in junior high, everybody should play. Once they get to be freshmen, maybe not everybody is going to play. Having a good staff is the key to having a good program."

Hamlin enjoyed much of the game and the work involved in preparing for each game, but he found some of the responsibilities to be unpleasant.

"In this day and age it's not a lot of fun sitting in open gym just watching kids play. This wasn't at Fort Loramie but I have a former player who is now a coach and he said to me, 'Man, you used to come to open gyms and sit there and read a book when I was trying to impress you.' I told him I always knew what was going on, even though I was reading. The weight room was something else, too. It's not fun for players and it's not fun for coaches, but you have to do it. I didn't like the paperwork and statistics and answering the same questions from reporters.

"I remember talking to Jack Albers who called me when he took over at Marion Local and asked if I had any advice for him. I said, 'Jack, the biggest thing I can tell you is not to allow the other stuff to get in the way of your coaching and your relationships with your players.' People don't know all the things a head coach has to do until they become a head coach. A lot of guys will lose some of the contact with their players or not be teaching the game the way they should. The most important thing is your players and if the rest doesn't get done, it doesn't get done. A coach has to be a good communicator. You have to be willing to listen and you have to be willing to say what you believe. You have to do what you perceive is the right thing. That doesn't mean you won't ever make a mistake, but you have to do what you think is right and it takes a lot of self-discipline to do that."

These points help a coach to remember what it takes to have success as a team. In addition, Hamlin includes the team criteria necessary for achievement.

"If you have talent, you have a chance to be pretty good, but I talk a lot about chemistry and accepting a role. I don't know that you can develop chemistry. Maybe if the team chemistry, on a scale of one to ten, is at a three, you can raise it to a seven, but you can't develop chemistry that isn't there. Part of chemistry is accepting team roles, but it is important to clearly communicate. 'Here's what you need to do. Here's your role.' Then hold them accountable to those roles. You have to get kids to play together, and I don't mean like each other, because sometimes they like each other too much and that isn't good. I mean you have to have a good blend of personalities and people who accept their roles. John Havlicek [NBA player] was a good example of that. For a long time he was a sixth man and he accepted that role."

Hamlin believes that these qualities can be found in abundance in western Ohio and that's what makes for the strong teams in the area.

"Basically, it comes down to great families, good values, the structure that kids have, and the discipline at home. They are taught how to work. So much of this area is farm kids and farm land, and even if kids don't live on a farm, they know what it means to work. They have a work ethic. In Fort Loramie, especially, they had a lot of big families and they had to learn to share and get along. There are the genetic things with size and athletic ability but the personal qualities come from the home. That's why they have good schools. Fort Loramie was a great place to teach, and that doesn't mean we didn't have our idiots like everybody else, but you liked to be in there because you liked the people and you liked the kids.

"I think this is true of Anna, it's true of Botkins, it's true of Minster, and it's true of Russia. Sports are important to these people. It's not that school isn't important; it's not that they want a school where kids aren't taught the right thing. It's that they want excellence in everything. That was something they were looking for when I came to Fort Loramie. They wanted excellence and discipline throughout their teaching. They wanted it in everything, and it's a community thing. In some of the bigger areas, I'm not sure community support in those locations is as strong as it is in western Ohio.

"My career began at the end of a lot of the school consolidations, but it was a long time before some of those rifts healed. In some ways, athletics helps heal those rifts because it gives them all a common purpose. In Newport and Fort Loramie there was always a tension there. In McCartyville and Anna there was always a tension. By having good athletic teams, it gives them common ground. When a kid gets a thirty on his ACT, it isn't much of a unifying factor. A lot of people don't realize how important athletics are in places like Fort Loramie. I'm sure it's hard for Anna people to accept that they've never won a state championship. Some of Bob Anderson's teams should have. That just shows you how much luck is involved. You can talk all you want about how good you were and how well you coached, but you have to have a little luck, and unfortunately, he didn't. And look at John Kremer. I'm not sure Fort Loramie truly appreciates John Kremer. You know, he never once said a negative word to me that whole year, and I'm sure there were times he had to bite his tongue because I was so different. He had never won a district championship and here it was in my first year. We had John cut the nets down when we won the regional. It was his right. He should have done that. I wanted him to sit on the bench at the state tournament, but that wasn't John. He didn't want to do that. Shelby County basketball was built on the backs of John Kremer and Bob Anderson."

Hamlin recalls the rival teams that fed the enthusiasm for basketball in his community.

"I would say the rivalry with Russia was probably our biggest. There was a rivalry with Anna, but Anna kind of dominated the series so probably it was more of a rivalry for Fort Loramie than Anna. Russia was French and we were German. They would throw cabbage heads out on the floor. Once in awhile the Fort Loramie people would put a frog on the floor, although I don't remember them ever doing that. I do remember the cabbage heads being rolled out, though. Being so close [in distance] and being strong, Catholic communities, and with a lot of intermarriage between the two villages, I'd say Russia more than Anna. There were some things we used to do that now aren't politically correct, but they were fun. It wasn't like some rivalries where fights break out in the parking lot. I don't remember any of that stuff. Minster was a rival just because of the proximity. Maybe Anna had the biggest home-court advantage because they played in the gym they practiced in. They had a nice facility. Fairlawn had the second nicest facility in the county back then."

Since Hamlin began his coaching career, the game has changed, and so have the rules.

"The biggest and the worst changes in the game are the three-point shot and the AAU teams. The three-point shot has hurt the game because kids don't learn to shoot the ball. Everybody wants to shoot three-point shots instead of learning the proper techniques. Before, there was no reason to shoot nineteen-foot shots. Now that's what everybody wants to do. You see little kids who can't get it up to the rim trying to shoot three-point shots. They should be learning proper technique and proper form. The unreality of the AAU situation is parents who think their son is a scholarship player. I'm a Division III college coach and there is no way. People get fed a lot of how good a player is and how many college coaches are going to come see them and that's why AAU is good for them. A lot of those coaches are coaching for themselves. They are not that interested in the kids. They don't discipline the kids and make them do things. Those are the two biggest changes in the game."

Hamlin played against some of the historic names in area basketball coaching and respected his opponents.

"We [coaches] were so close and we competed so hard that we respected each other. You obviously had to respect Bob [Anderson at Anna]. He was the dean. We had some interesting times. I respected Fred Nuss. He didn't have a lot of talent to work with. He didn't have a great situation to work in, but his kids were always competitive. Very seldom did you beat their brains in. I had a lot of respect for Jerry [Harmon at Jackson Center] because he came into a situation that was awful and five, six, seven years later, he's the state champion. We had epic battles in that little gym over there. One night we were getting ready to play for the league championship. They opened the doors and our fans walked in, but the gym was ninety percent filled. They had let their fans in the back door. Our fans couldn't get in the game. But he had come into a situation that was awful. I came into a situation that was pretty darned good. Two other guys were Chuck Blair and Kim Rank at Fairlawn. Kim's teams came into the games so well-prepared and hard to play against. We won those games by thirty points, but not because we played better. It was a situation that if they beat us once in ten times that was great, but they never thought they couldn't beat us. They fought us tooth and nail. Kim was a great coach."

Developing the whole player was a key to Hamlin's success as well.

"A good player is someone who is willing to commit at both ends of the floor. Everybody wants to score and everybody wants their picture in the paper, and you don't get your picture in the paper when you are defending or rebounding. Someone who is willing to give of himself for the team is really important. I think back to the players who did that and Doug Brandewie is probably the best player I ever coached. He's probably not the best athlete, but he is the best player. Here's a guy who had already made a reputation for himself in Shelby County and if John [Kremer] had stayed, he would have averaged twenty-five points a game. Yet, he welcomed me with open arms. He defended. He was willing to commit to that. Tom Steinke only scored twenty-five points in his whole career. And then he averaged twenty or more in the tournament. Charlie Quinter was probably told that he should be starting because he was the best guard we had, but it wasn't in the best interest of the team for him to start, and he accepted that. I've coached a lot of kids who fit my description of a good player over the years, but Doug is probably the best player I've ever coached.

"I was an intense coach. I was what you would call hands-on. I was not always easy to play for and I know that. And that's sometimes lonely because you are doing what you need to do. With a couple of exceptions as a head coach, I've always had competitive kids. If you are going to play for me, you have to be competitive. You have to be willing to give up something to get something. You have to see the big picture, the greater good. You had to be willing to be coached and be criticized and those are two different things. If you do something right, I'm going to tell you that. If you do something wrong, I'm going to tell you that, too. I will always listen to what players have to say, but they have to be willing to listen to what I have to say. They don't like it because I tell them the truth. Have I been wrong? Of course, I've been wrong, but I'll tell them what I think. That [state tournament] team was willing to do those things and there were some rough spots. There was a situation when I almost dismissed a player from the team, and it would have been an integral part of our team, but he responded. He was willing to win.

"Trust is extremely important and it's hard to build. You can't lie to kids. I don't think you can fool them. They may not call you on it, but they see through it. I've had players come back and tell me they didn't understand it then, but they get it now. They're high school kids and they're going to lie to you sometimes, but even your own kids will lie to you. Trust is the most important thing between a coach and his players.

"Experience and putting kids in pressure situations helps kids handle pressure. Bob Knight always said that games should be easy compared to practice. We did a lot of disadvantage stuff, the five-on-four or four-on-three. We had consequences. Anything you could do to make your practices hard and make them competitive is where you teach them to handle pressure. And then in games if things go well, you point out that they handled it well, and when they don't go well, you point that out, too. You teach from those experiences.

"Leadership is responsibility. I'm a believer that seniors have to take responsibility for their team. Coaches will tell you that teams that have good seniors are good teams. That's been my experience. You also hold players accountable. If you want something done a certain way, they continue to do it until it's done that way or there is some consequence. The way to build competitive drive is striving for perfection. Competitive drive is hard to teach. You can be a good player and not be very competitive. You can't be a great player and not be competitive. You can tell if a kid is competitive if you say, 'Let's do X.' The kids who jump into it are competitive. The kids who won't or wait around to see what everybody else is going to do aren't. I look at an open gym, and the kids who want to get out there, do it. Some people would call that leadership, but that's part of competitiveness, too. There are kids who are willing to sit on the bench, but you want the one who is not willing to do that. There are kids who aren't good enough to play, but they are competitive enough to want to stay and play. That's part of competitiveness, too.

"Drills should be cumulative. Start with the base and keep adding layers. We use a lot of four-on-four shell drills. Those are defensive drills, but they could be offensive drills. We use disadvantaged drills. When you do drills, you want them to be harder than game situations.

"I absolutely think that if the coach is interested in the whole person you coach kids to go beyond what they think they can do. If I saw a player I thought could play at the college level, I called coaches and I sent tape. We are educators and we want kids to be in those situations. I don't think it's your job to do it for them. It's not my job to get you a scholarship. So many parents today think their kid is a scholarship player and that's not realistic. Unfortunately, I think that's why a lot of high school coaches shy away. They don't want to tell a kid he isn't going to get a scholarship and he isn't good enough. As a college coach, I know that we send out letters to high school coaches, and you would be amazed at how many don't send them back. It's important to do that. It's good for you, your players, and your program.

"Parents and fans should be supportive. They should give their kids unconditional support. The worst thing a parent can do is criticize at home. It tears the kids down. If there are things they question, and playing time is not something they have a right to question, then it is okay to come in and we'll talk, but parents are too involved in their kids' lives. I've told kids that it's us, right here in the gym, against everybody else. You have to let go of what everybody else says, and that's a real tension for kids if the parents are critical. It can be destructive to their son or daughter if they do that.

"I never felt pressured by the fans in Fort Loramie. You can be vocal and disagree but that never bothered me because I knew what I had to do. I always felt accepted by those fans. Sometimes I think Loramie fans gave me more credit than I deserved. I always consider the 1981 team that went to regionals more of a personal accomplishment than the team that went to state because when I went to Fort Loramie, the pieces were already in place. They were talented kids with a lot of history who knew how to play the game. I just gave them a little different focus and a little more enthusiasm. That was a great situation. It's a great place to coach, but they have expectations. You better work hard and you better be demanding of the kids. Fans today are a lot more critical and that's because of ESPN and AAU. They see the guys on ESPN criticizing Bob Knight and Mike Krzyzewski and Rick Pitino. What right do they have to do that? How can they say those things? In AAU, it's a whole different ball game coaching against Joe Smith than it is coaching against Fred Nuss [Houston High School coach]. That's a big part of it. We've all become experts."

"The media at the state tournament can be overwhelming. You have people who form opinions of you and your team with no basis in fact. They are generalists, not specialists. One guy at the Brookville Star, Ted Landis, followed us around and had great articles about our kids and our team. My best relationship, though, was with Dave Ross at WMVR. I've never had great relationships with print media, but I've always had good relationships with the radio. If they would ask me a question I didn't like, I could talk it out with them. I tend to ramble and if a print person picks up on something, he could put it in a context I totally don't mean. On the radio, most of the time, you can correct that right away. In print, it's the next day. I would always sit down with a print reporter but I didn't like it and most of the time I didn't like them. They'll tell you I was hard to deal with, and I'm sure I was.

"A rule I don't like is three officials. It has allowed some guys to stay in the game longer than they should have. It gives them a false sense of security about coverage. They don't have to be in condition as much. Some officials don't even work up a sweat in a game."

"A lot of people are afraid of the shot clock, but I'd like to see maybe a forty-five-second shot clock. Watch a college game and see how many times there is a shot-clock violation. You can go to games and not see any. Very few high school possessions go longer than thirty-five seconds. It's not as big a deal as some people think, but I'm not advocating it for high school, though."

Hamlin's experience as an assistant coach at Denison University is a contrast to his days as a high school head coach. He isn't the person who has to make the hard decisions, and because he knows how difficult those decisions can be, he is satisfied to serve in an advisory position to the coach and in a supportive role with the players.

"I have college players who say to me, 'I wish you were the head coach,' and I say, 'Oh, no you don't. Be careful what you wish for.'"

Chapter  Two

FRAN GUILBAULT

ST. HENRY HIGH SCHOOL

1991 STATE CHAMPION
1990 STATE CHAMPION
1979 STATE CHAMPION

*"It's more fun to shake hands with the other
team after you win than after you lose."*

In 1961, Fran Guilbault arrived in St. Henry where he began his career in education and his life in coaching. The first three seasons produced a total of only thirteen wins for his varsity team, so with a "get better or get out" attitude, Guilbault chose the former, embarking on a fourth year that was to be the first of his 35 consecutive winning seasons until his retirement in 1999. Raised in the Upper Peninsula of Michigan in the town of Ontonagon, Guilbault recalls clearing so much snow off his backyard basketball court that the piles formed walls around their playing area. When he was in the seventh grade, a new varsity coach came to town and brought with him a style that Guilbault admired and later emulated throughout his 38 years of coaching. Guilbault, often cited as a source of knowledge and encouragement by many of today's outstanding coaches in Ohio, identifies his inspiration as Coach Guss Lord and traces his own dedication to the game back to those years when he challenged Old Man Winter and won.

"I had an older brother who was a sports nut. He was three years older, so I followed him around. They built a basketball court that was in a field right in our back yard. We were always out there and, of course, up there, you always get two or three hundred inches of snow every winter. We'd be out there shoveling snow and when

we got it cleared, we got a lot of company to play ball. When the wind started blowing, you had to wait until it subsided to see the basket. We didn't have television or anything like that, so whatever was in season was what we played.

"When I was in seventh grade, Guss Lord came to town. I eventually ended up playing for him. He was never an individual who yelled or screamed or anything, and he treated us all well. He made the game fun and I just kind of followed his philosophy. He was the varsity coach there at Ontonagon High School and I copied the way he handled kids. I always wanted to coach although I was more into football when I started. I played freshman football at Western Michigan, and that was when I looked at it and I saw that the head football coach had all these assistants and he didn't do much coaching. In basketball you did your own thing. I never had a varsity assistant, so I did it all.

"I joined the Marines right out of high school. It was right when we were in a kind of recession. I had a football scholarship to North Dakota State University, but finances were a problem since they didn't have full scholarships then. My older brother was in the Marines, and I came pretty close to staying in, thinking I might make it a career, but I guess I wanted the teaching and coaching a little more. Plus, in the service there was always at least one person who outranked you and could make you pretty miserable. I found it wasn't much different in coaching. There was always someone around who could make you miserable, too.

"I enjoyed teaching just as much as coaching. I taught college prep English and American history when I started here at St. Henry. I had my bachelor's degree from Western Michigan and in 1960 I came to Ohio on a one-year teaching assistantship at Ohio University. I was looking around, then, for teaching jobs and at that time, they didn't care what you taught. As long as you had a pulse, they hired you because they were so short of teachers. I was unusual because I had three teaching majors of English, American history and government, and because I was a jock, I had health and physical education, too.

"We looked around in 1961. St. Henry had contacted me. I turned down two or three interviews before I finally came up here because I really wasn't interested, but the athletic director, Art Brophy, eventually sold me on it. I always kidded that he said St. Henry had such a strong basketball program that if you just threw out the basketballs, we would win half our games. Well, I threw them out, but I found out that not many could catch them. So what I thought was going to be great turned into thirteen wins and forty-five losses in the first three years. They were ready to run me out of town. I had an offer for a job I had applied for in the Panama Canal Zone, and I was going to take it. Our superintendent wasn't much into sports, but several people encouraged me to go to the board of education, so I went to the board meeting. There was one board member that I thought was sleeping through it, but finally he looked up and asked what kind of a teacher I was. The superintendent told him he thought I was one of the better teachers, so the board member said, 'I don't know what we're talking about, then. Give him what he wants.' So they gave me a three-year contract. Of course, I guaranteed them I could get them a winning record, and then we ended up with thirty-five winning seasons after that."

Guilbault's coaching methods weren't so much paper and pencil as they were guided practice.

"I never felt I was a good strategist. My idea of coaching was to really work during the week and prepare those kids and then on game night I just literally turned them loose and let them have fun. I never did much coaching during the game because I felt they were prepared. I never diagrammed a play in the thirty-eight years I coached. At practice, we'd walk through it. We'd give the plays names, and then if we needed an out-of-bounds play rather than sit down and diagram it I just told them what we were going to run. I often wondered how a coach could diagram during a time-out because some of the players would be looking at it upside down. So I never did that, and I never used a whistle. I just used my voice.

"A lot of people would say to me, 'Boy, if you hadn't started out with those first three seasons, think what your record would be.' I always told them, 'If I hadn't started out like that I probably wouldn't have the record I have.' I wanted to make sure it didn't happen again. I made it a twelve-month job. When the season ended, I had interviews with kids and went over things. I took care of all my own open gyms. I did all my own scouting. I didn't trust anyone.

"I've had administrators and other people call and ask how I managed to keep the program strong. I told them one way not to keep it is to hire a new coach every other year. When I wrote the history of St. Henry basketball in my eighteenth year, I figured that I had coached against eighty-some different coaches in those eighteen years. Some of these schools change coaches every other year. There's no continuation. I had a reputation of being a hard-nosed so-and-so, and I suppose the Marines helped me there, but I very seldom had to cut players because they knew what I expected and it just kind of took care of itself. I had a philosophy that you had to play all four years in the program. If you quit, you're only going to quit once. I'm not going to let a kid do that and come back and beat out another kid who had been with me all along. Once they dropped out of the program, they were done. I had a lot of them mad at times and we lost some good ball players, but you still had those kids that stuck with you.

"I never thought much about philosophy. The basic idea was to work and have fun. It's more fun to shake hands with the other team after you win than after you lose."

Guilbault began coaching before film was used as a scouting tool or an educational method.

"I read anything I could get my hands on that would make me a better coach. I subscribed to a coaching magazine. I went to clinics. Of course, no coach has anything original. Everything you use, you get from somebody else.

"When I first started coaching, if the ball went out-of-bounds, the clock didn't stop. When they began to stop the clock, you had longer game times. Even before that, a player was given only one free throw, and it was only if he missed the first one that he got the second one. The coach had the choice of shooting the free throw or taking it out-of-bounds. There were some kids who never shot a free throw unless they were first given two.

"In the 1970s it became an up-tempo game. To be honest, now I get bored sometimes because I was an up-tempo coach. I coached over eight hundred games and we averaged over seventy points a game. Of course, there was a reason for that. I never felt I was a very good defensive coach, so I told my teams that we were going to beat any teams we could hold to sixty points or less. We ran, we fast broke, and we pressed all the time. It used to drive me nuts when we'd play Jack Albers because he would slow that down at Marion [Local] and he'd average maybe fifty points a game. Even our own fans would get critical. They'd say, 'Marion plays good defense. They're only giving up forty points a game.' But they were averaging forty-five. We were averaging seventy-five and giving up sixty. I look at the point spread. In my total career the point spread was over twelve points a game, so I felt we were doing something right.

"My philosophy was to press and keep the tempo up. If I wasn't pressing, the game seemed to slow down. Wherever the ball came in play dictated what press we were going to be in or what defense we were going to drop back into. I always told the kids, though, that the best defense was a good offense. I was certainly an offensive coach.

"I did all my own scouting, unless I couldn't see someone [because of a schedule conflict]. Once we got in tournament play, I had to send my junior high coaches to scout, but you hate to assign something like that when it isn't a paid job. One time I tried to get a scouting budget and that got shot down pretty fast. When I scouted, people would want to come up and talk. I couldn't do that because I had to watch the game. When I first started, the ball players would all go with me. It was kind of neat because you had one relationship with them as a teacher, another relationship as a coach, and another in the car. I was kind of like a buddy, but they never forgot who I was. Later on, my own kids went with me and once in awhile, I could talk my wife into going if I was going by myself, but I enjoyed high school basketball. I would keep five newspapers during the season and those were for scouting purposes. I kept a file on every team, and I'd have all their schedules and all their players, and for each game, I'd write the score and what each player scored. Then from the scouting report, I'd deal with the strong points and the weak points of each individual player. I had a scouting part on offense and a part on defense and a part for comments. That would end up being an eight to ten page scouting report. I would run that off over the weekend, and if we had two games, I had two reports. I'd give it to ball players Monday morning. They'd come in and pick it up. I'd have who their starting lineup was and the assignments. So I never went to a game and told them that night which players were our starters. They knew Monday morning. The kids had the report all week and very seldom did I go over it with them.

"We never studied videos together. I was lucky because there was a little storage room across from my classroom and once we started using videos we raised money to buy our own equipment, and I gave them passes to get out of study hall for them to come watch video in that little room. They would go in and study the video, but once in awhile I stuck in a tape of basketball funnies or the *Hoosiers* movie. I'd check up once in awhile to be sure they didn't sneak one of their buddies in. It was for basketball players only. They were usually pretty good about that.

"I never criticized a player in front of others. If I had something to say to them, it was in my office one on one. I didn't talk to the players after a game other than to tell them good game or tough luck. It was too easy to be mad, so I had enough time over the weekend to think about it and take notes on what I wanted to say without being mad. Kids responded to that more. The only reason I had a kid in my office to give him heck is if I thought he was loafing, and we didn't have that situation very often."

In 1979, St. Henry won its first regional championship and the usual excitement of tournament time intensified.

"Every game was a big game. I never looked ahead. Probably the biggest games were Friday nights on a double weekend. If we won that game, it would carry over to Saturday. If you got beat on Friday and had to come back on Saturday, it was tough. St. Henry had good teams before I got here, but they had never even won a district championship. In 1970, we went to the regional for the first time and we got beat in the first regional game by Bowling Green.

"The biggest thrill, though, was probably the regional championship in 1979. In 1979, we won two games at Bowling

Green, and then we came back and there were fire trucks out to meet us. All that was probably because they knew we were going to state for the first time. They were running a bond levy at the same time to build a new addition to the school along with the new gym. They didn't think it would pass but they were going to run it the first time. We came back and they were selling tickets for the tournament on the Tuesday of Election Day. They had a seventy percent turn-out that day. The levy passed easily and we got a big, new gym. I started coaching in the typical, small gym, which seated eight hundred people, if that. After the first couple of years you could have come in and lain in the bleachers because there weren't too many fans there when we were losing. Then they gutted that. What was the length became the width and they put the new addition on and that seated about sixteen hundred, but by then we were really going to town. Then they built the new gym, which seats about two thousand, so I've coached in three gyms here.

"Tournament time is always exciting, especially when you are winning. People get all fired up. In 1990, we moved up to Division III for the first time. It took one hundred and thirty-nine students, and that's what we had. Of course, nobody had heard of us in Division III, so we went down to Columbus and set a new record by winning by forty-some points in our first game. We set the record for the worst beating any team had ever had. The next night we played Youngstown Liberty who was undefeated and ranked number one in the state. After we won that game, then the pressure was on. We went to Division IV the next year and had most of the guys back. Of course, those teams probably could have won in any division. We always had good kids, but it seemed that they became the favorites of a lot of fans down there. I don't know what it is. A booklet from the state tournament was put together here and some guy from Akron had sent a poem, 'The Red Wall,' which was published in it.

"I never raised heck with an official. If I had something to say to an official, I'd wait until a time-out and I'd walk over and tell him what I thought, but I didn't want to do it in front of everybody or try to embarrass him. I don't think officials really influence the game that much. I've seen good ones and mediocre ones and I've seen bad ones, but I don't think I've ever seen a dishonest one. They work at it. We had a JV official once who gave me three technicals for going out on the floor when Chuck Stahl was badly hurt. Three technicals meant I was out of the gym. After the game, I wasn't angry, but I wanted to know what had caused him to do that. He wrote me up for being out of control after the game and I had a heck of time trying to convince the [OHSAA] commissioners that it wasn't like that.

"I was never used to losing as a player, and then as a coach I was 4-15, 4-15, and 5-15. We won one more game the third year because I played my good friend, Al Souder [the first coach in Mercer County to win a state championship in 1971], who was 20-0 with Fort Recovery. Since then I realized that if you're going to have any success, you have to work at it year 'round and you have to sell the players on hard work, which would pay off. We even went around town painting orange squares on the basketball backboards to make them look more like a basket. After that, we put together thirty-five straight winning seasons. It got to the point that if St. Henry had two or three losses in a season, the fans thought there was something wrong. I guess we set the standard and that's where Joe Niekamp had it tough. When I stepped down, Al Summers had a lot of good ball players back, although I don't think I would have gone to state with them. He put in an open-post offense, which I didn't like at all. Those kids could shoot because we always did spend a lot of time shooting, and it really paid off. He had all seniors [who made it to the state final game that year]. Joe had been an assistant and took over after Al's one year of varsity coaching. Then, Joe, in his first year had his work cut out for him after my thirty-five winning seasons and Al's one. I think in his first year, Joe only won about six games. Losing is a big lesson for every coach. An interviewer asked me once about retiring and when I thought I might do it. I told him that I thought about retiring every time I got beat.

"A coach is the worst second-guesser there is. Every time you lose, you think about something you could have done differently. It's a strange business anyway because you put a kid in and he hits two or three threes in a row and you look pretty smart. If he throws it away two or three times, you're a dumb so-and-so for putting him in. There are a lot of instances I can think of that I probably should have done something differently, especially if it was a close game. We've had a lot of those and fortunately, we didn't get beat really bad when we did get beat. I never took players out of a game for making a mistake. I see some coaches who, if kids make a mistake, put them on the bench. I don't think that helps their confidence. If a player was hurt, I would get him out as soon as possible, but otherwise, I'd wait until I could take him out on a positive thing, or he'd be at the end of the bench with his head down. I would more or less take the positive approach. Some coaches really criticize their kids which is fine, but you have to tell them how to do it right. It's easy to chew someone out, but you have to tell them the right way. That's what coaching is, I think.

"When you coach as long as I did, there are a lot of games when things go well. I remember a game against Loramie at Piqua. We were both undefeated at that time and we beat the heck out of them. It just seemed like everything we did went well. I always felt lucky since I had seen teams play in the state tournament and they didn't play very well because of all the pressure. It seemed like the more we advanced, the better we played. We played six games in Columbus when I was coaching and we won them by an average of more than twenty points."

Perhaps his emphasis on offense gave Guilbault his most difficult challenge in practice, and that was teaching defense.

"I would have to force myself to teach defense. I would work on a practice plan to have so many minutes on this and so many on that. All my practices were run with a stopwatch. If I was going to work on certain things for ten minutes, I set the watch. If I thought the other team had a good press, then we'd practice against a seven-man press to make it tougher. Defense wasn't as much fun for my kids. We always practiced full-court, never half-court. If a group was pressing and stole the ball, they would fast-break to score. If the group was on defense and got the ball, they would do the same thing, and then you had to hustle back, so everything was full-court. Our kids always thought practice was harder than games. I was criticized by fans for being a six-man coach. I thought kids had to know what every teammate was doing on the floor, so I never subbed in two or three kids at a time. We played one game against Celina

Immaculate Conception that went into five overtimes and I subbed only one time. It was the only game I ever did that. I remember that game, too, because Wally Post's son, John, was playing and Wally and Joe Nuxhall would come to the games and Joe happened to be at that one. I'm sure the kids got a little tired out and it got to be a long night. People would complain that the players on the bench never had playing time and they wouldn't be ready if they had to go in. I felt that in practice they were going against the best players around and they'd be ready the next year. And they were. Oh, sometimes we'd have to go a little deeper but never unless I really had to."

Guilbault believes that lack of preparation can put a halt to a team's success. Any distractions that take away from mental preparation can deter a team from reaching its goals.

"Lack of practice and lack of dedication are obstacles. I was never one who gave rah-rah speeches, but the kids knew how hard I worked at it because I did everything myself. Fans can be an obstacle by getting into the kids' heads during the season and even during a game. We had certain fans on the sidelines who would constantly yell at the kids, and these are the people who would come up after the game to congratulate them. The kids knew who they were and it was hard on them.

"It's an irritation to have critics who think they know more than you do, and they've never coached. They should come watch practice for a week. It was disgusting at times to hear the way some of the fans would yell at the players. A friend of mine who coached over forty years once told me that for every year you coach in a community, you'll have one person who actually hates your guts and will do anything to run you out of town, and I had them. I used to tell people that I knew I was going to heaven because I'd had all the hell a person could ever get after thirty-eight years. I have former players who got into coaching who said they didn't realize all the trouble and all the work that goes into it.

"So, I never told my coaches what to do. They could run the offense and defense they wanted. I could learn from them, too. I didn't want them to scout. I just wanted them to coach.

"When it stops being fun and starts being a job, although I never got to that point, it's time to give it up. When I had my open-heart surgery in September of 1991, I thought, 'Uh, oh. My wife is going to be after me to give it up.' But after I was at home here for a couple of months, she was all for me staying in it. I convinced the doctor I was healthy enough to go back to work, so I could be at the first practice in November.

"I decided to give it up when I found myself working harder at teaching and not doing a very good job. I always took pride in my teaching, but I couldn't really get into it. The board and the administration agreed to let me coach one year without teaching, so that took care of that. I was on the bubble in my thinking about it, and the board helped me with that decision. I believe, though, that you have to be around the kids during the day, so I only went one year like that.

"Being around the kids and working with them were the biggest rewards of coaching. After we won a game, it was seeing them celebrate, although the more we won, the less they celebrated."

From Guilbault's perspective, the personality of a coach can make a big difference in the direction a team goes.

"It's funny. I never tried to give any advice. I've never been to Joe's or Al's practices. They have to do their own thing. Your personality has a lot to do with how you coach. I used to kid Al that I had to go up in the fifth row of the bleachers to watch his games because he stood up all the time. I never did. I probably got criticized by a lot of people because I never got excited during a game. I remember getting the tape of one of our state championships and the radio announcer said, 'Uh, oh. Fran is getting excited. He just uncrossed his legs.' I felt good because I got complimented by commissioners who told me that was how coaches should act.

"I've seen mediocre coaches win a lot of games, and I might be one of them since I wasn't much of a strategist, but I've seen some very good coaches lose their jobs because they didn't win, and they were good coaches. They just didn't have the horses and that's the key. I always felt that I was successful because I worked harder than most coaches I played against. I may be wrong, but I heard them talk about their assistant coaches covering things like open gyms, and I did all that myself.

"You need dedication and loyalty from your assistant coaches. Those are the two keys. It's always nice if you have a staff that's been with you for a long time. I learned things from my coaches, too. Junior high coaches need to be able to teach the fundamentals. That's the problem with schools that change coaches so often.

"I was nervous before games. There is no doubt about that. I never tried to show it and I tried to relax as much as I could. The toughest part of game night was coming home and having that dead time between the end of the school day and the trip back to the gym. Most of the day I was teaching and I had a period at the end of the day when I could fill out the scorebook and go over the scouting report. I always packed all my own equipment. My wife laundered varsity, JV, and freshmen uniforms all those years so I knew they would be ready. I'd check all the equipment before each game and be sure it was ready. I'd come home for a quick lunch and try to relax. Late in the JV game, I would start to feel nervous. That nervousness was thinking about losing. Even going to Columbus, you really wanted to win, but you hoped you never got trounced or you embarrassed yourself. I always remember beating that team by forty-eight points and reading in the paper the next day that their coach had been asked how he felt. He said he knew one hundred and eighty-some other coaches who wouldn't have minded being in Columbus getting beat by forty-some points.

"I never gave a rah-rah pre-game talk. I would go over their assignments one last time and remind them of what we were going to do on offense and defense. I'd tell them what was going to be our primary press and our secondary press and what defense we would drop back into from that. I basically ran a motion offense. Some people call it a passing game. When I was in high school, they called it freelance basketball. The more you run, the more you get open. If you want to get loose, just keep moving. I never called a play or never ran a pattern. We had a motion offense based on the three keys of pass, cut, and screen. If they didn't get the ball, they'd pop back out to keep the floor balanced. I told them what I thought the keys to winning the game would be. After one pass, there is a twenty-five percent chance you're going to throw the ball away. After two passes, there's a fifty percent chance you'll throw it away. After three passes, it's a seventy-five percent chance. After you make the fourth pass, head back on defense.

"I didn't care who shot and most years we had four or five guys score in double figures. The only times I felt we had bad shots were when someone had a better shot or we didn't have any rebounders. Our goal was to take seventy shots a game. Now they take about forty. If you hit fifty percent of forty shots, you have forty points. If you take seventy and hit thirty, you have sixty points. We put them up.

"At halftime we'd go in the office and look at the stats. We cut up oranges and had orange slices for the kids to chew on. We'd go over the things we had to work on. It's so easy to criticize, but if you don't correct it, you don't gain anything. We just went over things we had to improve on and tell them things they were doing well. I was more the back-slapper type because I gave them more positives. Our kids could switch defenses on their own, so I'd tell them that if they wanted to switch, they could, but if I wasn't happy with it, I'd switch it back. I still wanted them to play the defense they were convinced would work for them. I gave kids a lot more leeway than most coaches did.

"I never gave a post-game talk. Win or lose, I'd wait until Monday when everyone had a chance to cool down and I could think about the game and watch the video and mostly go over statistics. I kept every kind of statistic. I could look at some numbers and figure out percentages in my head.

"Most good coaches I know who got out of the game, left it because they were criticized. They just couldn't take it. They don't shoot coaches, they fire them, so when it was tough those first few years, I knew I might have to find another job.

"The feeling after a loss is tough. It's when you do all your second-guessing. Every year in Ohio, all but four coaches end their season with a loss and they have to live with that loss until the next season. That's the nice thing about winning it all, but that doesn't happen to too many. The toughest thing for me was putting the equipment and uniforms in storage until the next season. I'd take the inventory and pack it away and think about what could have been and the players I was losing.

"You look at the number of schools who have won a state championship and compare it to the number of schools there are, and it's a small percent. We're almost in a class of our own because we've won four, the three when I was coaching and the one with Joe. [At this writing, according to the state tournament souvenir program, Middletown has won seven titles, Columbus East has won five, and St. Henry joins six other schools with four.] The funny thing about it is that when we won the championship in 1979, people were just happy we finally got to Columbus. Then, we broke the ice here by being the first team in any sport at St. Henry to win a state championship. There is no pat answer for how to win a state championship. You have to have the horses and you have to have some breaks along the way. At times, it takes a little luck. It seemed like after we won the district, it was easier going for us in the regional and the state. It seems like once we got to the regionals, we beat the heck out of teams.

"You have to have fun in those games. The first time we went to the regionals, I made a mistake in my approach. I thought 'we got this far and nobody else ever did. What we get from now on is gravy,' and that wasn't a good approach. After that, our goal was winning the state, but still you have to take it one game at a time. And you want them to enjoy it.

"I didn't enjoy the first championship as much as the others because it happened so fast. It all seemed like it was a big dream, but the more I thought about it, the more I realized there were a lot of nightmares in there, too.

"The first time we went down there, I had never coached a Protestant. We went to the state tournament on Thursday and didn't play until Friday so I had a big fish dinner planned for the kids. All the other teams were private schools, so they told me I could get a special dispensation. I told them no because I didn't want to leave anything to chance. Every year that we went down there, we had our fish on Friday. On Saturday, we played for the championship, so we had our steak dinner early in the day and I had never seen so much wasted steak. They were probably a little nervous. That's the toughest part of going to the state tournament, the planning when to eat and getting enough sleep and eating at the right time. It's really tough. I wasn't a great one on diet. My high school coach didn't like to see me eat a candy bar or popcorn, but I didn't even know what my kids had for supper. We never had team meals. I wanted them to go home and eat their normal meals. The only time we ever ate as a team was at the state or maybe after another tournament game. Those kids knew what they liked and maybe even some were a little superstitious about what they ate before a game.

"It used to be that once you had a twenty-point lead, you felt safe in a game. The three-point shot came in and then it was hard to decide when to clear the bench. If you had a twenty-point lead, they could hit a few threes and they were back in the game. We once had a big lead and I cleared the bench, but then the other team came back and I had to put the regulars back in. It was tough for them to get started. I made up my mind then that I would rather be accused of running the score up on a team than blowing a game for my kids. I played it safe."

Guilbault planned his seasons and his practices carefully. He made certain that his players were ready to play every game knowing that the game conditions would be easier than anything they experienced in practice.

"I never had a basketball camp. Camps can get expensive, so I told the kids it would be open gym, and those didn't cost anything. If they went to camp and spent their parents' money, but then they didn't do anything else, it was money down the drain. We had open gyms every Monday and Thursday. There were times I had both gyms going cross court, I had so many kids. I kept attendance records and gave the winners old warm-up jerseys, T-shirts or old uniforms.

"Every summer I would give the kids a jump rope and a pair of ankle-weight spats. I set up a program for them. The biggest thing was jumping rope to build up their legs for rebounding. You'd see kids mowing the lawn or riding a bike with those weights on. In preseason conditioning one year we were running steps. All the others were getting tired, but one boy was running very easily. I stopped him and saw that he had taken all the weights out of his ankle spats.

"I scrimmaged the same schools year after year. I didn't want these tri-scrimmages. I wanted to scrimmage one team. I didn't want them to scrimmage a quarter and sit out a quarter. We'd scrimmage twelve quarters. The first four quarters, we'd play the regulars, the second, we'd play the bench, and the third, we would work with combinations. I usually scrimmaged Russia and Anna, but I also tried to find someone who had many of their players still in the football play-offs as we did.

"We would shorten practice as the season progressed. Even though we did that, we always did two shooting drills, the give-and-go and spot shooting. We wanted to have a weak-side rebounder in the give-and-go because all the studies showed that three out of four shots go long. We spent ten minutes on that drill. Later, we'd do spot shooting in positions all around the key. I had my post players go through that drill, too, because they needed to know where the rebound was going. We were always blessed with good shooters and we put a lot of work in it. Our free-throws were thrown at the end of practice. If you made both shots in a one-and-one, the ball went to the next guy. If you missed the first one, you ran three laps. If you missed the second one, you ran one lap. By the time you got back from three laps, it was your turn again, so you were tired like you would be in a game, and the pressure was on because you didn't want to run again. I'd get a bunch of candy bars, and whoever made the most free throws at each basket would get one. They always had fun with that.

"We tried to set up pressure situations in practice and get them used to it, but it still wasn't the same. There are always some players that like pressure. They want the ball in pressure situations. Other players will kind of go and hide. Leaders, then, naturally seemed to rise. Some led by example. Some were more outgoing. For example, Bobby Hoying was a leader on the championship teams, but when they took the floor, there was no doubt that Scott Brunswick was the leader. He ran the show out there. Everything we did in practice was to get as much competition in there as we could.

"Thursdays were fun nights. We would have shooting contests and they'd take me on, double or nothing. I would shoot the old two-hand set shot. I'd go way out and end up shooting from half-court. I could still slop it in and that just made it more fun for them.

"When we went to the big gym, I always used the jump ropes. Whenever they ran laps, they ran with the jump ropes to work on coordination. I didn't like running lines back and forth. We used basketballs in every drill we ran. I planned the practices and ran them with a stopwatch. Everything we did was full court. We'd start with the first team on man-to-man defense and they had to hold the second team to twenty percent. If you held them to twenty percent, you would go into a two-one-two zone and hold them to twenty percent. If you did that, you would go into another defense and if you held them to twenty percent, you'd go on offense. When you were on offense, you had to hit fifty percent, or you'd go back on defense. Everything was full-court transition all the time. Kids would say that games were easy after practice. Games were thirty-two minutes and we were going for a couple of hours."

While he was coaching his team, it meant that he had less time at home.

"It's tough on a family, and I'm sure my wife wished I'd gotten out of it sooner. I had two sons, twenty-one years apart with five daughters in between, who played for me and they were pretty good ball players. It was even tougher on them because I was tougher on them. People still accused me of playing favorites. Being so dedicated to coaching year 'round made me a pretty mediocre father and a mediocre husband, if they would describe it that well. The girls would say I cared about the ball players more than I cared about them, and I'm sure I was spending more time with the team then. My wife basically raised our family. During basketball season I was home on Sunday nights and Wednesday nights, and those were the nights I worked on my scouting reports. Your social life is basketball. We had friends we'd go to bring-your-own-bottle dances with, but all we talked about, even then, was basketball."

Good teams are built from the team concept. Talent is the cornerstone on which championship teams are built, but no team excels without understanding the importance of each player's role.

"You have to have talent, and you have to convince them that the team comes first. I remember people telling me when Bobby Hoying and all those guys were coming along that I wouldn't have enough basketballs to go around. All five of those guys averaged in double figures. The highest average was around sixteen points a game and the lowest was around twelve points a game. We worked a lot on the team aspect. At least three of those guys could have averaged thirty points a game for somebody else. Scott Brunswick was our point guard. He'd steal a ball and start down the floor. He'd see Bobby was coming and he'd wait so Bobby could slam dunk it. Bobby had sixty-some slam-dunks in his career. He's a good example of working at it. He had an adjustable backboard at home so he'd set it at a lower height when he was young and work until he could stuff it, and then he'd raise it up. A lot of coaches don't encourage it, but I always told the kids that for every slam dunk, I'd buy pop. The kids loved that, and sometimes, they didn't have to buy pop all week long. I always had gimmicks like that, whether it was a candy bar or a dinner, and that's what made it more fun. When we started the season, I told the kids that the first double weekend that we won both games, I'd take them out for a steak dinner. Eventually they wanted all-you-can-eat chicken, so if we won our first five games, that's what we'd do. Then it was every five wins. And when we got into the locker room after one of those games, boy, they'd let me know. That was all I'd hear. Some of those years, what with all the dinners and the pop, it took a lot of my salary. I used to go with them, but they had more fun without me, so I'd give the co-captains the money and tell them to go where they wanted. They ended up most years going to the Casey Jones restaurant in Celina."

Guilbault believes the small school environment contributes to building team chemistry.

"There were so many small schools around a long time ago and you didn't need much equipment to play basketball. That's where it started, and it quickly became a major sport for everyone. I used to say that basketball in St. Henry wasn't a life or death situation, it was more serious than that. That was their weekends then. Football is big now, but when I came to St. Henry, it was only basketball and baseball. With all the fan support, and the gym only held four hundred people, you sold right out. The biggest gyms around when I came here were at Coldwater and at Marion Local. We had such big players like Vern Hoying and Ron Niekamp that we said they would get in those little gyms and touch fingers and that was the whole defense because you couldn't get by them. Coldwater was our biggest rival when I began coaching, but the more we played all these teams around, the more they all became big games. So many times I felt our kids played better on the road than they did at home because we didn't have our fans all around the floor putting pressure on them. When we went to Columbus, I told the kids that it was just like playing at home because St. John Arena had the red lines and markings on the floor."

Even though Guilbault believes the three-point line was the biggest change in the rules during the years he coached, it didn't have a big effect on how his team played the game.

"When we ran the motion offense, we'd set up three-point shots at times, but we weren't a team that shot a lot of them because I used the double post. I wanted my two big men near the basket. In a motion offense they were high post and low post and just moving around there. Really, the biggest effect it had on me was when to substitute. If you wanted to get those kids in who weren't playing, you were a little leery about how quickly that could change the whole complexion of the game."

Guilbault has seen many changes in the game and has had plenty of opportunity to assess their influence. He has mixed emotions about the three-point shot but is convinced that a shot clock is needed in high school.

"One good thing is that they now stop the clock when the ball goes out of bounds, so now kids are up and down the floor for thirty-two minutes. They clocked football and it showed that kids only actually play twelve minutes, so basketball is a different kind of conditioning. People think you're going to be in good condition if you play football, but it's different.

"I've had mixed emotions about the three-point line. At times I liked it, and I really enjoy it now, but I always worried about it at the end of a game. It hurt my bench because they didn't get in the game.

"The biggest change is that for some reason the game has really slowed down. I think sometimes a lot of these young coaches want people to know they are coaching, so they slow down the game to show that they have everything under control. Maybe it's more emphasis on defense, but I just turned them loose and enjoyed it.

"Of course the biggest change I favor is the shot clock. That would speed the game back up. I'm sure they'd want longer than thirty seconds, but that's what I'd like. I also think the game has gotten more physical because the officials referee more like a college game.

"We never really had a booster club for many years and our first boosters were for football, but they always treated me well. We had a shoot-a-thon and raised quite a bit of money. I'd give that back to the kids to help with the cost of their shoes, and we put red carpeting in the locker room and put in a stereo system. So we never actually did anything with the boosters because we had our own money. It was kind of nice that way. All our equipment belonged to us.

"League voting for the All-Star team is terrible. Most coaches are going to vote for the best, but some want their own kids to make it so they vote and give some kids a bad deal. If you're going to pick an All-Star team, there's no fair way. If every coach would do it the same way, it would be fair, but that's not the case. All-Star teams never excited me as a result. Voting for state teams was the same way. Some coaches would send out pages of information on their players and a lot of it wasn't related to basketball. I never did that. If our kids made it, fine. I never really worried about it, though. I voted who I thought the best players were.

"I'd like to have teams seeded at tournament time by records instead of by voting. I always messed it up at the drawing because our kids never wanted a bye. If we were lucky enough to get seeded first or second, I'd jump in and play right away.

"I always said the more successful you were as a coach, the less you got paid that season. I'm happy that I was able to get the board to pay a coach a little more each time the team advanced. You're spending more time practicing and you have more games. I got them to put in a longevity pay increase, too, for more years coaching."

Since Guilbault coached against so many other coaches, he saw many different styles and respected them all.

"You really had to respect every coach you went against, or you'd be in trouble. Some became better friends. I think Bob Arnzen is a top-notch coach and a top-notch individual. When Al Souder was at Fort Recovery we became good friends because we went to every clinic and every meeting together. Some you didn't like but that didn't mean you didn't respect them. I'm sure there were plenty around who didn't like me."

An even, steady, persistent confidence characterizes the good coaches to Guilbault's way of thinking.

"A good coach coaches the same way all the time. I hardly called time-outs because I felt we were in better condition than the other team was. We were going to run, and we were going to press. I didn't want to call time-out to rest them. When we won the state championship in 1979, I called two time-outs in the whole tournament and that was after we were way ahead at the end. Our practice time prepared us, so I didn't have to call a time-out. If someone was making a run, once in awhile I might have to, but I didn't run into that problem very often. It was the same with technical fouls. I had maybe three of those in my whole career. I never wanted to let a team score because of me, and as far as using them to fire up kids, I never believed that.

"Our pace was up-tempo. We always attacked on defense and we always attacked on offense. We wanted to press and we didn't want to pass that ball around too much. If we had to set up an offense, we were still going to attack them. We made the fewest passes we could possibly make. We just wanted to go at them. I always wanted a fast break. We never walked the ball up the floor. We always pushed it.

"I get a kick out of listening to people who interview for a coaching job who say they'll see what kind of personnel they have before they decide how they're going to play. My personnel had to fit to me. I didn't fit to them. We worked and even when we didn't have the type of team that should do that, we managed to get it put together. I couldn't coach slow-down basketball for nothing."

The players who could play this type of game for Guilbault had the key qualities of dedication and willingness to work.

"Players had to be willing to work. And you have to be careful because you have kids who play three sports. You can't have them doing something that will affect what they have to do for the other sports. Naturally, you want someone who is coachable. You want a team player and that was never a problem for me. In all the years I coached, I only had a few players who averaged more than twenty points a game, and we scored a lot of points. It's always been balanced. If they all weren't that type of player, I wouldn't have had the success I did. What always impressed me about our kids was that the seniors treated the underclassmen as equals. Each year, the new seniors always treated the new freshmen the same way. On the bus the cheerleaders would lead the Rosary and the basketball players would answer. Before a game, the last thing we would do before we took the floor was join hands for an 'Our Father' but not to pray that we would win. In those first few years when I started coaching and we were getting beat, oh, I was down on my knees praying, but it didn't do any bit of good at all. You don't pray for wins. That's selfish. We just prayed that we would play our best and that no one would get hurt. We were a public school and there might have been someone who didn't like it, but it's just something we always did."

Guilbault had several favorite drills that covered a number of skills.

"We had a hamburger drill that was a three-on-three around the bucket. I would throw the ball up, not wanting it to go in. They'd have to rebound and anything goes. We had guys bleed at times. It really got physical. Whoever got the rebound tried to score and all the other five would try to keep him from scoring. We had five-and-go jumpers and spot shooting. Our transitional basketball was full-court. We also had free-throw shooting drills."

Some of his players went on to play college ball but Guilbault never felt it was his responsibility to get them to that level. He was part of a broad network of coaches, though, and he worked the Miami University camp for many years, so he was able to make contact with college coaches quite easily when necessary.

"I don't think our job as coaches is to develop college players. Our job is to make them the best basketball player and person they can be. I sent out letters to colleges with information on players if I thought they were good prospects. Today, you can help the kids with videos that we didn't have when I started."

Guilbault credits the small schools and the parental support as the underlying elements of success for a team. He was a parent of players, as well as their coach, so he saw both sides.

"For a coach, you want the parents to encourage the kids. During a time-out, I only had sixty seconds, so it became a dictatorship. I didn't have time to get players' advice and I didn't have time to go up in the bleachers and get their parents' advice. You hope parents don't second-guess the coach, but it's a problem because they do. I was lucky. I didn't have too many of these around. When you had them it was difficult at times. I see myself as a parent and it's hard to look at it objectively. I always told my wife that if I lived a real good life, my reward when I die will be to coach in an orphanage. I won't have any parents to deal with. I had one parent who never had a good thing to say about me, even though I coached several of his children. Fortunately, other people didn't pay any attention. Early in my career I had the reputation of being bull-headed and unwilling to listen to anybody. After awhile, it starts getting to you. When I had my heart surgery, the doctors told me it was stress-related, but I was just coming off two state championships. They explained that the most stressful jobs today are coaching high school basketball and high school football in a small town because you have all those people who are going to be on you. You get in a city school and they don't have that big of a backing. But then I retired and got rid of all that kind of stress. Now it's a computer and a cell phone to try to figure out.

"I think I understood how parents felt, but I'm not the sympathetic type. My youngest son broke a training rule when he was a freshman. I realized it when he came home one night, so I made him turn himself in to the athletic director. I expected more from my sons. I told them I believed in a second chance. I told them that my talking to them was their first chance. The fans get on them more quickly so it was hard on me."

These sons, though, were his presenters when he was inducted into the Ohio High School Basketball Coaches Association Hall of Fame in 2001. This honor came amid the other distinguished achievements which include the AP Coach of the Year in 1980, the UPI Coach of the Year in 1991, The NFCA Coach of the Year in 1992 and 1993, the Paul Walker award in 1991, and the Bob Arnzen Award in 1979. He was named League Coach of the Year eleven times and District 8 Coach of the Year six times.

"Parents all want their kids to play and most treated me well. The hard thing was the parents that were really nice. I did establish a rule that I wouldn't get friendly with any parents that I would visit with, because it makes it tough on the kids. There are a lot of nice people around here that we could have, but it was only after it was all over that we did.

"We also had a great relationship with the press here. I always cooperated with them because I knew that we wanted positive coverage. As you start advancing in the tournament, though, you get phone calls from people asking the dumbest questions, such as, 'What do you have to do to win?' Well, the answer you'd like to tell them is that you have to score more points, but I went through the spiel of rebounding and cutting down on turnovers. One was kind of funny from the first year [1979]. A paper from Mansfield called and said it was really something to have four parochial schools playing for the championship and they had put together a two-page spread on the story. I had to give him the bad news that St. Henry was a public school. Jim Lachey, one of my former players, said he was watching one of the tournament games in the 1990s and the fans started yelling, 'Recruiting, recruiting,' not knowing we were a public school. When you get in the press room in Columbus, they're mostly asking you about your team. One time, though, we had won our semi-final game and the other one had yet to be played between Tri-Village and Columbus Wehrle. They kept asking me about what I thought of Wehrle because they were the big team from a parochial school. I said, 'Hey, you know what? There's another team down here that's going to play the game against Wehrle and they're pretty good.' The [OHSAA] commissioner complimented me on saying that about Tri-Village to the press, and then Tri-Village won and we played them for the championship."

And a very good team won.

Chapter  Three

JACK ALBERS

MARIA STEIN MARION LOCAL HIGH SCHOOL

1984 STATE SEMI-FINALS

"I always consider the odds that indicate the best percentage of success. It's all a matter of checking the numbers. Being a mathematician in coaching is really helpful. It's a game of numbers and probability."

In his seventeen years of coaching, Jack Albers compiled an impressive record of tournament appearances, recalling that many of his losses in that span came at the hands of eventual state champions or runners-up. Albers became the head coach at Marion Local in 1979, succeeding Irv Besecker who had led the Flyers to a state championship in 1975. As Besecker's assistant coach, Albers had a taste, then, of what it was like to get to the state level, and he understood what it took to get players to perform at their peak.

Monroeville beat Marion Local in the state semi-finals in 1984, in the Flyers' only appearance at the tournament under Albers, and went on to win the championship. In the following year, the Flyers had only had two losses the entire season and they were both to Jackson Center, who then won the championship in 1985. Albers felt sure his team would beat Jackson in the regional semi-final game, even though Jackson had prevailed in the regular season, but a repeat appearance at the state tournament wasn't to be.

Albers, the epitome of intensity and perseverance, gleaned as much as he could from Besecker, college coach Bobby Knight, and professional coach Del Harris who on one occasion sent Albers a personal note recognizing his success at Marion Local. Albers began immediately in his first year of coaching to search for ideas and learn as much as he could.

"I went to many clinics. The first one was at Walsh College. It was Adolph Rupp's last clinic presentation. I felt incredibly privileged to be part of that. Bobby Knight was there, along with John Wooden and an incredible lineup of coaches. Once I listened to those people and their stories and their ideas and their thoughts, a lot of it was reinforcing. My common sense was telling me those things, but I didn't know if what I was doing was right or wrong, and when I heard these people say it, it just excited me about the prospect of coaching basketball. I went on to serve as the president of the District 8 Basketball Coaches Association, the largest association of coaches in the state of Ohio. I remember Randy Ayers was coaching at that time at Ohio State. Bobby Huggins was at Cincinnati. Also, I was fortunate enough to work Ohio State clinics beginning back when Eldon Miller was at Ohio State. The fraternity of coaches is pretty broad in terms of the contacts I've been fortunate to have."

The game itself is instructive, as well, Albers has learned.

"In a three-way scrimmage, we were playing Van Buren. I had a junior who struggled. Every time he made a mistake, he'd follow it with a mistake. He was a pretty talented player, though. We were playing defense and this player stole the ball, went down the floor, and missed a wide-open lay-up. This was near the end of the quarter and a few seconds later he stole the ball and missed another lay-up. When the quarter was over, I went out on the floor, put my arm around him, and said, 'I don't know what happened, but you're going to be a great player. It's what you did after you missed the lay-up that is going to make you a great player. You went down the floor and played as if nothing had happened. You're going to make those lay-ups because this is pre-season, but the attitude you had after you missed those epitomizes what it takes to win in this game.' He ended up, at the state tournament in Columbus, being my point guard.

"In our district final game against Minster, with only a little time left on the clock the same player looked at me in a way I understood. What he was saying was that it was late in the game and we were down by four in the fourth quarter and he wanted to go late-game defense. He had emerged as this coach who knew the game and understood it. It was too early for that move, and he understood that, too, but we came back and beat Minster in overtime. My nephew was playing on that Minster team, and it was tough. These family connections between these opposing teams make you appreciate the effort given by both sides."

Albers learned from respected mentors and his experiences how to establish high expectations for his players and his teams.

"One of the things I expected was incredible intensity on the defensive side of the floor. It was inexcusable not to provide optimum intensity. There are two totally different personalities necessary for success in the game of basketball. The defensive end of the floor requires sheer, absolute intensity. The offensive side requires confident poise and a good decision process. With my own personality, being as emotional as I was, I felt that it was difficult to get a kid to really know that he needed to do things with every God-given talent he had and to keep in mind that a whole different personality has to emerge on both ends of the court. I found it a real challenge to get kids to understand that and appreciate that.

"Unless you had a good rationale for something, you needed to do things the way I expected them to be done, and I was pretty relentless on that. There were certain things that could only be done the way we asked you to do them. There were certain areas where we just weren't tolerant. I didn't care if you were the only player on the floor; individualism is something we just weren't tolerant of. Training rules required sacrifice for the rest of the team and failure to follow them indicated selfishness which was not going to provide optimum performance for the team.

"Anytime you put your own statistics or your social life ahead of the team then it was time for you to pursue other avenues, and for us to keep you on the team would not maximize our abilities. It's difficult to see an individual becoming individualistic and breaking down the team chemistry. When that happens, it's time for the coach to say, 'We may be better off not playing you because we may be better without you.' Sometimes you can justify that with statistics.

"As a math teacher, I was a numbers guy. Statistics can be misleading, though. A parent might come to me and say that a player had a high efficiency rating and wonder why he wasn't playing. Well, he was playing at the end of the game when there was less talent out there on the opposing team. You can get misled by what you see. Putting statistics in the hands of those who abuse them can be dangerous, and posting statistics in the newspaper doesn't really lend itself to good team chemistry.

"I remember an outstanding defensive player who set a record for steals, but he gambled too much. I told him he had to stay in the framework of our defense. You're jumping out there, and when you miss that steal, you give up a wide open shot, and in our defense we cannot do that. He listened to what I asked him to do, and his senior year he stayed within the framework of our defense and became a much better defensive player. Statistics can be misleading, and this is an example of a statistic that was actually bad. He set a record in steals but killed us by giving up too many open shots. Shooting percentage is another thing. A parent once came to me saying, 'You told my son not to shoot.' I said to the parent that I told him not to shoot in certain locations because he was only shooting ten percent. He needed to get where he could make a shot.

"The overriding principle was that I expected my players to give all their God-given talents every second of their performance. We have one shot at life. It's not a dress rehearsal. This opportunity to compete in these high-interest communities in Mercer, Shelby and Auglaize counties is incredibly exciting.

"When we played in the holiday tournaments, we'd go to Dayton and scout where there were only sixty people in the gymnasium. That isn't fun, but you come in here, and people are hanging from the rafters. It's excitement. And to be quite honest, my players' parents over the years have been very good. It was a wonderful experience that I enjoyed immensely with my players and my assistants. God blessed me in the sense that he gave me the opportunity to coach, and he blessed me by allowing me to coach in this particular area. There can't be any more exciting basketball than there is in this area. It was a ball."

Albers grew up in neighboring Minster where he had seen the same excitement for basketball that he experienced as a coach in Maria Stein. He was a farm boy and an admitted sports nut.

"Competitive drive came from my being a fourth child with three older brothers. It was competitive in our family from the get-go. I tried to carry that over to my team. We had this one shot to put it on the line, and when they didn't, I was extremely demanding that they bring a higher intensity level than they were giving."

Even when he was in college in Rensselaur, Indiana, the environment was much like that of home, so he came back to the farm country that was a comfortable setting for him.

"The ancestral background here breeds a large person. The genetic background is typically a lot of tall Germans and a lot of these people stayed here. The work ethic and the ties to family are important to really developing the unselfishness necessary for team success. I remember when I was the District 8 Basketball Coaches Association president and Bobby Hoying was playing for St. Henry. His statistics, because he was playing with such a great St. Henry team, were not that phenomenal since he was such a great team player. He had good statistics but his points weren't that high. One player of each division was selected to play in the state All-Star game, and he was not the person who won the vote from his division. There were two at-large nominations for the state All-Star game, and I thought he was deserving of playing in that game. The coaches listened to what I had to say and selected him as an at-large player. And guess what? He was selected the MVP of the All-Star game. That typifies the kids from this area. They aren't just looking for their own personal statistics; they're looking for what's necessary for the team. That unselfishness certainly lends itself to the athletic success of this area. That stems from the home life. It certainly doesn't hurt to be a little bigger, either. That's advantageous, but the family and church ties are important. That experience epitomizes the team play our kids in this area exhibit."

It is difficult for Albers to rank in order of importance the big games in his experience as a varsity coach.

"There were a huge number of big games. Every team I coached had a big game. If I say, 'This was the biggest game of my career,'

I do a disservice to every player I ever coached. Every game we played was the biggest game at that time, and we were going to give it everything we had to win that game. It didn't make any difference if we were playing in Columbus or the regionals or the district or the regular season.

"When the game is over, though, it's over. It's foolish to second-guess yourself. It is a game. All fans have the right to critique and second-guess the coach, but if you set a tone in your community that makes the players second-guess what's expected of the coach, you're part of the problem and you're no longer part of the solution. What makes it enjoyable for fans to watch is the energy that's given by the players on the floor. When I made my decisions, I made them based on my experience as a coach. I didn't see anyone else out there who had the same kind of experience and the contacts and the expenditure of time that I had to be able to make the kind of decisions I needed to make as a coach. Unless I was a full-time coach and wasn't a teacher where I could spend even more time, my life wasn't coaching. It was teaching and coaching, so when it's over, it's over. I rarely second-guess myself. Now, is there something that if that same situation or scenario would come up again, I would do differently? Very possibly."

Albers recalls a situation that still is difficult for him to understand why and how it happened.

"We played St. Henry in the district final in my first year of coaching. We had been in the match-up zone from beginning to end. They had two All-Ohio players who could hit the downtown shot. They were stroking everything. With ten seconds left in the game I decided that there's not a chance in the world that anyone would go man-to-man, but that's what we did. We went man-to-man. I think it was a mistake on Fran's [St. Henry coach Fran Guilbault] part to devise a play that would only work on man-to-man. Our zone would have stopped that play cold, but they got a lay-up. Did he second-guess me? I find that hard to believe because we had hardly played man-to-man all year. I'm not sure. I don't know. Sometimes, you're rolling the dice out there. Based on the probability, as a mathematician, I thought it was the best call for our team to make. It's foolish to go back and say you would change it. I always consider the odds that indicate the best percentage of success. It's all a matter of checking the numbers. Being a mathematician in coaching is really helpful. It's a game of numbers and probability."

Some games are good examples of when talent and probability mesh to create a seamless, fluid performance. Albers recalls a few of those times that the team seemed to be demonstrating clinic-level performance.

"We were at our best when we put our God-given talents on the line to the utmost. Sometimes we overwhelmed teams, but that was secondary."

One time, in the deep winter, Albers gave Mississinawa Valley all they could handle – and, with a couple of unusual events away from the court, more.

"The game began with everything our JV team was putting up going in. After the game, one of our players made some derogatory comments and a lady came up to me just ripping on me. I apologized and said that was not typical of our players, but I had to excuse myself to get in the locker room for the varsity game. She wouldn't let up. She was really upset. I promised her I would take care of the player. She was adamant because the comment just really, justifiably, set her off. So in the varsity game, we came out there and it was the same thing. Every one of our balls went in the hole. We smoked them pretty good. After the game, their coach and I were talking and the lady who had ripped on me came into the room. The coach introduced me to her. She was his wife. She had settled down by then, though, and everything was pretty cool. Well, that day was very cold, and I was the bus driver, too. They had told me to park near the locker room because it was so cold and it would be closer for our kids to get into the building. After the game, I looked around and didn't see anything, so I got in the bus and backed up. And then, bam! I hit something. The kids in the back of the bus said, 'Coach, you hit a car! It's a white Cadillac!' I got out of the bus. The windows were all frozen over. I saw the Cadillac and I saw some kids from Mississinawa walking out. I asked them, 'Do you know who owns this car?' They said, 'Yeah, that's the coach's car.' So I sent my assistant, Keith Westrick, in and he said to the coach and his wife, 'We backed into your white Cadillac.' She looked up at him [in exasperation] and asked, 'What are you trying to do to us?' There are so many of those types of stories that you can laugh at now.

"I remember getting upset on the bench with an official's call. Bill Elking was my assistant at that time, and both of us came up off the bench at the same time. I swung my arms, hitting Bill in the head – and almost killed him. Another time, when I was the assistant coach, we were playing Indian Valley South in the state championship game at St. John Arena. They had church-pew benches there. There was a call made that caused all of us to come off the bench at once. I was the last one to start up, but the back of my sport coat was caught in a crack of the bench that was created when everyone was sitting on it. When they all jumped up, the crack closed on my jacket. It jolted me like a rocket, and there I was sitting on the bench with a ripped sleeve. It seems like every year something like that happened. I remember when I was just a young coach and probably pretty brash. There was a terrible rule change that coaches weren't allowed out of their seats. Before that rule was implemented, I was in Lima with a bunch of officials and coaches. I [slid off the edge of my chair, holding on to it with one hand] and asked if that was in my seat or out of my seat. There was no answer for that, so I was ignored. That rule did get changed, though."

These lighter moments came after the preparation and work, which wasn't easy. Albers found that the most difficult part of the game to teach was good shot selection.

"It's true that what is a good shot at one time, isn't a good shot at another, but good shot selection was always something that players had difficulty understanding. When is it a good shot and when isn't it? We have to feed on the situation and momentum.

"A coach has to make sure players have the confidence and reassurance to make good decisions while they are playing. If players believe in what the coach expects, then you have the chemistry necessary for success. When you have hesitation and doubt, that's when there's a problem.

"I gave this advice to young coaches. We aren't paid enough to make it a livelihood. It's a hobby. When it becomes such that is causes problems with your family, it's time to hang it up. I did not retire under those circumstances. It was a tremendous time factor and when I began to have grandchildren, it was time to give it up. It was time for me to prioritize my family, although I had been doing some of that all along. On my twenty-fifth wedding anniversary, I had our assistant coach take the team to the holiday tournament. When my daughter graduated from Ohio State on a Friday in December, I did the same thing.

"Another time, I grabbed a kid for a substitution. And when I did that, the kid stumbled. He and I both knew it wasn't because I took hold of him, but on the tape it looked awful. The bad part about that incident was that my parents were there for parents' night. They didn't say a word, but the fans' perception was such that it was appropriate that I showed I disagreed with what I saw and that I did not feel good about that. I felt it was appropriate for me to suspend myself for one game.

"I always ran technical fouls. My players weren't supposed to get technical fouls, but they ran if they did. So I ran my technical fouls to discourage that kind of thing and promote the behavior we wanted.

"Wasting time bothers me, too. It's the same thing as in the classroom. I'll never forget in practice one time I heard one of my players say, 'Hey, Coach isn't looking.' That sent me through the roof. What kind of incredible stupidity is that? Coach isn't looking so you can screw around? The more you screw around, the more you become less of a player than you could be. Then you wonder why you are on the bench. What kind of nonsense is that? I shouldn't have to be in the proximity for you to be following the instructions we've set. Players should do that simply to become a better player. I can't fathom why in the world you would waste time and not optimize your ability to play basketball. Life is too short for us not to give the task at hand everything we have. Who have you cheated? You've cheated yourself. Getting that across to my players was a high priority and when that didn't happen, I was irate.

"For new coaches, I would say not to prioritize wins and losses as the most important. If you keep your focus on optimizing the abilities of your players, and you stay on task, you might finish at 2-18 but it will be a wonderful season. Records don't dictate lifelong learning which can be far more important. Sometimes I question how much you really get when you win that state title. Some teams never have to overcome the adversity that really transpires in people's lives. When you think of the ups and downs in people's lives, when you overreact to the joys, the fall down is so far that people can't handle it. When you get that state title, don't jump too high, so that when the deaths and some of the real tragedies in your life occur, you can deal with those. Successful people minimize the highs and maximize the lows. Get them all up to a nice even pathway in life.

"Nobody is living or dying with the outcome of the game. It makes no sense to me not to give it everything you have, but when it's over, it's over. The priority is family and if basketball is invasive to that, it's a problem. One of the things that bothered me about some coaches is that everything was basketball. That's not right. Kids need time with their families. You should ask what you can do to make yourself better for the next time you compete. Most families understand that. Family is important. We try to work around that schedule because it's number one. Whatever schedule families had, we tried our best to work around that schedule. [On the other hand], I've seen coaches who have let parents get involved in the program, and that's a mistake. Their role is to support their kid while they are playing. Anytime that you bring in people who have not had the same training you have and you give them a role in your program, it interferes with making good decisions. Definitely allow a network of respected colleagues to be people you can communicate with to bounce things off of. The bigger circle of knowledge you have, the better it prepares you."

The fraternity of coaches is a close one for the most part because other coaches are often the only ones who can fully understand the complexities of that role.

"I remember as a JV coach playing Fort Recovery. Nothing was going right for them, so their coach called time-out after time-out. Things were still going really badly for him, so he looked at me and said, 'Jack, how about a time out? Will you call a time-out for me?' So, I did. That's what coaches do for each other. In the heat of that competition, we are incredibly competitive, but we are very close in terms of the respect we have for each other. It's an unspoken thing that you can't put your finger on. Bob Arnzen at Delphos was a real inspiration to me. His demeanor didn't change after a game. He was always complimentary of you and your team. He was the kind of guy I really enjoyed coaching against."

For Albers, game days were a time to focus. His expectations for himself and his players were at their peak.

"I focused on success. Failure was not an option. It didn't mean you weren't going to lose; you just knew that when you went out there, you expected to win. If you give it everything you have there is no consideration as to the possibility for loss. Regardless of who we played we felt we were the best team and we were going to go win. At least, I always felt that. I never felt that we were going to play and get our butts beat. I probably should have felt that way, playing St. Henry with Hoying and those guys. I felt that if we did what we were supposed to do, by golly, we were going to be right in there and have the chance to win the ball game.

"One time we had a terribly late game in the tournament against North College Hill, but my expectations for players were always high. I expected their social behavior to be a model for the school. Negative modeling of behavior was not tolerated. I expected them to be at school after that late game. They were all there. On Saturday, we played Dayton Jefferson and we only got beat by four points by a team that was blowing people out. My expectations for players were higher than those for any other kids in the school. In fact, it was quite the opposite from the usual idea of players as prima donnas. They were expected to be the leaders. Any misbehavior spoke contrary to the expectations of the team concept."

Albers had a general plan for his teams before, during, and after the games. Prayer was the focal point, but focus on playing the best possible game followed close behind in those discussions.

"Our pre-game prayer asked God for us to play to the best of our ability and to protect the teams. During halftime we made adjustments. If we were getting hurt inside because we weren't physical enough, I would tell them, 'The officials are allowing the game to be physical. You have to get after it. You have to play the game according to how they let you play.' If they were running a tight game out front, players had to quit the reaching and get their feet there. Offensively, we tried to provide insights, but if they were doing something I didn't see on the scouting report, I'd tell them and we'd make adjustments based on what we saw in the first half. The post-game talk was never dictated by wins or losses. It depended on performance. We always had a team prayer, and then we looked at the good and bad of the game and what we needed to do for the next game.

"But always remember that coaching is a sacrifice for your family. I remember that if I had a discouraging loss, I would get home and see one of my little daughters and it would make me think, 'What am I getting excited about?' You can't make it so important that it invades what is really important, and that is your family. When you see it impacting your marriage you better start looking at if it's worth it. I have had fans come back and say they couldn't sleep after a loss. I always slept like a baby. It was over. You can't change it. We had a great season. We had fun. If we'd won the state championship, maybe that wouldn't have been as good a lesson for the players. Now when adversity hits, they know what adversity is. We went through it, and it's OK. The sun came up the next day. Did we look at the season as twenty-five wins or did we see it as a regional loss?"

A person interested in coaching should have the essential qualities of resilience, perseverance, and enthusiasm. Establishing high expectations and being respectful to the players are additional needs for the potential coach.

"Some people misconstrue that word, 'respect.' They think that ripping on a kid is not respecting a kid. My contention on that is that if I'm telling your kid, 'Here's how it needs to be done,' I'm trying to get more playing time for your son, so I'm respecting your son as a potential player. I'm pretty strong on my expectations, so I came across sometimes as domineering, and maybe I was, but this is the way it had to be done to be successful based on my experience and listening to people who had already had that success.

"Success comes when every player plays to the optimum of his teammates' abilities. In other words, if your strength is being a shooter, then we're going to get you the ball in the position where you can shoot it. If your strength is a rebounder, we'll get you in a position to display that. The really good teams were the ones who were able to recognize all the strengths of the team and play to the strengths of every one of the players on that team. A lot of people call that 'team chemistry.'"

The biggest rivalry for Marion Local in Ohio's breadbasket of basketball was St. Henry.

"St. Henry was our biggest rival simply because we had some great games in full gyms and because of their proximity to our school district. We'd play two games in the season and usually play again in the tournament. The first year we played, there were some really strange things in that gym. A guy who sat behind me kept catching my hair in his hands when he clapped and I didn't know if he was trying to intimidate me as a coach or what. And then he must have kicked a water bottle so the back of my jacket was completely soaked. I kept thinking, 'Jack, keep your cool.' I think that might have been a good experience because I never did anything as bizarre as Bobby Knight did. I had the demeanor very similar to that, so I had to be cautious. Woody Hayes and Bobby Knight had the same personality I had. At that level you really have to govern it and be careful."

True to his development as a coach, Albers attempted to coach all his players to their potential in every game, regardless of the score at any given time in the contest.

"Once the game was determined, and I didn't care when that was, I coached every player to the optimum of his ability. I remember an acquaintance of mine, a Fort Loramie fan, the year they won the state tournament, leaving our gym and [being critical] of my calling a time-out at the end of the game. I had called the time-out because the kids were not playing up to what my expectations were. I believed that our kids deserved to be coached as much as the ones who started the game. Those kids gave me their heart and soul. I shouldn't bother to check their performance? That's nonsense. I loved every kid I coached, and they all deserved to be coached. I called a time out because they were embarrassing themselves and I was going to be sure they were relaxed and comfortable on the floor. Just because they weren't starters was totally irrelevant. It's easy to play when your name gets heralded in the newspapers, but what if you're the player who gets the very rare playing opportunity and you've stayed there all the time and practiced all the time? I think those kids come out much stronger because they are ready for life. They went through it. They put all this time, energy and effort into it. Their part in the success of the team is really neat because our team was fortunate enough to have some success. Some teams never get that chance, and yet those kids stay in there, day in and day out. Those kids are ready for life. Some parents think their kids don't get a chance to play so they encourage them to quit. That's foolish because their kids can benefit unbelievably. They are busting tail not getting any notoriety, so when bad things happen in life to someone like that, they're resilient."

Albers freely admits that he prioritized his season by setting his goal to win every game.

"A couple times I remember my players went to play in summer leagues, and I couldn't stand to watch them because they were doing stuff that I thought ran counter to what I considered good team play. I was really bothered by those leagues and discouraged my players from competing in them. The discipline we modeled in our program was anything but that. The kids thought those leagues were fun, but I told them that if they played like that, they would embarrass themselves in the regular season, and I didn't call that fun. This is nonsense. This is not the way the game is meant to be played. Gambling on defense by attempting to steal all the time and hot-dogging was absolutely ludicrous and I couldn't stand to watch it. I guess I'm a control freak because when my kids were out there, they needed to be doing the good fundamentals of basketball, so if you were doing something counter to that, I got distraught.

"I had open gyms in the summer and a camp for the younger kids. High school kids didn't go to camp. They could go to camps they chose to go to. I worked camps at Ohio State and Ohio Northern. I did take them to Cincinnati my last couple of years coaching. Team camps weren't really that commonplace at that time. I've been retired twelve years and team camps only started surfacing at the end of my career.

"I was one of those who didn't have a lot of pre-season conditioning. I always felt that if you get into it too much, you wouldn't be hungry for it. Plus a lot of my kids were in football anyway.

"My practices were break-downs on everything. There wasn't a lot of scrimmage time. Everything was broken down into scenarios. Defense was half-court when I could emphasize what needed to be done. Offense was the same way. Full court drills. If we needed to practice press offense, then we would practice press offense. If we were going transition we would practice offensive transition. There was very little time when we would scrimmage because it was hard for me as a coach. I could only watch certain things. If I had to see whether or not you were playing solid defense, I had five guys I was watching. I don't know how people can see all that. I can't do that. I thought I had to have control of everything my players had to do for me. If they weren't meeting our expectations, we had to stop, correct it and let them know what was necessary for them to do it correctly. My practices were typically eight minutes of this, eight minutes of that, eight minutes of that, eight minutes of that. The only time we went longer than an hour and a half or two hours was when a drill went long. Then it messed up my time schedule.

"One of the simple drills had a lot of fundamentals for throwing the ball with intensity because I wanted really, really hard passes. When you throw a pass hard and you have your players stepping back to the ball it was impossible to intercept it. We would run it competitively so it was a lot of action with a lot of intensity and it promoted good fundamentals. Another drill was just running the post defensively. It was kind of a boring drill, but every time the ball would move on the perimeter, the defensive man would have to beat the offensive man to the ball. If you allow the offensive man to beat you to the basketball, he's going to have you on his back and have the dominant control and allow the ball to enter the post. In terms of our thinking, we owned the post. Nobody gets the ball in the post. If you get the ball into the post, somebody broke down. The post was ours and you can't allow that to happen. It taught that when the ball moves, you move. If you have to think about it, you're too late. It has to be an automatic reaction. Jump to the ball, jump to the ball, jump to the ball. The kids hated it, but it was a powerful fundamental drill. Then we did rebounding drills. I felt rebounding drills were something that should be done strictly as a matter of turning your head when you saw a shot. It doesn't matter how you check that person out. Do everything you want, but it's just flat-out turn your head and go get the guy. Shooting alone in a gym can be counterproductive to that because that's not the natural setting of the game. Shooting during the summer should be a two-person activity."

Albers thought in the early years of his coaching that certain teams had home-court advantages in terms of the officiating.

"I thought most leagues did a good job of hiring commissioners and minimizing the home-court advantage. Sometimes I felt that certain teams were hiring some people who were providing advantages for those teams. I never restricted our athletic director at all in terms of who we hired. One thing that gave us the tournament success we had was the ability to play according to how officials were going to officiate. If you hire the same officials over and over, you never get the diversity you need for tournament play. Having a league commissioner to assign officials is good. Officiating today is as good as it has ever been. There is much less of an allegiance of an official to a certain school, which should never happen. It's a basketball game and you have to get out there and play, whether it's the cozy confines of Delphos St. John or St. Henry's old gym. Every school can say at certain times every gym can be hard to play in. Shut up and play.

"My best scouts were Bill Elking, Keith Westrick, Jeff Griesdorn, and Jeff Luebke. They knew what we looked for. They knew how to take away their strengths and how to promote our strengths. We didn't focus on variables that could be quickly changed.

"We broke down responsibilities among the assistants. Given what we'd seen, we might focus on offense. They had the same expectations of their players that I had of mine. We tried to provide consistency from the JV to the varsity program.

"The biggest change in the game during my career was the three-point line. I wish they'd added the shot clock. That would have been an advantage to us the way we played defense. That would have forced early shots. The three-point line caused us to make some adjustments to our defense. It caused us to come out farther.

"Fran Guilbault, Bob Arnzen, Jim Niekamp, and Dan Hegemier were coaches you knew that when their teams hit the floor they were going to be well-prepared. Whatever happened out there, you knew you had to complete they game. If you let up at all, they were going to be right there. There was no let-up from their players.

"One of the things you had to recognize, when you were ahead in those games, was the opposing momentum and you didn't feed it.

When you were ahead and you sensed the opposing team coming back, it was very important that you took your time to get a good shot, were poised, and didn't get rattled. Reading momentum is a really big part of understanding the game of basketball. You control momentum by great defense and patient, good, shot selection on the offense. If your team isn't doing that, you need to call a time out and get your players to see the momentum. If you are behind, you don't panic. You do the things necessary to allow your team to come back. Sometimes you get good shots, but they just don't drop. You certainly don't want to try to do something you aren't capable of doing in an attempt to get back in the game. When things are going your way, and your three-point shots are dropping, you keep running it. Now, when you miss one of those three-point shots in a moderate flow – the momentum is not swinging to one team or another – you have to go back to a more disciplined offense and get the shots we considered to be part of our normal offense. Controlling momentum is tremendously powerful in the game of basketball and you control it by patience.

"The state level games always bring out an adrenalin rush because you know that your kids are on that huge stage. To be the focus of that is pretty incredible. Even [at the state tournament], I never wanted to overemphasize any individual in press coverage. Most of the media understood that and most of the press coverage I got over the years was pretty decent.

"Most of my players who didn't necessarily connect with my personality, understood where I came from and they played according to that. To minimize pressure, kids need to stay focused on doing the best they can. Let's say there's a possible winning free throw at the end of the game and you're shooting a one-and-one with one second to go. The idea is to think that you have been given this great opportunity. Do the best you can, follow the form, work on it every day, and do what you're supposed to do, and if you do, and it doesn't go in, what the heck more could you do? You did everything I asked you to do. So there shouldn't be any pressure. That helped with our tournament success. I don't think anybody missed a shot because they felt they had to make the shot. It was never a consideration. They just did the best they could.

"Leadership is recognizable from the importance they give to basketball. Leadership is not just on the floor. It is lived. It is something that is done in terms of how you live your life and the goals you have for your team. If you are doing something that contradicts your goal, then that contradicts good leadership."

Leadership carries over to other aspects of life and Albers has seen his former players take those skills and basketball abilities beyond high school.

"A lot of players play college basketball. It's just a matter that preparing them academically had them well-prepared for what the college expected. Playing basketball attracted inquiries, then, from coaches that allowed kids to get those opportunities to play. I was proud of Nick Bertke who was player of the year at Ohio Northern in that conference and went on to play pro ball in Japan. Many others had great college success because they gave a great sacrifice. In some cases, those colleges have no scholarships, so it's hard work. My players were disciplined kids and I'm quite proud of their careers.

"The rewards of coaching are the camaraderie and these relationships with players. It was life-rewarding and something they could carry with them throughout their lives. I would like to think that maybe daily, they think back to what we did as a team and how they can use that now to make life the wonderful journey that it should be."

Chapter  Four

JERRY HARMON

JACKSON CENTER HIGH SCHOOL

1985 STATE CHAMPION

"Perfect practice makes perfect."

Growing up in a steel mill town in eastern Ohio during the 1950s meant that kids had to find their own entertainment, as Jerry Harmon recalls. Television came later to his neighborhood, so the elementary school playground was the center of activity. It was in those early years that he discovered his love of basketball. It was a challenge that he enjoyed on the playground in the 1950s and a challenge that was to become a daily way of life for him in the ensuing decades.

"I liked the challenge of putting the ball in the basket. I liked the challenge of keeping someone else from doing it, so I played a lot of one-on-one. The elementary playground was only two hundred yards away. It was a slanted playground that went uphill, making that a shot difference of about a foot from top to bottom. The basket was only nine feet anyway, so you could have an eight foot six shot or a nine foot six shot, depending on where you were."

Then, as Harmon left his childhood, the slanted playground became the level gymnasium. His love of basketball continued to develop until he took his first teaching job at Lexington High School and was the assistant to varsity coach John Barr.

"That is truly where I learned the intricacies of basketball. I thought I knew basketball. I really loved it. I wanted to be a coach coming out of college but after two or three practice sessions with the Lexington team I thought, 'I don't know a thing.' I had a lot to learn. He's still my mentor to this day. He moved on to Grove City College in Pennsylvania and that's where I took my teams every summer. He's the single biggest influence on my coaching and my career.

"The person that replaced him at Lexington, Dan Roseberry, was quite different from John, but his drive to win was so tremendous, that he taught me an awful lot about exploiting match-ups. Some coaches are stubborn from the standpoint of, 'I have a philosophy. I have a pattern of play and I'm going to do it, no matter what the other team does.' Dan went at that a little bit differently. If he saw that [there was] some weak player on our good player, even if it wasn't our star player, he would isolate that person and just drill him and drive him into the ground until they would call a time out or just stop. John's teaching philosophy was great; however, Dan showed me that in those little segments of a ball game, I have to just go at the disadvantages they have or the advantages I have."

Harmon has also drawn insights from books and publications by college coaches John Wooden, Bobby Knight, and Dean Smith.

"I think I came up with something that's a mix of all of them. My coaching style is quite different from John Barr's. We've discussed that years and years on end how I would play a zone defense and he would never, ever use a zone. I kind of used the

Dean Smith approach that now and then you use a zone just to throw teams off. One of the big things teams need to do is make adjustments during the game. Sometimes they'll see us in a two-three zone and other times in a man. That just taxes their players' overall ability to adjust, and many times you can win a game there."

Then came the move to Jackson Center, a school that hadn't seen a victory the previous season. One of his first assistant coaches was

Don Thogmartin, a person Harmon credits as being so valuable to him because he had an "unbelievably analytical mind," teaching Harmon the little nuances of the game.

"He could see little intricacies and he could predict, 'If we do this, this is what's going to happen here or there.' He really affected the way I looked at things the rest of my career."

Both Thogmartin and Gregg Gooding became Harmon's best scouts because they were able to relate what they saw to the Jackson Center program and the coaching style Harmon employed each year.

Harmon knew early in life that his destiny was beyond the steel mills that surrounded him in his youth. He was determined not to repeat the life and death of his father in those mills.

"I was going to be an undertaker. I worked in a funeral home when I was in high school. That was one of my part-time jobs. I knew for sure I wasn't going to work in the steel mills because that's where my family worked, and my dad was killed there. Even before he was killed, I was going to get a college education, and I wasn't going to hold up the lamp post downtown.

"Then I switched courses and wanted to be a coach. I knew you had to teach to be a coach back in the 1960s. You couldn't coach and work at Stolle's or Honda. You had to be a teacher. I really wanted to coach."

And coach, he did. Over the years Harmon has read books and manuals to be a constant learner. He accepts that, today, the material he learned from print sources can be found in videos and on the Internet. The best coaching instruction, though, came from interaction with good coaches. He learned from his mentors and from experience that some of the essential principles of basketball aren't really about Friday night games. They are about teaching and about preparing players for the challenges of life.

"I've learned that the best players are going to play. I came from a situation in Lexington where they fired Dan Roseberry because he had cut a [board member's] son who wasn't good enough as a junior. That wasn't the place for me. They actually fired me from my JV coaching position. They said I'd have a chance to get it back when they hired a new head coach, but I didn't want any part of it. I knew it was a bad situation. I had already committed to building my house there and living there. When I came here, to Jackson Center, Betty Scoggin was on the board and she had a son who was going to be junior. She gave me a hypothetical situation, and I said, 'I play the best kids. I don't care if their parents are on welfare or if they are doctors. If that's not what you want, don't hire me.' I told them about that [Lexington] situation that night when I was interviewed and that's why I had to leave there. I don't play favorites. I play the best kids."

They must have liked that approach because Harmon was offered the job that night. He wanted to be a head coach, and he and his wife had decided that they would accept the first job from the two or three he had been pursuing. The first offer came from Jackson Center.

"I was after a head coaching job. I had an opportunity my second year out of college at Canal-Winchester and I turned it down. I went another five years without being offered one. The year I got this one, I had about two or three in the hopper. My wife and I, through prayer, decided that we would take the first one that was offered. When they offered me the job that night, then, I didn't even have to call her. I knew this was where we were coming. That got tested a little bit later that summer when one of the other jobs came through. On paper it seemed like the ideal job, a little closer to home, a great returning cast, and all that kind of stuff. This was actually the worst of the three. Things were so bad here, and not just that they hadn't won a game the previous year. Their team picture included a kid with blue Chuck Taylor All-Stars-for the Jackson Center Tigers, orange and black. Now come on. The locker room was so bad. I often joked that even the cockroaches wouldn't go in there. That first day in October, the team and I spruced up the locker room and the gym. I got hired here and that's why I'm here.

"Another philosophy I've had for a long time is that perfect practice makes perfect. If you practice something wrong over and over again, you get good at doing it wrong. Not 'practice makes perfect.' You have to learn how to do it properly. After you learn how to do it properly, you train and train until it becomes automatic and then you make it part of your game. Perfect practice makes perfect. That guided all of my drills, so you have to do meticulous teaching of fundamentals from footwork up. You must have proper form in all fundamentals. From the very beginning when you are teaching something to your young players you teach them the right way so at least you can fall back on it and say, 'Look, remember how your elbow always has to be under the ball? Your elbow is way out here, so you're practicing wrong every time you shoot. Get it under.' It's meticulous detail.

"And getting more into the life philosophy, I learned that a kid is not trying to mess up out there on the court. There has to be some compassion from the coach to the player. Kids mess up and don't do what you asked them to do, but there is no kid who goes to the free throw line and says, 'I'm going to try to miss this.' No kid goes into a ball game and says, 'I'm going to do everything my coach told me not to do.' It's helped me most times, although some of my players might disagree on how hard I was on them, to give kids a break but then build on it.

"I always tried to relate the things that happened in practice or a game, whether it is success or failure, to the things they're going to come across in life. I've been through some of them. 'I've been down that road, kids, and this will help you in college when this happens, or this will help you when your dad dies or when you wreck the car and you have to go tell your mom and dad.' Through a lot of the things, success or failure, the struggle, the goal-setting, I've really, really tried to make that a priority, to make that more than just games and headlines. If that's all you're working for, a lot of times you're going to fall short."

Harmon's team, however, produced many headlines in March of 1985 when the Tigers won the Class A state championship. The final match-up between Graysville-Skyvue and Jackson Center was the biggest game of Harmon's career, but he quickly adds that his first victory as a head coach when the tiny Jackson Center gym was packed to the rafters created a response in him that was very much like that of a state championship.

"Most people don't get the chance to win a state championship and when you do, you're in elite company. Honestly, there are other games that have come pretty close, though. What an elation and what a feeling that first night at Jackson Center. It was our first victory and the first night that I coached in Jackson Center. That gym was packed clear out through the hallways. The stage was packed, and I thought, 'Oh, my goodness! These people like basketball.' I knew they did, and we won that game in overtime, I think. Kreg Huffer had an unbelievable night. He came out and hugged me after the game. It was like we won the state championship. You see, these people had only won two games in two years. That was important, and so was the first time we won the league championship. We did that in 1980, even though we tied. The next year, we won it by ourselves. I could talk about that one forever. Danny Sosby had a big role in that. Plus, it was our homecoming.

"The regional final against Fort Loramie in 1985 was, come on; you can't get a bigger game than that. Our first district championship in 1984 was big. The big one we really didn't get to relish was the state semi-final against [Columbus] Wehrle. They were the sixth-ranked team in the entire nation in all classes and we beat them. Then we had to come back and play within forty-two hours. Then [Harmon's son] Jason's first varsity game in 1986-87 was an important game.

"But the state championship and the circumstances by which we got there and being down about nine with 3:47 to go was big. There's a story in that whole thing. In the regional semi-finals, for instance, Loramie was the game right before us and they had already won. We were going into our game knowing that, and we were thinking, 'We can't let them have this.' They were already there. So here we were in the regional semi-finals against Marion Local and Loramie is already in the finals. And then to beat Loramie in that final on Saturday afternoon was unbelievable. We played Loramie ninety-six minutes that year, and we came out ahead by about three or four points, total.

"You know, there wasn't one second of those games that I wasn't totally on top of it. I wasn't overwhelmed. I didn't panic in any of them, even though we were behind. I knew the situation. It was totally planned. There were no surprises. The kids knew what was going on. I even had the songs picked out to play or reference. "One More Night" by Phil Collins was the song after we beat Wehrle. I knew we were going to do one more jingle [a running drill used frequently for conditioning] when we won the state on St. John court. I also had a plan for the picture of the ball and the trophy sitting on the O. I had it planned. I truly believe that if you can conceive it, and believe it, it's possible to achieve it. Oh, it was a good ride."

Despite the frenzy and the ultimate glory of winning it all, Harmon doesn't readily display the spoils of victory.

"If you walked into my house, you would never know I'm a coach. I don't have stuff all over the place. Do I have anything in my office...? It's one of those things that people would say I'm not humble enough, but I try to make sure I don't flaunt it. Yes, I'm proud of it. The one thing I have is my license plate [JC 1985] which I got about eight or nine years ago. I don't wear my ring, but then, I don't wear jewelry anyway. I thought about wearing it to the state tournament. That would be the ceremonial place to wear it, but I'm a little sensitive to that. I'm thankful but sensitive."

The most exciting games in Harmon's career were the games leading up to the state championship, and, of course, the championship itself. The regional semi-final against Marion Local, which had been to the state tournament the year before, begins the list, followed by Fort Loramie, Columbus Wehrle, and Graysville-Skyvue.

Marion Local "was a returning team to the state tournament. We had beaten them by about ten in the regular season and we had to face them again down there [Dayton]. Their fans thought they got cheated here so when we beat them again by ten, [we were vindicated]. That was a big win. They were huge. They beat us the year before in the regional. That whole run was murderer's row. Plus, we had to beat CAPE for the district title. They were a physical education high school, plus they had Carlos Snow, who was a great running back for Ohio State."

In that same championship year, Harmon wasn't the only one delivering life lessons. Only a few weeks before the trip to Columbus, his team sounded a wake-up call for the coach.

"We had just beaten Riverside, who wasn't very good. We only won by about seventeen or eighteen points, and I was on the kids in the locker room a little bit. It was late in the year. I was saying something to the effect of, 'Guys, we've got to play better regardless of our opponent. We played sloppy out there and if we play sloppy against good teams, we're going to get beat. We can't afford to get beat. We have high goals and we have big things we want to accomplish.' While I was saying that, I was thinking I was putting it in the right context. One of the rules I have is that kids have to listen to me. They can't be doing something else. Well, while I was talking, there was Tony Meyer untying his shoes, and the body language was there. I noticed it right away, and being the person I am, I said, 'What's the matter with you, Meyer? You're back there untying your shoes, acting like you're not listening to me, acting like you're ticked off. What's the deal?' He very clearly said, 'Coach, we're sixteen and one, and you're treating us like we're one and sixteen.' I was ready to explode, but something inside me told me not to do it. I waited about fifteen to twenty seconds and there was dead silence. The kids had to be thinking, 'Oh, Meyer's lost it, and that car wreck he had last summer was nothing compared to this. Harmon's going to stuff him in a locker and that's going to be it.' And then this is exactly what I said, 'Fellas, it's probably best if I don't make a comment right now. I'll talk to you on Monday.' Over the weekend, I could see what he was saying. If I don't think I'm riding them, but they think I am, then I am. On Monday I told them I needed to take a pass on Saturday night in the locker room at Riverside, so we spent about ten minutes that practice just talking about getting better. Without that experience, we might not have won state."

Harmon can put the state run into perspective because he experienced the pain of other games that turned out differently.

"We were ahead nice at Loramie in 1984 playing for the league championship, maybe up seven or eight with three minutes to go and we lost it in regulation. It was devastating to me and devastating to the kids. To make it worse, I was one that always waited around for the press to come to talk, but he [Ken Barhorst, sports reporter for the Sidney Daily News] spent so much time in the other locker room I was thinking, 'Come on, Barhorst.' I was alone lying on the bench in the Fort Loramie locker room when he finally came in. The kids had been on the bus for fifteen minutes. I think I was a very good sport, gave him all the answers, and was courteous, but that one tore me up.

"I still can't figure out what I should have done differently. It seems like there was something I should have done to stem the tide, to stop the momentum.

"Another one was the Loramie game from the 1979-1980 season in the sectional tournament over at Bellefontaine. We were the number one seed and ended up with only two losses, both to Loramie. That was Donnie Sosby's senior year. We were great. We were a great basketball team, but I messed up at the tournament draw. I made a mistake and got myself positioned in Loramie's bracket and I didn't have to be. It was a bitter defeat."

To brighten these moments, Harmon enjoyed a victory over Anna in the sectionals at Piqua a few years later.

"That was one of those where they had beaten us late in the season of I think 1983-1984 because Deron Sosby and Steve Ryder were on that team. Anna was crowing about the fact that their one-three-one zone had really gotten to us. I knew it wasn't, and I couldn't hold my tongue in the newspaper. When we started the game against that one-three-one, we hit our shots. We scored the first ten or eleven times. It was like, 'Forget that one-three-one.'"

The toughest part of the game to teach, though, isn't the X's and O's, according to Harmon. It's the balance between a player's mental state and its effect on performance.

"Sometimes kids definitely have the ability. You've prepared. You've practiced. It's that whole balance there that's an inexact science. Sometimes you think you're going to play rotten and you play great. Sometimes you think you have it right down to a T, and you go out and lay an egg. Some coaches like to think they're the gurus of the mental aspect of the game, but how much of this is luck to see if your team is going to perform at its peak? I guess you measure that by how many times your team plays at its peak. If you play at your peak ninety percent of the time, you can say we played as well as we could play tonight. That's how you probably measure it. I do know it's a hard thing to maneuver through.

"After that, the biggest obstacles to success are distractions when individuals or a team lose sight of the team aspect of the game. Distractions can be a host of things like girlfriends, cars, and jobs. I have a whole speech about the male high school athlete and those worst things. Even though there is an individual aspect to it, it all has to be in the team concept of a team pursuit. If anything distracts you from that, then that affects you in a negative way and that's no good."

In the end, Harmon decided to finish his coaching career in 1989. He compared that decision to the story of the farmer who said about Sundays, "It's better to be sitting on a tractor thinking about church, than sitting in church thinking about being on a tractor."

"When you're doing something that's an absolute, essential part of your job and you wish you were somewhere else, you better start considering it. If you are wishing you were going out to dinner with your wife on a Friday night instead of going to a basketball game, that's an early sign.

"When the pressure is such now that it becomes more desirable to be somewhere else, that's it. I had tremendous pressure on me. My most satisfying season was the season following the state tournament. I had one returning letterman and we won the league championship. The year we won state, we only tied for the league. A kid like Jeff Teeters, who was the hero obviously, of the state tournament, making that shot, was a such a dominating influence against Anna when we won the league championship over there the next year. It was unbelievable. He had twenty-five points and he was five for ten against kids who were 6'6" and 6'4".

"We're fanatic about all sports here in this area, but in our league people are nuts about basketball. They start talking about it the first day of school. They can't wait until Meet the Team night. People ask me, 'What else is there? You won the state championship.' The point is, that isn't all there is. If you're only going to be in it for state championships, most years you're going feel that you were a failure. A driven coach is still going to do the same things this year that he does during a state championship year, even if that challenge is not there. You're still trying to build character, and help kids set goals and make plans. Coaches have been doing these things for years. The personal and spiritual growth you have as a coach makes you hope your players are getting it, too. Even in adversity, if you are alert, you can learn something. Those are the real rewards of coaching."

Those rewards must offset the minor irritations that certainly accompany a job like this. For Harmon, the work he disliked most was the pre-season busy-work: handing out uniforms, ordering shoes, deciding on shooting shirts, and taking the team picture. He also found that practice preparation, when there was no game the next day after a loss, was particularly distasteful. Outside interference or the distractions that diminish a player's focus obviously peeve Harmon, but the thing that created a true headache for him was always the weather.

"It's already agonizing enough the night before the game without the snowstorm that's predicted making you think, 'Are we going to play or not?' It's not like playing outside where you're freezing like football or baseball. You know you're going to be warm and maybe overly warm, but when the weather is turning bad, that's a pet peeve. It's one of those nasty, pesky things that aren't overly important, but to me, it was. It could set me on edge."

What Harmon sees in today's coaches is a relentlessness to continuously work players with few breaks during the year. Despite his efforts to discuss a "less is more" approach, the pattern continues.

"Coaches today are doing way too much in the off-season. They are doing way too much with kids in the summertime. They are robbing them of their youth and the playful time in their life to just be a kid and not have all the structure. Every chance I get, I try to tell coaches that. I can't convince them that they shouldn't be doing all this stuff. If they win a state championship they'll say that's why they did it. You know what? We won a state championship and we didn't do that stuff. I'll tell coaches that most people don't win a state championship, so are we allowed to blame that, then? I know it's true from the bottom of my heart that coaches should do a lot less. The way we coach high school sports today is insane. It's foolish.

"A future coach better be a great teacher and a great learner. If coaching is what you want to do, you'd better know the game inside and out and be able to teach it from the very first step kids take on the court, or they're going to do it wrong. All drills build up from the very first step to the most intricate thing you do. Those drills that you teach them when they are fourth and fifth graders are the basis and foundation of being able to do that properly when they are juniors and seniors. If they have bad footwork, they're going to trip and stumble, and then when the big play comes, they fumble the ball out of bounds. If you drilled that the last four or five years, it probably wouldn't happen."

Each coach discovers methods of teaching that work for him or for his team and no one would be surprised that most gyms are full of kids working on fundamentals, ball-handling drills, or game situations. In a coach's life, however, there are some thoughts and experiences that only other coaches understand.

"I don't think anybody understands the mental stuff you go through in the day leading up to the game – the twenty or twenty-four hours before the game. It's like a nightmare. You're walking in a void. You don't want to hear anybody. You don't want to talk to anybody because you are focusing yourself to have everything down pat. I'd have things written down on a little piece of paper because in the heat of battle you can forget the things you want to do. Also, those times when your team is underachieving and you just can't get that little secret or that little thing that will turn it around just eat you up as a coach. Nobody understands how much of a war goes on inside you if you are a driven coach.

"When your team is underachieving you get a little paranoid. You develop a whole conversation between you and all your relationships that isn't even taking place. It's probably not even in their brains, but you've developed a dream world. People know when to leave you alone."

In order to be alone on game days, Harmon never went home between school and the game. He spent those hours working out to work off some nervous energy, reading devotions, and finalizing game plans.

"Keep your eye on the dot. I tell kids, 'No distractions. Nothing to the right, nothing to the left. No girlfriend. You have a job to do tonight and that's what you have to do.' I sent Matt [Meyer] a note after he won the regional [in 2008], and that's all I put, 'Keep your eye on the dot.' It would be real easy to get undisciplined and just go laissez faire and let it go. Then you lose by six when you could have won by three.

"I'm single-minded and that's to my detriment, sometimes, with my relationships. All my relationships were affected negatively. I can't prove that, but in my own family, I believe it did affect that, although I think we've overcome that over the years since I've been out of it. It wasn't good. I think it affects some of my relationships now because some people still feel like I'm trying to beat them down. I'm not.

"I got to the point where I thought people just tolerated me. I just felt, 'I have a job to do and that's your problem, not mine. You're not in the pressure situation I am. You're probably going to go to the Holiday Inn tonight and have a few drinks and a nice meal, and then you'll come to the game and whether we win or lose, you're going to sleep tonight. I won't.' That affected those relationships and it wasn't good.

"I remember a time talking to some parents in my office in the elementary school. I'd never met them before. We were talking about their kid and when it was over, they were walking down the hall and they didn't know I was following them. The guy made the statement, 'That wasn't too bad. I always heard he was a prick, but he seems like a pretty nice guy.' If I had any misconceptions about how I was received, in many ways, that was Lesson A. People from other schools have found that out, too. When you talk to them they'll say, 'You're sure a whole lot different. I used to scream and shout at you, but you aren't that bad.' So I can laugh about it, but it was negative. Now it's turned into positives. People can see I'm still there. I'm a helper. I haven't thrown in the towel."

When game time came, Harmon was prepared to give last-minute instructions to the players. He reminded them of the keys to winning the game, eschewing the pep talk approach.

"The kids know the three to five keys that are vital. I downplay the rah-rah stuff and that's a John Wooden thing. You don't want kids to be too high. If adversity comes, then they drop too low. They have to stay pretty much on an even keel. Keep your eye on the dot, do what you ought, make sure you know what we're doing.

"At halftime, I began by reviewing the keys to the game. It's imperative that you start by saying something positive about the first half. You can point out the negatives, but not in a ranting and raving way. If you really get on them at half time, they're going to fall flatter than a pancake in the second half. If a team comes out and plays great, you know what the coach did? He said, 'This is our game plan. You guys aren't doing it. I'm really disgusted, but I'm not going to say anything about it. You guys get some water and get rested up and let's go out and play.' Before you send them out again, if you started with something positive and pointed out the negatives in a constructive way, end with another positive.

"Then in the post-game, and I knew this before the incident at Riverside, you need to keep it brief, whether you won or whether you lost. If you won, get out of the way. Let them have a little bit of fun. 'We did what we wanted to do tonight. Here are a couple of things we have to work on. Enjoy it.' Then get out of there before you say something you regret. Have some clear plans about when you're going to meet next and mention the curfew. It's not rocket science. It's important but not as important as some of these sportscasters who have never been there think it is – the post-game and pre-game talks."

Ultimately, the essence of an outstanding coach is to be a great teacher.

"It's a Bobby Knight and a John Wooden thing. You have to be a great teacher. And this is where, I don't care what anybody says, I'm a great teacher. I can take somebody through the process of not knowing something, to practicing perfectly, to learning how to do it and drill, drill, drill until it's automatic, to making it part of your game. I can do that. You also have to have the knowledge and the skills. You can't be a great coach if you're just a paper tiger. There's got to be some substance there. You have to have good personal skills. You have to be able to relate to the players, the staff, and the parents. Finally, you have to be single-minded. You can't let any distractions get in the way. First and foremost, though, you have to be a good teacher."

Becoming a good coach is one thing. The criteria for a successful team are different.

"You have to have talent. It doesn't matter who's coaching. If you don't have talent, you're not going to win. Once the talent is there, then team play comes in. You need to be able to play together, and there needs to be a clear line of authority. Then you need to have focus and have fun. But it's hard work. There's an old Loretta Lynn song, and the kids don't feel this way, but the line goes something like, 'There's no amount of money could buy from me the memories I have of then, but no amount of money could ever make me go back and do it all over again.' You couldn't pay me to go back and do it again, but that's not the way the kids think. They'd love to do it again.

"When I was an assistant I said that kids were kids anywhere. Good teaching and good coaching can make a good team. That's why I wasn't afraid of this job, even though they didn't win a game the year before, because I knew they'd been to state in the past [1963]. But I think it's genetics. Kids are big around here. Those kids in Mercer County are big. Bigger, faster, stronger wins state championships. There's also tremendous competition between these little towns, and you have to stay on top of it. That breeds good success and achievement on everybody's part. There's a tradition here--an expectation that we're going to have good talent. You go to northwest and west central Ohio and you can't get better, as far as the number of teams, anywhere in the country. The MAC is approaching one hundred state championship teams in that league alone between the girls and the boys. There are some leagues in places where they've never had a team at the state tournament. And the MAC alone is in the nineties. Think of Minster, Marion Local, St. Henry, Versailles, Coldwater, and Ft. Recovery, all of them. I don't think there's anyplace to compare anywhere in the country."

If that's true, then team rivalries, which must be among the most storied elements of Ohio sports history, have developed here over the years. Rivalries, in general, can ebb and flow, depending on year to year talent, but in this part of Ohio, the clash is deep and long-lasting. Players from these schools are sometimes close friends off the court, but on the court, no prisoners are taken. Jackson Center's biggest rival in the Harmon years was Fort Loramie.

"Some people here might consider Botkins and Anna bigger rivals, but not really. When it comes right down to it, it's Fort Loramie. I knew Fort Loramie's name before I got here because I always looked at the state standings. Every year, they'd be [at the top] in the polls. They never did anything in the tournament, though, until my first year here when they won the state. They were the best around, so we needed to do what Loramie was doing. They and Marion Local were our standard. The Loramie rivalry has been respectful, but it's been a little bitter at times, too. Generally, it's been good. They've usually been the better team."

For Jackson Center, the route to a state championship required keeping an eye on Fort Loramie and getting into position to be ready for the opportunity to advance in tournament play.

"All coaches will tell you that. Put yourself into position enough times and you'll have a chance to win. Out of my thirteen years, there were three or four when we had enough, if the right things went our way, to win state."

Harmon had a sense for when things were going right and when they weren't.

"Every now and then I'll talk to Dan Roseberry and he'll say, 'What's up, Har-mone? You've got that seven-down-and-nine-seconds look in your eye' and that was before the three-point shot. If you're in a four-possession game with nine seconds to go, you're beat. You know you're beat. In that situation that's very obvious.

"But here's where some arrogance comes in. After about half a quarter or at the end of the first quarter, I knew when we were going to win. If we had done exactly what we wanted to do, if we stopped what they wanted to do, and if they had called two time-outs, and we kicked them both times after those time-outs, I could just see it in the coaches' faces. If I had them scouted well enough and my game plan was good enough, I could take away their strength and attack their weakness to the point that they would take a time out to make an adjustment. After that, we were ready, too, because I would know from my scouting report and I could say, 'This is what they're going to do,' and then we'd have a counter for how they were going to stop us. That's when I could see their coach thinking, 'Let's just not get beat by thirty.' So sometimes I knew within the first quarter.

"There are other times when you're up eight at half and you aren't sure. When it gets late in the game and the tide is going your way, you know it's over.

"If I were still coaching today, my season would still be planned this way, and we'd be winning fifteen or sixteen games a year. When we have good talent we'd be winning districts. I'm absolutely confident of that.

"I didn't do everything everyone else was doing. I started with a meeting in May after the season was over. I'd have kids sit down, reflect, and get some goals. Then, I'd meet with the team and give them the schedule. The rest of the summer would include open gyms but not to interfere with baseball. I wanted kids to play baseball. I tried to schedule open gyms so it wouldn't conflict with ACME, but if it did, I told kids to go to baseball. Then we went to Grove City camp the first week of July and after that I had my captain, based on my pick and the team pick, then that was it until the end of September. We started conditioning and still had the open gyms and then practice began in November. We took a week or so off at Christmas. We didn't play over Christmas because I wanted them to be on the rise before tournament. The first week of January we only had six or seven games left, so I gave them time off so they would come back and perform at a high level and be rested and refreshed. That's how I organized the year.

"Practices were totally detailed minute by minute. I didn't just say, 'work on rebounding for twenty minutes.' I had rebounding as a heading but then I listed four or five drills with two minutes doing this and three minutes doing that until I had twenty minutes. Towards the end of my career, [Jackson Center superintendent] Don Knight stopped me when the kids were out for a drink, and he asked to see the practice plan I was carrying. He said, 'That's amazing. You won a state championship. You know basketball inside and out, yet you still have your practice plan written down minute by minute. That's the mark of a good teacher.' After practice, I wrote notes, then, to remind me what worked well and what didn't."

Preparation and attention to detail consumed Harmon in those days leading up to and including the state tournament.

"I had everything planned out to the minute from the pep rally before we left for Columbus to the return on Sunday. The kids don't know this, but, someday maybe my kids will put it in a scrapbook and give it to the school here, I had an alternate plan. That plan was what we were going to do if we got beat by Wehrle on Friday. I gave the team my itinerary: we're going to the arena, watch Skyvue and Vanlue, beat Wehrle, shower, leave the arena, and go to Worthington Christian's gym the next day. I also had that completely different itinerary that I never showed to anyone else."

One of the factors that led to success but he couldn't use it in the tournament was the Jackson Center gymnasium itself. Within a few years of his arrival at Jackson Center, the varsity team was able to move from the small gym in the old building to a brand new facility.

"We had the biggest home court advantage in the league. I'm not happy that our orange walls have now been painted white, and the tiger that Barb Sailor [Jackson Center art teacher] painted is gone. A coach left here one night after we beat them when Scott [Elchert] was coaching Jackson, and he didn't know I heard him, but he said to one of his assistant coaches, 'Let's get out of here. I'm sick of this orange dump.' It was a planned thing that we wanted it to be orange. Plus, people just didn't want to play us over here. I kid you not, kids would come here and argue about who would take the ball out of bounds. Out of bounds! They didn't want to be the one inbounds with Tony Meyer or Danny Sosby coming after them."

The biggest changes in the game since Harmon came to the scene have been the year-round immersion in the sport and the three-point shot.

"We were on our way to a clock back then and the three-point shot has actually eliminated the need for one. Smaller teams have a chance to win. It used to be that if you were playing a team that was huge, you'd stall the game a long time. You'd try to get the lead and just hold the ball and make them come out of their zone. There used to be a hundred games in the Saturday paper and you'd see those scores, maybe nineteen to thirteen or something similar, and you knew they stalled the game, but you only see one or two of them a year now. Teams that are little feel like they have a chance to win, even if they're outsized."

Harmon describes his role as head coach much like a mother hen. He had duties he assigned to the assistants, but he managed everything. He expected loyalty from his coaches but he also wanted his coaches to aspire to a position as a head coach, with one stipulation – not his position. They'll work harder and want to be the best. They will want to learn everything they can about the game and about how to instruct players. Harmon began that lesson by putting all players together for instruction.

"We had stations for freshmen through varsity to be sure everyone was getting the same instruction. Coaches today separate kids into their own individual practice time. The kids are in their own world. Freshmen need to be practicing with the varsity. Many times you'll have a freshman who's quick, and you think he's quick so you put him up against one of your mediocre varsity players. Then the mediocre player is better than he is, so you know the kid is good for a freshman, but he isn't close to being able to compete at the varsity level. Sometimes, though, I like to put a Keith Doseck, who is a couple years [younger], up against a Deron Sosby and say, 'Keith can hold his own there and I don't have to be afraid if I ever have to use that.' I gave my coaches a lot of responsibility but I was always double checking and making sure they did it exactly – it had to be exactly – the way I wanted it done.

"There were an awful lot of good coaches around here back then. I don't mind mentioning these names, but if I leave anybody out, it's not that they weren't good; it's just that these people were exemplary. Number one was Bob Huelsman at Covington. His preparation and his coaching style were so good that if you were playing against him, you were really worried. They played a controlled style of basketball. They didn't care if they won twenty-eight to twenty. If they had you down by four or five before the three-point shot came in, you were in deep trouble if they had the ball. They were a great free-throw shooting team, as well.

"Fred Nuss at Houston was always on top of everything and what a great competitor he was. He could run a game plan against you.

"Bob Anderson. Unbelievable. Love him or hate him, but to beat Bob Anderson, you weren't going to go in there and just beat his primary defense. Let's say you had a good game plan against his man-to-man or his two-three zone, Bob Anderson would do some switches or make some change-ups. If you beat him, you had to beat everything he had in his arsenal. He was going to use all his weapons and if you beat him, you knew you won.

"Those are three, but the fourth is Dan Hegemier. Dan Hegemier is a great coach. Part of it is the fact he has big talent, but at the same time he's a good game coach and good preparer."

All the preparation finally comes down to the game itself. The decisions that have to be made within a few seconds are the result of hours, and sometimes years, of coaching experience or accumulated knowledge. Knowing what to do comes down to time and score.

"Coaches will understand this time and score point of view. Sometimes when you're behind, you still don't make any changes, even if you're down five or six points. If you've got a quarter and half to go and you know your philosophy is sound and you've had a couple of things happen and you have a player sitting on the bench with three fouls, you stay with your plan and eventually it all plays itself out. The idea is don't panic. Don't get overconfident the other way if you're running it up on somebody.

"And a sixth sense I had, and I don't know what it is or where it came from, is that I knew when to make an adjustment at just the right time. To this day, Steve Bunke will ask me why I didn't put him back in when Keith Doseck fouled out and Tony fouled out [in the state final against Graysville Skyvue]. I put Jeff Teeters in. That wasn't as mystical as it seemed at the time because we were behind. Steve Bunke wasn't going to be a good person to chase the ball. I had to put rats in there to run everywhere, and Jeff and Marc Wahrer were rats. I remember running over to the radio station after the game and yelling 'How'd you like that substitution?' I was crowing a little bit, but it was a good substitution. Who can say I was wrong?

"We went in to games with the idea that we were going to set a frenetic pace. We were going to be pressure defense, up-tempo offense, and the John Wooden philosophy, which is so, so true, especially against teams that you were better than, to increase the number of possessions for both teams to have more rebounds, more passes, more ball-handling opportunities, and more shots. The lesser team is going to make more turnovers and miss more shots. So just in that, you're going to win because you have better talent if you get the possessions up. Conversely, if we go in way under-matched, you want to limit it. You want to take a shot only after several passes.

That's where Covington would get in trouble with such a slow game. They would keep a bad team in the game with them. They might be up with five minutes to go by only five or six points. Generally, that would be good, but if a team got lucky, they could whip you."

Harmon had a number of good teams during his 13 years of coaching, with many of the best players in Jackson Center history coming through the program in that era.

"A good player needs to know his own talent and how it fits into the team concept. For instance, a kid who is a twenty-eight percent shooter can't be shooting the ball eleven or twelve times during the game. You might leave him in for defense, though. I once put a kid in and told him not to touch the ball. I needed him out there to rat. It was a big victory, but his mom wrote me a letter to tell me how awful it was not to let him have the ball on offense. But he was in there for a specific purpose and it would have been an instant turnover if he touched the ball.

"Players also have to have that spit-in-your-eye mentality. They have to have that attitude out there. It's not as easy and Sunday School-y as everyone thinks. Competition is friendly, but it's nasty out there at times, too. They have to do that without getting a technical foul. They also have to be unselfish, but at the same time they have to be selfish. I read an article on Kobe Bryant that described how he doesn't believe anyone can stop him. He wants to be the one that gets the job done. So you have to be unselfish, but if something needs to be done, you need to want to take over and get the job done. If a kid is getting out of line and they're outside the game plan, the coach has to moderate that. We were down so bad against Loramie my first year here. They beat us one hundred eleven to ninety-six that year. We were down by about twenty-six and Kreg Huffer was just gunning it. I took him out and sat him down and said, 'Kreg, I know we're down, but you have to stay within the team concept.' With him on the bench, we cut that thing to eleven points with six or seven minutes to go, and Kreg looked at me and said, 'Coach, I understand what you're saying. Put me back in.' The coach has to moderate when the kids get outside the team concept, but you want kids to take charge, too.

"Players who fit that mold were Kreg Huffer obviously, and Tony

Meyer, Jimmy Gooding, Matt Meyer, Vince Wake, Brian Scoggin, my son Jason, Jeff Poppe, Keith Doseck, Scott Doseck, Greg Vetter, Tim Rostorfer, Steve Ryder who could knock your head off in a competitive way if he wanted to, and Donnie, Danny and Deron Sosby. Those players were just unbelievable.

"Some players might fit in a different system, but my style was to play up-tempo with lots of running and pressure. A player who might be described as a plodder would have a tough time fitting into my system on a large floor. Yeah, there are going to be times when we're going to go half court, or slow things down or work an offense inside to a bigger guy, but I had a system and the kids knew from seventh, eighth, or ninth grade where they could see themselves in that system. The parts would just fit and they would get right in line when someone graduated and they would be right there. The kids could see it pretty early on. I rarely did any changing from year to year. I'd make little adjustments based on talent, but basically we were going to press and we were going to run."

Harmon used a reward/punishment model to teach his players how to manage pressure. Leadership was another issue entirely.

"In practice you have to put kids in situations that are as realistic as possible, so you have to use the Pavlovian philosophy. 'Do this or you're going to run or jump.' My drills were based on change every three to five minutes. That's a Bob Knight philosophy. He would change without a big break. You could be running and he would call a change on the fly. It teaches kids to adjust without calling a time-out which stops the other team from getting time to play a trick on you. You can tell your kids this is the play I want with a one-word command. Or I'd move someone else in their position and say, 'You can't handle this,' and they'd have to earn it back.

"Competitive drive has to be there already. It's a matter of enhancing what's already there. Leadership is just a matter of letting them do it, but always with good oversight."

The best drills Harmon used were basic but effective. He liked loose ball drills when the ball was tossed onto the court and two players were told to go get it. He liked grasshoppers – two footed hopping up flights of stairs, and spot shots.

"Grasshoppers were just an early form of plyometrics. Footwork drills are part of the fundamentals. We did footwork drills the day we went to Columbus and it was the same stuff they did as fifth-graders the very first day. We did them every day. Every day."

Harmon doesn't believe the coach has a responsibility to get kids to play at the college level. He is only a facilitator.

"The fact is, Tony Meyer achieved the highest level in basketball here. He was All-Ohio Conference for two years and you look at all the good players we've had. Come on. You're not going to Ohio State – generally. In the county even, how many have played Division I? Loramie's had three or four; Anna's had a couple, but how many go on to play Division I basketball from our county? The MAC has, but that's up to the parents.

"The role of the parent is important. At the awards banquet we say we appreciate the parents; that is important. The fans are important, but Jerry Harmon would be driven even if there weren't any fans in the stands. But it's fun to have fans there. That first game here when it was packed, that was fun. But they cannot be distractions.

"I'm a little more cynical about officials. I've been in situations when the officials have affected the outcome of the game, and that should never be. It should never be. With league assigners, it's much better now. If you get a bad break, it's nothing you can point to that's intentional. No official was hired for that purpose. Everywhere back in the early years, it was a jungle. It still is with the MAC because their assigner doesn't assign non-league games.

"The best rule change is the three-point shot. I was opposed to it early, but it has eliminated the slow-down game. It shouldn't be plodding and almost boring. So I like the three-point shot. The worst rule change was this 365/24/7 thing that came about because of a soccer court case. I don't think it's been good for basketball. Also, the physical contact that's allowed has turned the game into high altitude wrestling. Basketball should be finesse and skill and graceful movement. It shouldn't be brutes holding you so you can't get off the proper shot when they themselves can't go to the free-throw line and shoot a free throw because they are a muscle-bound gorilla. They can play defense, but they don't have the grace and skill to be a great basketball player."

Harmon believes that if anything becomes a distraction or

interferes with the mission to be a coach and teacher to the players, and those distractions might get the coach fired, then it's time to move on. Booster groups and administrators are all important, but they have to let the coach be a person.

"The administration called me in to support me during that first year, and you talk about flying high. It was good to have them support me. Some schools, you go 5-14, that'll get you fired. I was allowed to grow as a varsity coach, and believe me, the eight minutes you play in a varsity game is a long way off from the six you play in the JV. If the administration backs you, you're in a good place.

"The first night I was hired, I asked Kreg Huffer, 'How do you think we're going to do this year?' He said, 'We're going to win the county.' They didn't win a game the previous year and they were going to win the county. Unbelievable. That's the type of player you want."

Chapter  Five

DAN HEGEMIER

NEW KNOXVILLE HIGH SCHOOL

2008 STATE CHAMPION

FORT LORAMIE HIGH SCHOOL

1993 STATE CHAMPION
1988 STATE SEMI-FINALS
1987 STATE CHAMPION

"It's always fun beating teams that are way on top, and you sneak in there and get them and get out. That's fun. When you are the top dog, it's a little different. You're taking everybody's best shot every night."

The secret to Dan Hegemier's success isn't much of a secret to any coach who has put a team on the floor against his. In addition to talent, it's absolute teamwork from beginning to end in every phase of the game and in every detail of preparation.

"You have to have everybody on the same page. Everybody from the players, to the assistant coaches, to the head coach has to understand that there is one boss and we're going to do certain things. Whatever that is, that's what you have to do. That's the first thing and it includes parents and the administration. It makes things so much easier because you don't want kids to have self-doubt when they are on the floor. You want them to respond to whatever is asked of them and do it the best they can. Everyone needs to understand what the program is trying to do."

Teamwork, on and off the floor, dominates the decisions Hegemier makes for his players every day. He believes teamwork builds a formidable defense and an offense that allows optimum opportunity for many players to handle the ball.

"We're going to defend people the best we can. I always went to Bob Arnzen's camps at [Delphos] St. John before there were team camps. We'd divide all the kids up and we'd play. There was one team one year that was absolutely horrible and got drilled by everybody. For some reason on the last two days of the camp, the coach of that team had to leave, so Bob took over. They won the rest of their games. We sat back and wondered what he did. He didn't have a locker room speech. He just kept telling the kids, 'Let's play hard. Get in their face. Let's defend them.' It was a constant feeling he gave to those kids. 'Let's go pick them up at half court, and then we'll turn them, and we're going to play as hard as we can.' I was in awe right then and there, and that was one thing I wanted to do.

"I wasn't a great player in high school, but I always wanted to defend, so that carried over, too, and now we're going to try to defend people. You can look at the teams that win in high school, college, and the NBA. The ones that win, they all defend. They all defend. Having everybody on the same page and defending people are two big keys."

Other keys to being successful still center on the team concept.

"I don't care who shoots the ball, just remember that if you shoot, you better make some, or you aren't going to shoot. That's just common sense. To keep people involved, to keep kids happy, even the ones who don't get to play a lot, you have to give them the opportunity to put the ball in the hole sometimes, but it's basically like this, 'Son, if you don't work on your game and you can't shoot it, the type of shots you get aren't going to be as abundant.'

"The team concept is probably the reason I've run the flex all these years. Everybody gets to touch the ball. Team, team, team.

We have a saying on the bench when we see a bad shot. We say, 'Well, it must have been my turn to shoot.' I had a group this year [2007-2008] who had six guys who could play My Turn every time, but they never did. Those guys each averaged double figures, which is unheard of. If they wanted to be selfish or get a few more headlines they could have, but they never did. That's why we went 27-0. They were all good players who understood the game very well.

"They also know that I hate having kids turn the ball over. I don't like it. They know it. The keys to winning, especially in tight games, are defending, not turning the ball over, and not allowing offensive rebound scores."

Hegemier's basic principles of coaching stem from his love of competition that developed playing baseball and basketball and growing up with three brothers and three sisters on a farm near New Knoxville, but the direction his coaching has taken was influenced largely by other coaches.

"I went to college because I didn't want to stay around the farm, and I just liked being around the game. It is high energy and a lot of action. When I was a junior and senior at New Knoxville, we coached the little kids' teams and I really enjoyed that. My high school coach Gene Fries was a great role model on how to act, how to dress, and how to prepare. He was a great influence. I was 1-18 my first year of varsity coaching at Waynesfield-Goshen. I thought I knew everything and it wasn't pleasant. You have to work at it, copy some things, and get little nuggets from people in the coaching profession. I watched Fran Guilbault, Bob Arnzen, and all the other good coaches in the area. Fran was a great offense coach. You knew what was coming at you, but you couldn't stop it. I hit the camps and the clinics and all those things to pick up anything that might work. For me, it was get better or get out. The second year, we went ten and twelve, so that was better.

"I went to Spencerville and we had four winning seasons there with nice people and nice kids. We won the Northwest Conference championship and we had some good things going there. It would have been tough to win a state championship there, though, with not a lot of big kids. The Fort Loramie job came open and they'd had a lot of success with George [Hamlin]. I took that over and went sixteen years there. Then I went to the [Wright State University] Lake Campus. It was a challenge to get going. We had some good years, but I missed the tournament so much. When the Knoxville position came open, my brother called me right away and told me to get over there.

"Don Donoher [University of Dayton basketball coach] had a lot to do with it, too. I remember when I was just starting out, Damon Goodwin of St. Marys was being recruited by the University of Dayton, so the St. Marys coach asked me if I wanted to ride along down to UD's practice. We went down, watched a great practice, and then the coach came over and asked if we had questions. Well, I did. He sat down with us for an hour or so and got films out and we watched them. It was a great clinic for me. The man did not have to do that, so I have a lot of respect for him. I took a lot of ideas from him that day. A lot of these coaches go to clinics and pay their money, but if I really want to get the nuts and bolts of what they are doing and how it's going to help my team, I go to college practices or NBA practices. You watch and take little notes here and there. You get a lot more out of that. Some don't want you there, but if you have kids they want to recruit, they always welcome you. A lot of the small colleges will give you better stuff than the large institutions, but what the Big Ten is doing, you just can't do anyway because they have much better athletes. I always make a habit of going to one or two every fall. I spend a lot of time on the road doing that, but I've gotten a lot out of it.

"I also use everything else I possibly can. I've read books. I've done the Internet thing, and I watch games on TV always with a pad and pencil right beside me, in addition to going to the clinics and college practices. One thing that's bad to do is to read everything by, say, Bobby Knight and then want to be just like him. Well, there's only one Bobby Knight. You have to pick and choose the things that are going to help you. You can't copy anybody. You have to be your own person if you want to be successful.

"If you want to coach basketball, Bob Knight's how to defend and how to run motion offense is good. Even if you don't run motion offense, at least you know what the other team is trying to do. In order to defend people you have to know just about every offense there is. We don't run motion much at all, but we at least know how to try to defend it. Coach K's [Mike Krzyzewski] stuff in how he relates to people and how he treats people is good. I got a lot of good ideas from Gary Williams when he was at Ohio State and from Gale Daugherty, Joe Campoli, and Jeff Coleman at Ohio Northern. I spent a lot of time up there. Ron Niekamp at Findlay, too, is part of the wealth of resources in this area. You don't have to drive too far. All it takes is getting on the phone and calling to ask about spending some time."

Hegemier has coached in the area for three decades because this is home for him. It's where he grew up and where he played.

"The high school coaching around here is very good. The crowd and the atmosphere at the games are very good. You aren't going to compete against the top fifty players, the great athletes, but you will run into some really, really good basketball players. This area doesn't produce the top one hundred players in the United States, but it's a blast to go into a gym when it's absolutely packed and there's a big game on the line. If you're on the road, you know most of the times people don't like you very much. That's called competition, and that's what makes it neat. I have kids that are being recruited from schools on the east coast and you have to explain what this area is like and how competitive it is. The recruiters usually go to games where there might just be moms and dads there. This is different. Here, you have small, little communities. The people all go to church. They all work. The kids come from solid families that take great pride in their communities. It builds competition because the administration, the parents, and the town take great pride in their schools. Just drive around here and look at the schools that these communities have built, and a lot of it isn't free money. It's like Loramie and St. Henry when they wanted a football program. They just put the money in the pot and they did it. They put their money where their mouth was. It's an outstanding area for living, raising a family and going to school. I explain to people from outside the area that every night we're in a gym that seats between sixteen hundred and two thousand and we have coaches who have been here a long time and they know what they're doing. Just look at all the state championships in the area, too. I ask if they've ever heard of Bobby

Hoying or Evan Eschmeyer, guys that got paid to play. Then their interest is piqued a little bit. I tell them there aren't a lot of top athletes, but the competition is absolutely outstanding. Mom and Dad don't like to hear that, but that's the way it is."

With his many years of coaching experience, Hegemier has no trouble recalling games that illustrate the high level of competition in the area. These games are spread out over several years, indicating that competing nose-to-nose isn't a new phenomenon.

"We beat Columbus Wehrle in the regional finals in 1987. They were the country's ninth-rated team in USA Today. When we first saw them play, we thought we were going to get killed. We saw them again and thought maybe. We saw them yet again and knew what we had to do to have a chance. So we did it. The kids believed in themselves. Everybody believed in themselves, and they did what they were told. Everyone tried to have that game plan or philosophy and we did it. Back then, every time Columbus Wehrle stepped on the floor it was a big game. They traveled all over the United States to play. In a game like that you have to play and you have to score a couple more points, and both teams did.

"Then in 1993, we beat Lima Central Catholic in the state semi-finals. We won twenty-one games the previous year and got beat for the first time by Botkins in the sectional final. We lost a lot of good players, but we had a lot of good players coming back. We went 16-4 during the season and then got on a roll in the tournament. We were playing the number one team in the state again, just like it was when we played Wehrle. We played LCC during the season at Loramie and got beat by fifteen and I thought our kids played great. Then we played them in the tournament and defended really well. We had some tough, hard-nosed kids and barely scored enough points to win. That was a big game.

"In 1998 we beat Jackson Center when they were undefeated at the end of the season. We walked in there just a little over five hundred and beat them in double overtime. That was a big game. Beating Ada at Ada this year [2007-2008] was a game between two high-profile teams [Ada and New Knoxville]. That was a big game, too.

"There are a lot of them, and I'm not doing my other teams credit. We've had some great battles at St. Henry and Marion. It's always fun beating teams that are way on top, and you sneak in there and get them and get out. That's fun. When you are the top dog, it's a little different. You're taking everybody's best shot every night.

"The most exciting games were when Jerry Harmon coached at Jackson Center and when we played Bob Seggerson at LCC. All those games were really exciting because their teams were so fundamentally sound. If you made some fundamental mistakes, you were going to get beat. Going against those guys was always tough."

Hegemier can also point to games that were instructive and gave him some on-the-job training.

"When I was at Spencerville in 1982, we were playing Ada in the sectional finals. We started terrible. I got them wired up at halftime when we were down maybe twenty points. We got back in it and took the lead with five minutes to go. By then, we were just too worn out. I had gotten them too wound up. We lost by a couple of points. That was a lesson I learned that you have to back off a little bit and save something for the end. It takes so much energy to get back into a game like that. In the last three or four minutes you have nothing left. You need to have something ready to change when you come back or even take the lead. That happened a lot at Spencerville. We could compete, but we often just didn't have enough to finish games.

"Jackson Center. Loramie. 1985. Regional finals. I called a time-out in the last twenty seconds. I should have let them play. I should have just let them go. We were playing that well. Our kids gave it the best shot they could, but we just came up a little bit short. It was one of the best-played games of one of my teams and we still got beat."

A trio of tournament-ending games during Hegemier's years at Knoxville caused him to take a step back and analyze why his teams weren't able to put the other teams away.

"My first year at Knoxville, we were just trying to play hard. We played Minster in the middle of the year and just got waxed by twenty points. I apologized to their coach, Mike Lee, it was that bad. Then we played them in the sectional final and we were up by about ten or twelve points with five minutes to go and couldn't get it done. We lost in overtime and Minster ended up at the state tournament.

"The next year we played Ada in the sectional final. We had gotten a lot better and we were up by seven points with forty-five or fifty seconds to go. We got beat by one.

"Then the next year we were unbeaten and we were playing Georgetown in the regional finals. We played about ninety seconds of just bad basketball. You have to sit down and look at yourself a little bit. What was I trying to do to help these kids try to win instead of lose. Georgetown ended up winning the tournament that year, Ada was pretty dog-gone good, too, and Minster had gone to state two years before. It was frustrating for me and my assistant coaches. If we were just getting waxed, we could go home and forget about it, but that wasn't the way it was. We did a few more things with our ball-handling and spent time talking to kids about how to make plays. Once you win big, it's easier to win the next time. For some reason, you get a little self-doubt in there, you get a stupid charge, you miss a little bunny, or you aren't focused, and you have to realize that in life things can go haywire like that. You have to just deal with it. Those were three tough losses for me. It was a big hump for Knoxville to get over, but we finally got over it this year.

"Most of the time in any tournament, you're going to have a game or two when you are going to have to fight and scrap and claw to win, but we didn't have that this year. We were only down four points once at halftime and that was over at Coldwater, not even in the tournament. Our best game this year was against Houston in the regional semi-finals. Our kids were extremely focused, and they could have named the score. They knew their challenge because Houston had a couple of nice players, and they shut them down. It seems that if our kids know the other team a little bit, we can really focus in practice on what moves they make and what tendencies they have. Our kids were really focused the last four games of the tournament against Houston, Seven Hills, Wayne Trace and Worthington Christian. In the previous three years we couldn't get over the hump, so we talked about that and our kids picked up on it. They didn't want to be denied. I felt very confident every game we played, and most of the time I don't. I watched the kids warm up and I felt extremely confident. Until you do it one time, it seems like that hump, no matter how small, is a mountain.

"We feel that we can get people to defend well enough to win a lot of games. There are a couple of things kids need to do on their own and that's ball-handling and shooting. They have to put it in the hole and they can't turn it over. There are years when you're just not going to win. We've won sixty-nine games in three years at New Knoxville and that's a lot of games. We've won the MAC, undefeated, for two years. It's unheard of. Even the St. Henry and St. John teams haven't done that. I feel very humble and very fortunate that we've done that, but shooting the basketball is a lot of it. Somebody has to put it in the hole for you. That just comes from kids liking the game and understanding the game."

All coaches need players who have a particular skill to contribute. Shooting would be the most desirable and it's something Hegemier has learned that players generally pick up themselves. Hegemier has had his share of shooters, some more orthodox and athletic than others.

"In these little kids' camps we might have fifty, sixty, or seventy kids, but out of each class maybe only three, four, or five at the max will play varsity, so to put that varsity uniform on, you have to be able to do something for us. When I was over at Spencerville, there was a guy whose sons played for us, and they were pretty good players. The dad was a walk-on at UC when Oscar Robertson and all those Hall-of-Famers were playing. He was the thirteenth man on the team. That's how good he was, but he was just a short guy. His kids were good athletes, but they couldn't shoot very well, so I was going through some shooting drills. He grabbed me and said, 'Coach, you're wasting your time. If kids want to learn how to shoot, they'll learn how to shoot. They'll go in the barn, the backyard, the garage, the driveway. They'll teach themselves how to shoot. You're wasting your time.' And he was right. Some guys can shoot it and some guys can't. We were fortunate to have guys who could shoot it.

"This year we had a guy who was about six feet tall and slow as a turtle. He couldn't run, he couldn't dribble, and he couldn't jump, and he didn't defend very well either, but, boy, could he shoot. When he was a JV player all he did was stand out on the perimeter and shoot the ball. He was our leading scorer most of the year and at about the four-minute mark he would go in. He could only go maybe two or three minutes. We run our kids, but that's all he had in him. I called him Meat Loaf because he reminded me of the singer Meat Loaf with that kind of body, and when he got in there, they knew to feed the Meat. Give it to him. For most of the year, I didn't say a word because I didn't want anybody to know about him. But after he made eight or nine threes in one game, they knew."

Despite the results Hegemier has been able to produce with his athletes, some aspects of the game remain difficult to teach.

"Being competitive every night and playing hard every night are the hardest things to teach. Sometimes, kids think they are playing hard, and I think they are playing hard, but they're not. I don't care if it's three o'clock in the morning. When the ball goes up, you have to play. A kid might have a twisted ankle or maybe he's sick but if he puts the uniform on, he has to play, and I don't want to hear it anymore. Sometimes you play tournament games at eleven in the morning. It doesn't matter. When it's time to play, it's time to play. That's the hardest thing to teach.

"In a game, it comes down to who has talent and who doesn't have talent, who can handle the ball and who can't handle the ball, and who can shoot or who can't shoot – home or away. In a season, it comes back to whether or not your kids want a successful season and if it means a lot to them. Granted, you can't do it every second, and the coaches can't either, but when you go out, give it everything you have. You don't want to be sitting on a bar stool saying, 'What if?' Ten years from now. You don't get another chance. You can't go back. That's a big obstacle for kids to overcome.

"We tell kids this is their opportunity and it's what they've been waiting for their whole lives. I tell seniors, 'This is your year. This is the year people will remember you by, not what you did as a sophomore.' For kids, what keeps them from success, then, is everything. That's why I'm a guidance counselor. All the little quirks and problems in life can affect the individual and every year it's something different, so I have to be fair and tell the kids the door to my office is always open if there is a problem or a concern. Then, there's always one of the biggest things which is if a kid is afraid to talk to you or doesn't want to be around you if certain things are bothering him. I try to make sure that wall isn't there. We have two other coaches around, and the kids know that.

"Sometimes we get a bunch of players who aren't on the same page with us. I think you can have one like that, but any more, and you're in trouble. It's very important for me that everyone has the same mindset.

"There are a lot of physical obstacles, too. We might have a 6'1" guard who's trying to defend a 6'7" kid from a team like Marion and the kid outweighs him by fifty or sixty pounds. That's an obstacle, but you just have to deal with that. More important are the mental obstacles."

Hegemier believes it's time for a coach to retire when it isn't fun anymore. When going to practice becomes a duty, then it's time to stop. Even though he hasn't approached that point, some aspects of the job aren't as pleasant as others.

"I don't like kids who are selfish, playing for themselves. I can just feel it. They don't guard their man. They make excuses all the time. They don't help their teammates. I don't think you can win like that, but you can't do a whole lot with it. You try to stress the team concept but they're clueless and you're not going to have a whole lot of success like that. Fortunately, you don't see that around here too much. I don't like selfish people and I don't like people who don't want to play hard and I don't want to hear excuses.

"I also don't like to do the paperwork which is all the stuff before the season like the rules interpretation meetings and first-aid. It's the same stuff you've been going over for how many years."

Many of the best moments in coaching actually occur for Hegemier years down the road when former players are still talking about their years playing ball.

"It's all about seeing the kid's faces when we've won or lost, but they've played their hearts out, and seeing them again five or ten years later and talking to them about the same game. It's being friends. Do you know how many weddings I've gone to? That's the reward."

For anyone who is willing to take on these various roles by becoming a coach, Hegemier has some advice.

"You better be ready to spend some time. It takes a lot of time. You have to do your homework, and you and your family have to be prepared to sacrifice. You aren't around as much, and I wasn't much fun to be around if we'd had a bad game. You'll spend a lot of time in the gym and on the road. You're just gone. There's really no off-time and you have to do it. The time will come, too, when you'll have to make a decision on a kid and it will be the right decision, but it won't work out. Kids break the rules. You'll have to make the choice as to what you're going to do and then that's it. If you're the head coach, you have to be willing to make the decision, and there can only be one captain of the ship. That's why I tell my assistant coaches to talk to me all the time. I don't want yes people. I want them to talk to me about any situation. Sometimes I'll listen and sometimes I won't, but they can't take offense.

"You'll have to work hard and spend the time. You can never be satisfied. Never. You should know you're there for the kids. The players are the only reason you're there, and you have to get them prepared to play. You have to do everything possible to help your team be successful and for kids to succeed on an individual basis as well. You have to be able to communicate with them and they have to be able to communicate with you. In other words, you have to listen. Everyone knows that you care whether you win or lose."

Hegemier's preparation for game day occurs on Monday, Tuesday, and Wednesday, not Friday.

"On game days, I get up, shower, dress and go to school. Maybe I'll close my door for a half hour to be by myself. Then, I'll go home, dress, and go to the game. That's it. I used to go nuts on game day, but as I get older I get smarter. I'm more mellow. Preparation for that game on Friday night is Monday, Tuesday, and Wednesday. It's not Friday. I can sit back and relax. On my drive to school for the game, my gut starts churning and moaning. I make sure everything is done. I've crossed all the T's and dotted all the I's. It doesn't quit churning until I get home. It's more of a competitive type of thing. I don't know if I'm on edge or so focused on just that one thing, but it doesn't stop until I'm home. I'm nervous and anxious during the JV game to be sure everything is done. When the ball goes up, let's just play. I'm focused on that.

"The pre-game talk is a time to review ideas for us to be successful against this team, how we're going to defend them and how we're going to score on them. Not too much rah-rah stuff because we don't have to.

"At halftime, we make sure the kids rest and get some water. I talk to the assistants, look at a couple of key stats, and sometimes I know exactly what I want to say. Sometimes, I don't. I ask a couple of kids how they feel and what they think we're doing right or wrong. We make a judgment and go with it. When we played Ft. Recovery for the district championship, they had a player we couldn't guard. My best defender perimeter player just couldn't guard him. I asked at halftime, 'Can we guard this guy at all?' And Tony Meyer said, 'I'll guard him.' He did it. He guarded him. I had the type of team you could do that with.

"The post-game talk is positive. I want the kids to go out of the gym feeling good about themselves. If we played badly, we'll talk about what specifics we have to improve. If we're on the road, we don't spend time in somebody else's gym talking about our problems. We go home to talk about them. We're the fastest people taking a shower. I tell the kids they have five minutes to shower and then let's go. Don't they have better things to do on a Friday or Saturday night than take a half-hour shower in somebody else's locker room? The press better get there fast, or I'm leaving."

A team's success depends on many variables from talent to team unity and that's something this part of Ohio grows as well as it does corn and soybeans.

"For success, you have to have talent and fundamentals. The kids have to like each other and run around together. Some of the best teams I've had might not have been the most talented, but the ones that got along with each other were the ones that won the most. We try to emphasize that. There are teams that get along on the floor, but outside the gym, they don't like each other. They usually don't win the big games. The more team unity you have, the better, even if you don't have as much talent.

"I love the small communities and the great pride each has. They are clean and well cared for. They have beautiful churches and great families. It's extremely competitive. It's a unique area as far as I can see. The proximity of these towns, like Marion and Minster or St. Henry and Marion, builds that competitiveness. Probably the first or second year I was at Loramie, I went back to the kitchen one day and one of the cooks said, 'You have Minster Saturday night, right? My grandma's got a hundred bucks on that. You better win that.' There you go. For some people you can win all your games and lose to Minster and it's like Ohio State losing to Michigan. That's the way it is. It's pretty neat.

"Plus, another thing is the good coaching around here. The guys work their butts off. You can't try to surprise them or do anything special because, well, it ain't gonna work. Period. If you don't win around here, you aren't going to be around here. People want to see, not so much winning, but being very competitive and fundamentally sound. All that is very important to these people.

"Most of the officials in the game want to be there and they enjoy being around the competition in this area, too. They do a pretty good job. You don't have officials out there who are trying to stick it to you, and the assigners today help tremendously. All I ask is that officials be fair and courteous and that they follow through with whatever the call is. I don't fight them because I'm not going to win.

"When I first started at Loramie, our biggest rival was Jackson Center. Anna was always a big game. Russia was a big game. Houston was a big game, and then Botkins got good and there were some huge games. When you went on the road in Shelby County, you were on your own and it all depended on who had the talent. At Knoxville, when I first got there, they had a real thing about Minster. The New Bremen game is always competitive and goes way back. The Ada game we just picked up last year will be competitive. We had the round-robin in Shelby County and I hated that because you sometimes played the same team three times. Plus, you couldn't get away with all the things you did in the first game. If I could get a couple easy baskets here and there the first time we played, the second time we played it wasn't going to happen. And we already knew that. Fort Recovery is getting to be a big rivalry right now. Any game you play in the MAC is a big rivalry. The rivalries here aren't as bitter as they were at Loramie. There were some bloody battles over there. Oh, and whatever you do, you can't lose to Anna. 'You're not going to let them beat you, are you?' Well, no. We weren't going to try. I mean, those guys were serious. With the type of kids I have right now, I don't feel that hate or bitterness. They just like to play. It's just good solid competition where they respect you and you respect them. Whoever wins gets to crow about it a little bit."

Taking his teams to the highest level of the tournament has happened more for Dan Hegemier than for most coaches, yet the explanation for how that happens isn't entirely knowable.

"I've had teams I thought should have gotten there, and we didn't. I've had teams I didn't think had a chance and did. Kids can get tired and bored, but you have to remain upbeat. They still have to be competitive and get on a roll and ride the roller coaster. If we sense it's getting boring, we try to change it up to liven up practice. Some people go to movies together and other things, but I don't want to take away from our routine. It's up to the coach to keep that competitive atmosphere going. We pretty much know what we're going to do in the pre-season and how we're going to go for the first five games or so. That's pretty much set. Then, if we're bad at something, we're going to work on it. If some of the things we're doing on offense or defense aren't working, then we'll change things a little bit. I'm always adding different offensive stuff we'll probably never use just to get kids to think a little bit. I don't think you can do the same thing in practice every day throughout the year. It would get boring for me, too.

"Our first goal every year is to win the league. Right now I have to get New Knoxville focused on winning the MAC, not winning the state tournament. That's a serious thing to consider because everybody thinks it's an automatic. People are putting sunshine up their butt and telling them how great they are and patting them on the back. It's not an automatic. It's the hardest thing we do, and it's going to be the hardest thing they ever do. You have to go after your league title every year. That has to be your main goal."

"One of my biggest phobias is to have a lead in a game I should win, and then lose it. I have to keep myself focused on that. I don't want to sub too early or maybe back off or just sit and relax. The kids are playing it, but I don't want to relax and lose a basketball game. Sometimes it doesn't matter what you do. You can have the greatest week in practice and the kids are all focused and pumped and everybody's ready to compete and then things just don't happen. The kids are trying and doing everything they can. The coaches are trying, but it's just not in the cards. Then you back off, go home, lick your wounds, and get ready for the next game.

"You can tell by three or four different things how the game is going. In the first quarter you can tell if you can defend someone or not. If they're going around you, shooting over you and they're running their half-court, you have to adjust your defense to try to stop it. If you can, you can carry on from there and try to score enough points to win, but you're probably going to have to slow the game down.

"I don't want to blow it when I'm ahead. When we're behind, we just want to keep scrapping and look for that little opening to gain a hold. We encourage the kids to keep playing harder and harder.

"I like to be the aggressor. If we're playing a team that's faster, then we'll back off a little bit and wait, but most of the time, we want to be the aggressor. Sometimes we can bring it back and run the flex and run it and run it and run it, or we can come down and run some sets or some high low stuff, or we get it down, get a quick look and go. I tell them to go as fast as they can until I tell them to stop.

"Sometimes, it's the ebb and flow of the game. The start of the first quarter, the middle of the first quarter, and the third quarter are big, too, to see how a team responds.

"We used what is called coaching protocol when we played Minster. They had gone to state the year before and beat us in overtime to get there. Our kids were really excited to play that game. Minster might have only scored ten points by halftime. The game was over in the second quarter. It was done. By the middle of the third quarter, their coach took his starters out, so it was time for me to do the same thing. We never want to embarrass anybody. If we'd wanted to score a hundred points this year, we could have done it eight or ten times. I never liked that when I first started out, and it will hurt you in the long run because if you have kids you need to give some time to, you need to do it. Once you feel secure enough that they can't get back in it, get them out. You don't want anybody getting hurt. What good does it do me to score those hundred points and Tony Meyer steals the ball and goes in for a lay-up, and because we're up by fifty, somebody gets mad and puts him in the wall and we have to peel him off of it. What good does that do me? What good does that do my team? When we step on the floor, we want to beat the other team and they want to beat us and both of us will try everything we can to do that, but when it's over, back off.

"I remember a game when we were waxing a team and they were scared and embarrassed. It was ten 'til nine with the fourth quarter going on and all they were doing was hacking. They were totally out of control. I told my kids, 'Let's just stand in a zone and go home.' We were out of there in ten minutes. If you know my teams, we don't do that. But that's not our goal to score a hundred and forty points."

Hegemier organizes his program from the off-season work down to the daily practices to be certain he's developing a competitive team. He begins his off-season in April with deciding on summer camps and shoot-outs. Open gyms are once a week and weightlifting is four days a week. In order for teams to be successful, they have to be in the weight room. We keep them entertained and keep them sweating. One of the biggest compliments we got after the state tournament was that Worthington Christian players said our players were just too strong for them. They couldn't drive around us.

"Keys to a good tournament run are being good, staying healthy and having a little luck, so we have some different things we do to keep them interested in the weight room. I don't think you can do the same exercise all the time and get bigger and stronger. We don't have a strength or conditioning coach, so Jerry VanderHorst, the physical education teacher at New Knoxville, devises some different routines, and we do that."

After the dead period in late summer, open gyms are on Sunday nights in the fall, and if the gym is available, maybe an open gym might be held during the week. Hegemier's players do a lot of running.

"We try to get a wide variety of people to scrimmage. We try to get good teams with good coaches. We don't want to play a bunch of stiffs. It doesn't do them any good and it doesn't do us any good."

"Practices start every day with defensive slides. We go into different types of running drills where they have to handle the ball, dribble the ball, catch the ball, and run. We do other shooting drills. We use the clock, and it's a great tool. They have to do certain things in a certain amount of time and if it isn't done, there are consequences. And they all know that. The clock makes them play hard all the time. It keeps everybody honest. There is no screaming or yelling. You do what you have to do and if not, 'On the line.' After that, we break down our defense to fifteen or twenty minutes at the most. That's it. We have certain drills we do and the clock is running. We do a lot of shell drills. We do one-on-one and two-on-two defensive work. We put time on the clock and you have to guard someone for a minute and he can't score. You have to have competitive kids to stop that. That's tough. We do five-on-five stuff then. We finish practice not running. I used to run the crap out of them, but I figure we get enough running during practice. Maybe we'll finish with competitive running games and then we'll shoot free throws. It's a lot of running if they don't make them, or it's push-ups or heavy ropes or just make something up so it's something they don't want to do."

Hegemier has played in the same area gyms for many years and believes his own gym has the biggest advantage for his team.

"I think Knoxville has the best home-court advantage. It's a unique situation. A lot of the gyms being built are big, two thousand plus, and you're away from the floor. Knoxville, they're right on top of you. They cleaned it up a little bit, but they're right on top of you. For me, going to Marion Local is my Achilles' heel. I've won one time at Marion and that was a few years ago in a couple of overtimes.

"I respect all the coaches around here. When I first started at Loramie, Jerry Harmon at Jackson Center made you do everything right or you were going to get beat. Mike Lee at Minster does a great job getting his kids to play so hard. Bob Seggerson at LCC, Mike Ernst at New Bremen and Paul Bremigan at Russia do outstanding jobs. Paul comes from a small setting and gets his kids to play, oh, so hard. Keith Westrick at Marion [Local] has kids that just battle you and battle you and battle you. All the coaches around here do a great job."

The scouting staff goes to games in those gyms and others. Hegemier has confidence in their reports because they understand the team needs.

"They know what I want them to look at. My assistant coaches Kort Fledderjohann and David Tinnerman do a great job of scouting. They go watch the game and tell me the game, and I feel like I've been there. They put it on paper, but they also call me and we talk that night."

"I try to give my assistants as much responsibility I possibly can. Kort does the offenses and shooting for guards. David takes care of the post play. I try to make them feel as much a part of the game as I can because it's critical to whether or not you win a game. If all you have is a stat book, I don't think it's helpful. I want someone who is involved. You have to get them involved in offenses, defenses and player selection. I've been fortunate to have had some excellent, excellent assistant coaches. At Loramie, Don Goldschmidt, Randy Bruback, Karl Ratermann, Keith Simon, Tony Brandewie, and Bob Kroeger were all excellent. Many of my former players have helped me. Good coaches do battle for you. They don't go uptown and cut your throat if something goes wrong. Good coaches have to trust one another and respect one another. Something that is often overlooked is junior high coaches. If they are good and they are fundamentally sound and doing what the program is doing, it makes it so much easier when they get to high school. Good junior high coaches are hard to find. I don't want to overwork my junior high coaches by having them scout, unless there is something special I need them to see. I appreciate what they are doing for me now, and I don't want to lose them. If they are good, keeping kids involved because you don't know who is going to be good in a few years, it's important to keep them happy.

The three-point line has been the biggest change in the game that Hegemier has seen in his years of coaching.

"People do a better job of defending you. Everybody does a pretty good job of that now. In the past, that was not the case. Coaching is very good around here. Otherwise, coaching is the same. Kids are kids and players are players. I've calmed down a lot over the years. I'm older, smarter and have more confidence in myself. If all you do is rant and rave, kids are going to get used to it. It's a waste of time.

"Every year at the rules meeting, I hear that they are going to clean up the inside game. They're really going to watch that. Well, I'm still waiting. They tweak the rules here and there on traveling, but I still think the biggest impact is the three-point line. Whatever they tell me I have to do, I do. I don't worry about it.

"I'd like them to allow coaches to coach a little more. Instead of worrying about whether or not a coach is a foot out of the coaching box, they should allow us to do what we want to do to encourage and instruct our players. That's what I'd like to see. I think league and district voting is solid with good, quality coaches doing a good job of getting the right players in the right places. What are they doing in Shelby County with administrators checking the votes of their coaches? If you don't trust a coach, why are you letting him coach your high school team?"

Hegemier has the distinction of winning state championships in three different arenas, an achievement no other coach will be able to attain, since the championships are now at home in Columbus at the Schottenstein Center. His first championship with Fort Loramie at St. John Arena in 1987 was followed by another state semi-final appearance there in 1988. In 1993, he led the Redskins to another state championship at the University of Dayton Arena. He returned to Columbus in 2008 with New Knoxville to claim the title, capping an undefeated season.

"After you win, you don't care if it happened in the worst gym in the state of Ohio. It doesn't matter. We were fortunate to have it in all three places and each time, at the end, it was such a great feeling of satisfaction. All that time and effort was worth it and it pays off. One of the biggest things you can give your kids, especially your seniors, is to tell them, 'You're very, very lucky. You have an opportunity to take that uniform off and be happy. Most of us never get that opportunity.' That's another big joy when those kids take the uniform off for the last time when they are seniors and they are state champs. It's pretty cool.

"The Knoxville championship was really neat for me because I'm from New Knoxville, I played there, and a lot of my family is still there. It was neat to see all those people up in the stands because you knew them all and I grew up with them all and they got to experience what a state championship is all about.

"The one thing I regret that happened after we won [at the Schottenstein Center] the media hustled me off to the media room instead of letting me go off to congratulate my kids. I really regret that. At UD, we went back to the locker room and everybody was all lovey-dovey. At St. John, it was the same thing. At the Schott, they just grab you and shove you off into this room. I didn't like that at all. I understand their timelines but they need to respect what we've just done.

"There were some other things, organizationally, that I didn't like there. Before the first game, I totally lost it. Most of the time you have a meeting in Columbus the weekend before the tournament, but because the weather was so bad, we didn't have that meeting and it was all done on a conference call. It was a tough thing for them to do, I know, but when we arrived to see the first semi-final game between Worthington Christian and Bedford-Chanel, we wanted to take our stuff to the game because we had the next game and there was no use leaving it at the hotel. We drove up about forty-five minutes before the game and were told we couldn't park there. I told them we had the next game. Now, maybe we might have been ten minutes early, but it still wasn't a good situation. The bus driver had to park in general parking, bringing the bus around later. Then they wouldn't let us put our stuff in a locker room. When I asked how many locker rooms they had, I was told they were being cleaned, but there were only two teams playing at the time. At the final game, they really took care of us, though. The kid who was supposed to be our host ran away, and I didn't blame him for not wanting to be around me. The conference call was the main problem there. They want it to be a positive experience and the OHSSA does a great job at that. Sometimes you just have some quirks that don't get straightened out."

Hegemier felt that in 1988 when his team lost in the state semi-final, the problem was that they weren't playing at their best.

"One of the things you want to do on the big stage is have your team and your coaches at their best. And we weren't at our best. We got beat by Kalida, a good team with a coach that is an institution. You give them credit, take you hat off to them, and move on, but it's pretty tough. You want to get to that final game."

In order to have a shot at that annual level of competition, good players must possess some basic characteristics.

"Good players must have athletic ability, fundamental skills, and no fear of working and playing hard. They must be good, unselfish team players with an innate [desire] to win and not accept defeat. Even if you have some players who are not very good athletes, if they can take instruction, follow instruction, and understand what you want them to do, they can be very beneficial to your team. Some coaches might say a kid is uncoachable, but I don't believe in that. You have to get on the same page or get on the same level with those kids and give them an opportunity. Then you pat them on the back when they take it. You can have kids who aren't very good basketball players and still win. I've always liked to have one lock-down defender that I can put on their best player and he's going to take care of him. I love those kinds of players. I'll sacrifice offense for that. I don't put my best five offensive players on the floor. I don't think I ever have.

"The group I had this year [2007-2008] wasn't as hard-nosed or as defiant in allowing another team to score, but they could just outscore you and defend well enough. I told the guys that if we could defend as well as some of my Loramie teams, we wouldn't be next to anybody. They heard that whining all year and sometimes I whine very well. I tried to get them to play harder on defense and focus on it.

"My style of coaching is that we're going to guard you, we'll try to be fundamentally sound on offense and defense, we're going to try not to make mistakes on either side of the floor, and we don't want to turn the ball over or give offensive rebounds. We'll try to get down the floor the best we can as fast as we can and try to get in position to score. How many easy shots you get in a game is critical. If you get two or three in a big game, it will probably win you the game. Most players try to get in that style.

"You can do certain drills in practice to put kids under pressure, but the best way to get kids to handle it is just to play. Play and forget it. We might have a two-minute drill where we're up five and there are consequences to losing. Our kids like running those two-minute drills because when the JVs beat the number one team in the state on one of those drills, then we start laughing at them, and they just don't like it.

"Tight games are what you want. The gym is filled up. It's excitement. When Derek Alexander came to Fort Loramie from Fairlawn, we played and beat Jackson Center. He was on the bench for awhile and he leaned over and said, 'Coach, this is why I came here.' Some kids can handle pressure, some can't. We try not to put them in a position where we draw up a play during a game and say, 'Go do it.' We practice it and practice it and practice it before we ask them to do it. It takes a week or two for it to sink in. They aren't NBA players.

"Most of the kids know the speech about being together and

winning together. The fun and success of your team will determine whether or not you have leadership on the floor. Tony Meyer was a natural leader and did a great job with that. I've had quiet leaders like Eric Fleckenstein and Scott Albers who just kept playing and there was no stopping them. Scott had his teeth knocked loose and kept playing. The next day I asked what the dentist had to say about his teeth. He hadn't been to the dentist. He said, 'I didn't need to go. They're just a little loose.' Leaders need to do the little extra it takes, not take shortcuts, and encourage their teammates to do the drills. Winners take the extra work and that builds leadership."

Hegemier has a number of core drills that assist in player development. He uses shell drills and likes transitional work, always looking for something unique to create excitement.

"We do one-on-one and two-on-two in defense, just to be sure their fundamentals are right. We spend time running, catching, shooting, and handling the ball the first part of practice. We do free throws; then we shoot, work on defense, and go five-on-five. I think it takes a lot of time for a good offense to develop. Bob Arnzen always said some people use the full-court press to get easy baskets, and that press will work the first part of the season but it won't work the last part. He's right. How many teams, who use the press as their basic way to steal the ball and score, press at the end of the season?"

When players are approaching the end of their high school years, Hegemier enjoys helping them make connections if they want to play at the next level.

"I think I have a pretty good feel for what level they can play. I know a lot of college coaches and I'll make phone calls, write letters, and do all the things that need to be done. My kids don't need to hire a recruiter to get to that next level. I enjoy that and I like doing that for them."

The advice Hegemier has for a parent is to come to the games and enjoy them because it's a time of life that goes quickly.

"I've been a parent and a coach, so sit back and enjoy. We ask parents to buy shoes, take them places, and spend money on camps. We take their sons, work them hard, and spend a lot of time with them. They can sit back, then, and relax and enjoy the games. That will make it easier for them and for everybody. It's not all positive and we hope it isn't all negative, but there is good and bad in everything. It's a part of life. I want them to have fun with it as much as the kids.

"The fans should come and enjoy, too, and be a positive influence. The kids don't need to hear all that negative stuff. Our boosters have always been great in Spencerville, Loramie and in Knoxville and they are all there to help the kids. I ask for certain things. They get it to me. I don't over-ask. It all goes back to the same thing. If you want to have a successful program, the more people you have on that same page, the more successful you will be.

"This is a fun game so be together, enjoy each other, be unselfish and positive things will happen."

Chapter  Six

BILL ELSASS

McGUFFEY UPPER SCIOTO VALLEY HIGH SCHOOL

1994 STATE CHAMPION

*"To win it all is complete satisfaction and excitement.
You feel so close to your players that you did it together.
That's real."*

B ill Elsass spent hours and hours during his youth playing basketball in the barn on the family farm near Jackson Center. When the barn was torn down awhile back, Elsass took some of the worn boards to place in the barn where he lives now.

"I just hated to see that barn torn down because we spent so many hours out there playing on the driveway inside the barn. We had a basket on one end and a basket at the other and a lot of kids in town came out to play.

"My freshman year, Fritz [Gross, Jackson Center coach] was the varsity coach and I got to sit bench for the 1963 tournament. Then he retired and Lowell Foote, who coached my sophomore and junior year, probably had some additional influence on my ambition of being a coach.

"In 1963, Jackson Center was the state runner-up, and the following year, I was a freshman. That 1963 tournament appearance had a big influence on us. We talked about the possibility of our group going to Columbus and we decided we wanted to do that. We ended up having a pretty good high school team, but we never did get there. Our goal was to make it, and it came from seeing that 1963 team go to Columbus."

The impact of that team as the first from Jackson Center to go to the state tournament and the first from Shelby County to accomplish that goal was enormous for Elsass. Basketball was in his blood for good. He played three years of varsity basketball at Jackson Center and all four years in college at Bluffton. After college, he continued to play in a league for men older than 20. It was a tri-county league that included Shelby, Mercer, and Auglaize players. Teams came from St. Henry, McCartyville, Sidney, and Jackson Center, among others, and showcased much of the best talent around. The league lasted about 15 years.

"I went to college to play basketball, actually. After a year or so, I had to make up my mind as far as a career choice, so I entered education. Coaching just seemed to fall right in with being a teacher. I was hired in 1972 as a junior high coach at Botkins. Jerry Klenke was the head coach at the time, and when he left, somebody asked me if I might be interested. I didn't have a lot of experience going from junior high coach right into varsity, but I went for it."

Elsass coached from 1974 to 1981 at Botkins, took five years off and then returned in 1986 and stayed another seven years. Then he left for Upper Scioto Valley in western Hardin County where he coached just one year, winning the state championship at the end of the 1993-1994 basketball season.

"The year before I went to Upper, my Botkins team lost in the regional final to Fort Loramie who went on to win the state tournament. I knew I had all my players coming back for the next year at Botkins. I felt, 'This is my shot, next year, to make it to state.' It didn't work out, but I went to Upper and they had a great bunch of kids. Both Botkins and Upper ended up making it down there [to the state tournament], but Botkins got beat in the semi-finals.

"I really didn't want to play Botkins in the finals, just for the fact that I didn't see any real good that could come out of it. It would have been nice for both of us to make it to the finals, but I just don't know. I made a comment to the news reporters that at least I wouldn't have to scout them; I knew everything they could do. Some people mistook that as a comment that we were so good we didn't have to scout, so you have to watch what you say, but that isn't what I meant."

The principles that Elsass kept in all the years of coaching came down to giving 100 percent in every effort. He attempted to give basketball its proper due without over-valuing it, though.

"I tried to go by God first, family second, and basketball third. Some coaches put so much emphasis on basketball that when kids wanted to do something with their family, they would say, 'No way.' I tried to bend over backwards for that principle. As years went by, I tried to treat all my players as if they were my son. In the earlier years, I didn't do that. I tried to be a tough guy and I did some things I regretted. After I had my own son, I mellowed out, changed, and always asked myself before every decision, 'What would I do if this were my son?' I also believed that if you can't enjoy every aspect of the game, then quit. And that's what I did.

I found myself dreading to go to practice and I knew that was no good. When I thought of my son being a freshman the following year, I wanted to follow him, so I informed the superintendent I was going to quit. He said, 'You can't quit. You just won a state championship.' But I reminded him that when he hired me, he said, 'Teaching is first, then basketball,' and that's what I intended to do. I don't regret it at all."

Elsass learned the lessons and strategies of basketball from clinics and a few books. He especially liked Iowa coach Tom Davis and his style of offense.

"I went to clinics and picked up a lot of information. I got a few books, but nothing I considered the Bible that I followed. I remember going to a clinic listening to Davis and he had a tremendous offense against a zone. I always struggled for years about what to run against zones. I picked up that offense and we ran it for several years. It was one of the big things I thought was really a factor in my being more comfortable playing against zones. I picked up the match-up defense from Cincinnati's Bob Huggins and we used it in the state tournament. The first day of practice at Upper, I told the kids they were going to learn the match-up defense. They did and we stuck with it and used it in the state tournament. We ran it the year before at Botkins, too."

Elsass believes he was in a good place to put his ideas to work as a basketball coach.

"It panned out that the teaching opportunity was here and of course you couldn't find a better place to coach than the western part of Ohio. I knew that it was a hotbed for good teams. The reason is the small communities and small schools. Logan County is a perfect example of the opposite. They consolidated all their small schools and they just weren't as competitive as they were when they had small schools. In the small communities, people get behind you and support you. That means a lot to the kids and they pick up on it. It makes for a successful area."

Elsass considers the regional final in 1979 as the biggest game of his career. He had coached the Botkins team at the junior high level and was then their varsity coach. The regional tournament started with an odd experience for Elsass.

"After the district finals, some guy came up to me and slipped me a scouting report of the team we were going to play in the first game of the regionals. I didn't know him from Adam. It was a good scouting report, but I didn't know if it was somebody pulling my leg. To this day, I don't know why, but it was pretty accurate.

"That 1979 team was a special group of kids since I started with them in junior high. Andy Counts, John Reed, Mike Yahl, and Tom Greve were among the players. Andy played varsity his freshman year. John and Mike stepped in their sophomore year. So I was with those kids a lot of years and we became very, very close. Today, those kids are probably my favorite. Several of them later coached for me. Ron Brown was a JV coach and Tom Greve was the freshman coach. In 1979 we were 25-0 and we had big expectations of making it to state. We had to play Summit Country Day in the finals. Dexter Bailey [drafted by the Denver Nuggets in 1984] played on that team. Back then you played the semi-finals on Friday night and turned around and played the finals on Saturday night. After the game Friday night, John Reed my point guard who was averaging fourteen points became ill and was sick on the bus all the way back to Botkins. The next morning I called him and he was still sick. We got back on the bus to play Saturday and he was as weak as a cat. He was sick with the flu, but he wanted to play. So we let him start. He went up and down the court about twice, but he was so weak, he couldn't play. We replaced him with Jeff Greve who did a great job, but it just wasn't the same without having John out there. We lost that game by one point. I had nine seniors on the team that year. We thought that was our year and we were going to do it, but it didn't work out that way. It's the hardest loss I've ever had and the biggest game I ever coached, including the state tournament.

"The most exciting game, of course, was the state final against Worthington Christian. They were a running team, so we put a half-court press on them to try to slow them down. It was pretty successful because they only scored fifty-four points. They had a player who hit seven three-pointers that kept them in the game. We found ourselves down fourteen with about six minutes to go and I called a time-out to tell the kids, 'We didn't come here to fold and be runners-up. We came here to be champs.' They went out, hit a couple three-pointers, got a couple of steals, and in a matter of two minutes, had it down to two points. We finally tied it up and with 5.6 seconds left, my guard went to the free-throw line and sank both of them. We were up two, but there was still 5.6 seconds to go. They had a really good point guard, and we knew he was going to get the ball. He brought it up the court and shot a runner just below the free-throw line. It bounced off the back of the rim, and that was the buzzer. It was exciting. What really made it more exciting was that our girls had won it all the year before in 1993 and everybody was talking about them. The boys were sick of hearing about it. The girls went back to state and won it again, and then the next week we won it. That made us the first school in the state to have both championships in the same year.

"To get to the state tournament we knew that scouting was essential since during the season you usually don't see the team you are playing. You have to scout three, four, or five times. When the tournament draw takes place, you know what bracket you are in and who you might face down the road. You look at who has the good records and you try to scout them a couple of times before the season ends and then when they are playing in a tournament game, and you're not, you try to get there to see them. They might get knocked off, though, and then you never end up playing them anyway. We played Bristol at the state tournament in the semi-finals, but we hadn't had a chance to scout them and they hadn't seen us. At the meeting before the state tournament we both agreed to trade tapes of our own teams.

"We played our games at St. John Arena and when you entered it, you were filled with so much excitement that you had to remind yourself to focus and not forget anything. I remember sitting in the locker room waiting for the previous game to be over. We got out there and saw the crowd in the stands and then I realized, 'We're here.' It's what every coach dreams of. At that point, you start focusing in and relaxing, just thinking about the task at hand. Once the game starts, it's business as usual and you kind of forget where you are. To win it all is complete satisfaction and excitement. You feel so close to your players that you did it together. That's real. It takes a lot to get there and when you finally accomplish your goal, you want to share it with everybody. I remember hugging my players and then wondering, 'Where are my wife and kids?' They came down on the floor and we just wanted to experience it with everyone. I still get the tape out every once in awhile. It still brings chills. My point guard, Brad Leonard, works at Henschen's and I was in there a couple of weeks ago. He stopped to tell me he was watching the game the other night. He said, 'It doesn't get old.' It was great.

Elsass remembers playing Triad in a sectional game in 1977. It was a game best forgotten, but Elsass took it to heart, learning lessons that he kept with him the rest of his career.

"In 1977 we played Triad in the sectional tournament and we had won the Shelby County Athletic League that year in my second year of coaching. We won the league three years in a row, 1977, 1978, and 1979, so we had some pretty good talent with Al Greve, Gil Bornhorst, Gary Poppe, and Andy Counts. We thought we had a good shot at doing something in the tournament, but their coach just plain out-coached me. They probably didn't even have a winning record. We had won something like eighteen games and they upset us. Part of it was that I don't think I was quite prepared, and it was a big lesson for me early in my career in that second year of coaching. I made up my mind that from then on, I would be prepared, even if on paper we were the superior team. You don't want to overlook anybody, especially in tournament play. It was a valuable lesson.

"Another thing I think about often is a time during the state finals when I was going to do something differently, but I didn't, and I'm glad I didn't. What would it have been like if I'd done what I wanted to do? There was 5.6 seconds to go and they had the ball out at the far end, and I called a time out after our two free throws were made. I wanted to talk about our defense. I was going to put two guys on Kevin Weakley, their point guard, in the zone and let somebody else handle the ball and not guard the guy taking it out of bounds. I figured if he threw it in, he didn't have enough time to get up the court and be part of the play. Our point guard said, 'Coach, let me have him. Let me have him. I'll stop him.' I had a lot of respect for Brad Leonard, so I agreed and told everybody else just to get a man and don't allow any three-pointers. A three-pointer would beat us and a two-pointer would tie us. So Brad took him and stayed in front of him. Then Weakley crossed-over dribbled and got around him with Brad on his side. He got down to the free-throw line and shot the runner but missed it. I thought that if it had gone in and we got beat, what would I have done? But what I wanted to do might not have worked, so the way it turned out was great. I play that over in my head, time and time again.

"In the district finals in that same year leading up to the state championship we played Liberty Benton. We were rated first in the state and they were rated third. As the year progressed, every time I looked up in the stands, there was Liberty Benton scouting us. They must have scouted us ten or twelve times, so we went head to head, but our game plan worked perfectly, and we beat them by three. They had an All-State player and we were playing match-up defense. We wanted to really key on him. We put one man out on the point guard and one guy back on the foul line. Every time they'd throw the ball over to the wing player, the person on the foul line would go over and take him automatically, whether there was somebody else guarding him or double-teaming him or whatever. It was a big key in the game because it took him out of it. One thing that frustrated me in that game was my center, Jason Williams, who was conference Player-of-the-Year all four years, sprained his ankle. I thought, 'Not again,' remembering back to when John Reed at Botkins got sick. We got him to the bench, re-taped him, and he went back in and played, but that was kind of an anxious moment. That game was a great game. Our scouting report was great. It all worked out well."

The match-up defense worked well in that game, but Elsass found that over the years, defense was the hardest thing for him to teach his players.

"I was always offense-oriented. I liked to shoot the ball when I played. I remember in 1977 when Jim Schrock was my assistant coach. We were playing Russia at Versailles. It seemed like everybody back then had two good scorers. We had Al Greve and Gil Bornhorst and they had two good shooters, too. The game was winding down and I looked up at the score. Both of us had scored over a hundred points. I told Jim, 'I can't lose this ball game and score over a hundred points. That would be terrible.' We couldn't play a lot of defense that year, but we could shoot.

Today's teams score half that because they play so much better defense, and they even have the three-pointer. We didn't have it back then.

"Defense was always tough for me, and I just don't know why. I went to a clinic and heard Bob Huggins [University of Cincinnati coach] talk about the match-up defense. After the clinic, we got back to Botkins and talked to his assistant on the phone who told us to call anytime we had questions. I called him two or three times after that, and they were always good to answer whatever we asked. We started putting that into our game plan in 1993. Then when I left Botkins and went to Upper, I looked at our personnel and thought, 'Man, this is perfect,' so we put it in up there. That was a turn-around for me because I was able to feel comfortable with our defense."

Getting past the teaching of defense, Elsass also believes there are other roadblocks to success. Individualism can wreck a team and most often that is evidenced when a player is concerned with his own performance instead of how that performance helps the team.

"Individualism is a big obstacle. If you keep kids thinking about the team, you're going to have a lot more success. At the beginning of a season, an individual and a team need to set goals together. I've had times when certain players were worried about their stats and so forth. There's nothing that tears a team apart more quickly than a player who is playing just for himself. I was always careful about individual stats. Even when I talked to news reporters, I always tried to be more team-oriented. I didn't like to bring one person's name up. No good comes out of it. One player doesn't win a ball game.

"Team preparation is important to success. I was always impressed with Bob Arnzen [Delphos St. John coach]. Bob would go to the game, sit on the bench, cross his legs, and watch his kids play. I asked him about that once, and he said, 'Bill, I do my coaching during the week. The kids know what I want.' He was always mild-mannered. It made me a little less fiery. I had a lot of respect for Bob, and I thought that was a good idea. Not that you sit on the bench and do nothing, but you just have to make sure you do your job during the week."

The biggest irritation Elsass faced as a coach was parents. It was difficult for him to deal with some parents, and when he got out of coaching it was at a time when he became the parent of a player himself. He has seen both sides.

"Although I hate to say it, sometimes parents can be a problem, and I've seen both sides. The 1979 parents were very supportive and they would do anything for you. It showed in the kids' performance. Kids didn't come with a chip on their shoulders. They weren't hearing one thing at home when I was telling them something else. There were other times, on occasion, when parents made it very rough. I remember Johnny Orr [University of Michigan and Iowa State University coach] saying at a clinic one time, 'You know, the perfect place to coach is at an orphanage.' I often thought about that. After I got out of coaching and my son played, it's pretty hard to sit back and be a parent. As I look back after my son graduated, if there is something I would tell parents, it would be to be supportive and one hundred percent positive whether you agree with things or not, because it passes by so quickly. The more you gripe and complain, the more it will be a miserable time for you. It's one of the best times of your life to watch your son or daughter play basketball. You might as well enjoy it because you aren't going to change it anyway. I probably did some things as a parent that weren't the best things to do, either, but as I look back now, I probably wouldn't have done those things.

"Scouting was the thing I really hated. You finally get a night off and you can't stay home and spend time with your family. You have to go scout. Or you play Friday night with a Saturday night off and you have to go watch somebody. The best scout I ever had was Jon Cook. When I was at Upper Scioto Valley, he was my scout. He was an Upper grad and had sat on the bench as sort of a student assistant at Ohio Northern. He knows the game and when he'd go on a scouting trip and come back, he'd have a book."

Satisfaction in coaching doesn't come at the end of the game when the scoreboard lights display a winning number. For Elsass, the reward occurs throughout the game.

"The satisfaction of seeing a game plan work to perfection comes from putting something together and on Friday night the kids carry

it out. Some of the most fun years I had weren't the teams that had
winning records. It was when we were the underdog. At practice,
we'd try to find something that would win us a ball game and once
in awhile, we'd pull one out. We had no reason to win. In 1980,
we had lost nine seniors from 1979. I brought in some kids that
had no varsity experience whatsoever. We struggled until we got to
the tournament and we ended up winning three tournament games.
That was a lot of fun. We played a lot of sophomores and juniors
that year, so our goal was to get better each game, wanting to be
better for the next year.

"You have to find something that works for you. New coaches
should be themselves and not try to imitate somebody else. I see
so many coaches who aren't themselves. They try to be somebody
else like Bobby Knight or Rick Pitino. It doesn't work. Kids can
see through that. A young coach should try to find something
that fits his personality. Everyone is different. Two successful
coaches aren't alike. That's what's neat about coaching. You can
be different and still be successful. You just have to find methods
that fit your personality, and of course, find methods that fit your
players, especially in high school. You can't recruit all kinds of
players, so you get all variations. Some coaches stick with the
same thing, year in and year out, regardless of what kind of talent
they have. I always looked at what I had coming the next year
and tried to find what fit with their physical abilities. You have
to be fair across the board with kids. You try to make everyone
feel important to the team. You try to keep it positive. So much
more can be accomplished."

Elsass liked to follow his normal routine on game day. He had
an established process for addressing the team before and after
games, but when it was over, if the team lost, he experienced what
only other coaches understand after a loss.

"You are there by yourself after everybody leaves the gym. The
players leave the locker room, and you replay the game in your head,
wondering what you could have done differently. Only other coaches
understand what you go through then.

"On game day, I would go through my normal routine at
school. After school, I'd come home and I always took a nap. A

lot of people couldn't believe I did that. I always relaxed and I'd be refreshed and ready to go. On the way to the game, I started to get excited and I got a little nervous until the jump ball. Once the ball went up, I was ready to settle in. The butterflies would go away and I'd be ready to coach.

"The pre-game talk would be going over the game plan. We tried to refresh the kids' memory on what to do. We tried to mentally prepare them by visualization. We went so far as to shut the lights off in the locker room and have the kids shut their eyes and visualize themselves doing things successfully. If you were a point guard, you were to visualize yourself bringing the ball up. If you were struggling shooting free throws, you visualized yourself being successful there. I felt it had a positive effect. Sometimes, we'd even do it in practice. Then we'd turn the lights on, do a little rah-rah and out the door we'd go.

"At half time, I suppose it was the same as anybody else. We'd come in and look at what we were doing successfully and what we weren't doing successfully and try to adjust. I always tried to change something, even if we were ahead by twenty points. You knew the guy in the other locker room was doing something to adjust to what you were doing in the first half. If we changed what we were doing, then what he told his players had no effect. We always looked at the stats. You can get involved in the coaching and get focused in on one thing and you look at the stats and suddenly realize the other team had a player who had scored twenty points. There were a number of times when we played man-to-man the first half and came out in a zone in the third quarter. They struggled to get anything going and then we'd go back to a man-to-man. There were other times when we changed something and the lead just dwindled away. More times than not, though, it had a positive effect.

"Win or lose, at the end of the game we tried to find something positive. You don't want kids going out of the locker room feeling bad. You try to find something individually or as a team and then learn from it. Sometimes, you learn more from a loss than a win. Have a huddle for some team unity, and then let them shower and get out of there. I didn't want to spend a lot of time at that because I wanted to go over the game film and the stats myself before we discussed what went wrong. A lot of times, your first impression after a game is that a player had a terrible game. Then you look at the film and see why, or you see that it wasn't as bad as you thought it was. So sometimes if you open your mouth right after a game, you can put your foot in it. I waited until Monday or Saturday morning when we had a chance to get the kids together to discuss it."

A coach's family and friends travel the same road with him and sometimes it's a good trip and sometimes it isn't.

"You put so much time in that even when I wasn't in the gym or at school, I found myself thinking about basketball. My wife sacrificed big time. One time when I was coaching at Upper, she went to our kids' games in Jackson in the morning and in Botkins in the afternoon. Then in the evening, she'd come over to Upper Scioto Valley for two games. The family puts up with a lot. The kids benefited from Dad's advice once in awhile, but it could get rough for them with their dad being a coach. I remember once playing Jackson Center and my son, Travis, was about a second-grader. Early in the game my manager said something to the official and got a technical foul. The official explained what happened and then gave me one. Of course, back then, if you got two technicals – and the manager's went on the coach – the coach had to leave the ball game. I walked across the gym and into the locker room. Travis didn't understand what was going on and he was in tears. That was a trying game. Kids go through some rough times, too, when their dad is coaching. It's not all glory.

"I have great friends who were former players. I still see some of my assistants and even opposition coaches. Your social life is basketball-related when you are coaching."

Success in a game or a season comes from a number of sources. Elsass can identify several of them.

"You have to have talent. If you don't have the horses, you aren't going to be good. The kids have to be team-oriented and dedicated. The most important is having the deep desire to be the best. The good ones have that. They put all kinds of hours in working on their own.

"This is a bed of Division III or Division IV schools. When you are in that small school, the community gets behind them and the kids pick up on how important it is to be a part of it. You get to the big schools and you don't see little kids in the gym. You don't see people in the community either. Teams out of Cincinnati and Dayton only have parents in the stands. Some of the communities around here have the big, German kids, but others don't. I think it's the small communities with the small schools. When the small schools consolidated in Logan County, those communities lost their school and the spirit that goes with it."

School spirit fueled the fire that brought rivalries with other team-oriented communities.

"When I started coaching at Botkins, Bob Anderson was at Anna and those two schools had a big rivalry. Bob played a part in that because he always referred to Botkins as, 'The school up north.' We were five miles away. He went so far as to tell his players they weren't allowed to attend the open gyms at Botkins or associate with Botkins players. I respected Bob and I got my eyes opened. He was very serious about Botkins and Anna. I learned pretty quickly that when you played Anna, you better be ready. Everybody in both communities thought it was the biggest game of the year."

Elsass has learned that the dynamics of the game and the decisions he makes related to the action on the court are, sometimes, a roll of the dice.

"You never really know when you're going to win or lose, so if you want to get some of the players in, you might gamble a little and put them in there, but I've seen games change in a hurry, especially today with the three-point shot. It's just a feel. It depends on how good your subs are. There are times when you don't have a lot of confidence in your subs and then there are times when your subs a just a little below the talent of your starters, so you have no problem sticking them in early."

As soon as one season was over, Elsass was planning for the next. He had a plan for his entire season and a plan for each practice.

"After the season's last loss, I began preparing right away thinking about returning players and our strengths and weaknesses. You had to improve the following season. We looked at our strategies and we went to clinics that focused on the area where we wanted to make changes. We organized camps and open gyms to get them ready to go. We tried to sit down with each player and talk about their strengths and weaknesses and what they had to do in the summertime on their own to assure them they would have more playing time the following year. We set some goals and gave them some drills to work on in the summertime, too.

"I was big on conditioning. I look back on how conditioned those kids were, and I might have gone overboard. My players were always in good shape. We'd start conditioning six weeks before the season started. We had all kinds of drills. We weren't allowed to touch a basketball, but we did everything but. We used volleyballs, ran figure eights, and ran a six-minute mile. I told kids if they couldn't run a six-minute mile, they couldn't play for me, and I had some pretty good players that couldn't do it. I tied a rope around one kid's waist and tied the other end to my car and went ten miles per hour to make sure he was going to come in on time. He might have not made it, but I said he did. I was the one with the stop-watch.

"Scrimmages always go back to the team you have. If we had a good team coming back, I'd search for the best team to scrimmage. Division I schools would let us in to a three-way scrimmage if we were pretty good. If I had a so-so team, I didn't want to scrimmage the best. It would demoralize kids. I tried to find someone they could be competitive with so they would go into that first game of the season with a little bit of confidence. Of course, then you always have your buddies from college you want to scrimmage.

"I broke practices down into ten-minute intervals throughout a two-hour practice. We'd drill and I was big on intensity. After ten minutes, if we didn't make any progress, down deep I wanted to go twenty minutes, but we couldn't. The kids would lose their intensity and then you're just wasting time. So I stuck with going hard for ten minutes and if you got it, fine. If you didn't, we'd try again next time. In the beginning of my career, I worked on something until I was satisfied with it, but the kids would loaf and get bored, so I learned to go from one ten-minute drill to the next. Kids weren't allowed to sit down. To run from one drill to the next, in two hours it's bang, bang, bang, bang, bang. Our practices were actually conditioning, too. I'd always break down our defense and offense. In our match-up defense I had a drill that was only for the guards out front. The other drills were for the post men down low. All players participated in guard drills and all players participated in post drills. When the big men saw the guards working their tails off to cover that whole outside perimeter, they had an appreciation for that guard out there. They might not be able to cover it when you have guards playing post or vice-versa, but they appreciate and understand what the other person is doing. Sometimes, in a game, you get a mismatch that comes into play. You get a guard that might be five inches taller than the guy guarding him, so you get him down in there and let him post up.

"One other thing we tried to do in practice was over-stack the second team. If we were doing some three-on-three work, the offense would have three players and the defense would have four. The second team would always get an extra man. The second team usually wasn't as good as the first team, so it was easy for the first team to perform in practice. In the game, it's not the same, so by going against more players in practice, it prepared them for the game situation. We tried to make situations game-like. Then the last thing we did was always a conditioning drill with a basketball. We never just ran."

Elsass believed that when his teams took the floor at home, they had a big, but dubious, advantage. His own players at Botkins and Upper Scioto Valley all knew the other teams were going to have difficulty when they arrived at those venues because they had trouble there themselves.

"We had that tile floor at Botkins. Everybody hated to come and play there. We always said that other teams only had to play there once. We had to play there ten times. I never told my players that because we wanted to make it a positive thing. We'd tell them we had a big advantage because other teams hated playing on a tile floor in a small gym. We made our kids feel it was an advantage. It really was an advantage for us, I suppose, because we could practice in there.

"At Upper Scioto Valley, they had a court that was smaller than Botkins. When I got there, the bench was on the sidelines and the kids' feet were out on the playing court. I changed it and put the bench on the first row of bleachers on the opposite side. The fans were upset because it took seating away from them. It was terrible."

Elsass has been out of coaching for awhile, but he recalls several changes during that time that today's fan accepts as just another part of the game.

"They did away with jump balls. A year or two before that, I went to a clinic and sat next to a guy who said he had a good play for jump balls. He gave that to me, and anytime we had a jump ball underneath our basket, we scored. The next year, they made that rule change and I was so frustrated that I had just gotten this play that worked great, and I couldn't use it.

"The three-point shot did two things. It opened up the inside game because the defense just couldn't sag back inside, and it added a different dimension to the game. You can catch up more quickly. I think it was a good thing.

"We should put in the shot clock because there are too many times when the superior team is at a disadvantage if the other team is holding the ball. You have to do what you have to do to give yourself a chance to win, but if you're that superior team, you want to play that ball game. I think the shot clock should be put in with maybe thirty-five or forty seconds on it to give the team a chance to run an offense. You don't want to turn it into a running match, but it keeps a team from holding the ball."

The number of coaches on a staff and consequently on the bench has risen over the years. Elsass began coaching when only a JV coach occupied the bench with him during the varsity game.

"At Botkins, I didn't have a varsity assistant. It was the JV coach who kept certain stats and gave advice. I was always open to their suggestions, and even though we didn't always do it, I listened. At Upper, I had a great JV coach in Andy Howard, who gave great advice. He sometimes suggested what personnel to get in or get out of the game. Sometimes it was changes in offenses or defenses. He had been the JV coach for several years under the previous coach, who left for a college position, and he knew a lot about our opponents which was good because I wasn't familiar with the teams we played up there in the Northwest Conference.

"You have to surround yourself with the best coaches. I think a lot of coaches are intimidated by having someone with a lot of coaching experience who wants to be an assistant, but you have to have the best. It will only make you better. If you have confidence in yourself, it shouldn't bother you. Communication is important with your coaching staff. Just don't have them there on the bench not saying anything with you ignoring them. You have to make them feel important. And, then your coaching staff has to be willing to put in long hours and scout."

Elsass remembers that playing in Shelby County meant facing some formidable competition led by some talented coaches.

"Early on, the coach I most respected was Bob Anderson, and later on, it was Dan Hegemier. Bob was so intense and he got a lot out of his players. It was a good rivalry and everything associated with him was good. He was a veteran and I was a rookie. It was always a big challenge to play Bob. Later, with Dan, it was his flex offense. His kids would run it, and run it, and run it to perfection. You knew what they were going to do, but you couldn't simulate it in practice because you couldn't do it as well as they did.

"I learned that when you have the lead, you do what you want to do offensively and defensively. When you are behind, you react and try to change the momentum. A lot of games were lost when the coach tried to slow the game down after getting the lead. Being offensive-minded the way I am, I always tried to maintain the pace that got us there. I had a stall offense I stole from Jerry Harmon. He used it against me and it worked, so I wanted to put that in my book."

In his evaluation of players every year, Elsass looked for qualities beyond athletic talent to build strong teams.

"Good players have a desire to be great, and many of them are coachable, too. They know the game. They spend extra time in the gym and the outdoor court working on their shots or playing pick-up games and lifting weights. The kids who do whatever it takes are special. If you get one or two of those on a team, you're going to be good.

"I look at coaches and you can tell that if he's a big guy, he probably played post and his game is oriented around post play. A guy like me, I was always a guard, is guard-oriented and probably has a running team. I fit that mold. I probably had three players that fit my style in Jason Wendel and John Reed at Botkins, and Jason Kearns at Upper.

"Some players can handle pressure, and some don't. You can simulate it in practice, but some never do. Some can't handle pressure, and others thrive on it. As a coach, you set those pressure situations up in practice and you see the players who thrive. When game time comes, you want those players to have the ball in their hands in certain situations. At the state tournament, we held the ball for the last shot. We took it to the hole and got fouled. Now, back when I got to Upper, Brad Leonard and Jason Kearns were talking to me one day, and they said, 'Coach, we've dreamed about going to the state tournament for years. When we were kids, we played out in a barn and pretended we were at St. John Arena.' Jason said he had dreamed about making a foul shot to win the state tournament. So here we were, at the end of the game. The ball fell into his hands and he got fouled. Worthington Christian called a time out and the team came over to the bench. I told Jason, 'Your dream has come true.' I can show you the tape of him walking up to the foul line. He had a smile on his face. He was living the dream, and he sunk them both. He was a kid who was a gym rat. He knew the game inside and out. His mom and dad thrived on basketball. They were just a great family.

"The kids on the team know who your leaders are, so if you try to put someone else in that leadership role, it won't work. You can try to build leadership by giving kids certain responsibilities, but you can't force a person to lead. Leadership is a natural thing. Kids are going to follow who they want to follow, and sometimes that's a good thing and sometimes it isn't.

"If you expose kids to competition early in their lives, it plays a big part in developing their competitive drive. You see little kids at the state tournament and they experience that and they want it. They see the success of other teams, and they see what happens when you put in hard work."

Elsass used several drills that focused on sound fundamental development and honed the skills necessary for versatility on the court.

"Correct shooting form is big. All the good shooters have the same basic shot. The elbows are in and the follow-through is there. If you can get a little kid to work with a smaller ball so it's not too heavy, he can develop the correct shooting form early. If you wait too long, the kids develop bad habits that are hard to break.

"Ball-handling is important, especially to develop the weak hand. Whether you are a guard or an inside man, you also have to develop post moves, particularly in high school when you have all kinds of mismatches. We spent hours shooting free throws, too. Many games are won or lost from that free-throw line. Finally, strength training is much more important today than it was when I was playing. Back then, they said that weight training would throw your shot off, but look at LeBron James and what weights have done for his game. He takes it inside and gets banged around. I watch the old games on TV and even the college players way back when are skinny. It isn't that way anymore."

Coaches have responsibilities off the court and some of them believe that assisting a player beyond the high school game belongs in that category. Dealing with other influences beyond the game is a part of the coach's world, as well.

"A coach is a mediator between a college and the player. The parents, of course, have to be involved. You have to prepare every player as though he's going to college because you don't know which one is. What usually happened, in my experience, was that an assistant college coach would show up at a game and after the game, he would contact me to say which player he was following. At that point, I would tell the player a certain college was looking at him and ask if he would be interested in going there. Most college coaches will talk to the high school coach before they talk to a player. If they want to talk to a player, they'll ask permission. They're pretty good about that. I remember when Josh Steinke and Jason Wendel were freshmen at Botkins. They were getting letters from colleges, but they changed that and now colleges have to wait until somewhere around their junior year. It used to be unbelievable. Those boys were getting letters, as sophomores, from UCLA, Brigham Young, Temple, Ohio State, Michigan, and Iowa. It was ridiculous. I can see why they changed the rules.

"The parents, overall, need to be positive. It's hard to do, but looking at what good can come of a situation and being supportive of the coaching staff is the best way out.

"The fans should just enjoy the game and stay out of the coaching aspect because they don't know the inside story of what's going on with the players. It can look totally different in the stands because the fans don't know what's been going on all week long. If fans have a problem, they should work through the school's administration. I had a fan hit me in the head one night at Triad. They had a small gym. I kind of leaned forward and looked around. He was mad. So I motioned the cop down and told him what happened. He didn't escort him out, but he did sit by him."

Elsass also believes that the officials should stay out of the spotlight. The game is for kids and when officials lose sight of that, the game suffers.

"The influence of the officials is very important. Some aren't out for the kids. There was one in the Southwest District that always made a big show. When I got to Upper, I thought I wouldn't have to run into him anymore, but in [one of our tournament games], I walked out on the floor, and there he was. I told the kids in the locker room 'Don't say a word because this guy will give you a T right now. I guarantee you, he's going to call a T on somebody, and at a crucial time in the game, he's going to call a big three-second call.' During the game, he called a technical on the opposing coach and he called a big three-second call right down the stretch. He didn't seem to be in it for the kids. If you've been in coaching for awhile, you generally know the officials."

A positive experience Elsass describes without hesitation was his interaction with the media, especially the local reporters from the smaller newspapers.

"I always enjoyed working with Ken Barhorst at the *Sidney Daily News*. I'm not the best speaker, and he would take notes and make it look like I had a little bit of knowledge anyway. If I said, 'Ken, this is off the record,' I never saw it in the paper. He was just first-class. You aren't going to find anybody better than Ken.

"Then, when you get to big arena, it's a lot different. The big newspapers are there and they are firing questions at you, and what you say is what's printed. After we won the regional finals in Toledo, a representative came down to the locker room and wanted the coach and two players. They took us to a room for a half an hour with about twenty-five reporters asking questions. The bad thing was, they were asking questions of the players, and you have no control over what the kids are saying. They're just kids. When we got back to the locker room, all the other players were dressed, and there were these two still in their uniforms. The bus was outside ready to go because we wanted to get to Columbus to watch our girls play that evening. We waited on them and then took off. After we won the championship, then, school was over for the year. Both teams were going everywhere. I bet we took five trips to places like the state capitol, plus there was always someone coming in to talk to us.

"In my experience with boosters and administrators, I've been fortunate that they let me do the coaching. As far as league and district voting goes, there are some flaws in it, but it isn't the place for grudges. If you vote against a kid because you don't like the coach, you're only hurting kids. I don't think those kinds of problems are prominent, though. I've had positive experiences throughout my career."

Chapter  Seven

TONY ROGERS

BOTKINS HIGH SCHOOL

1994 STATE SEMI-FINALS

*"Successful teams have expectations, and if they use
expectations in the right way it can be a powerful
tool to get them where they want to go."*

Tony Rogers grew up just down the road from Botkins High School where he coached the Trojans four years in the 1980s and two years in the 1990s. "Down the road" in Botkins translates to Anna, and that's where Rogers went to school and played ball for the father of Anna basketball, Bob Anderson.

"Growing up in Anna, I knew basketball was very important. I was lucky to grow up with a certain group of friends who were athletic-minded. It got me started into sports which were very important to my childhood and, later on, my career.

"I give a lot of credit to my wanting to become a teacher and a coach to Bob Anderson. He had a lot of good teams, but he never made it to state. He was one of the best coaches in Shelby County in my estimation. I knew there were certain things in his personality that I wasn't capable of doing. He was hard-core on discipline, rules, and regulations. I just didn't feel like I was that type of person. It took me awhile to realize I wasn't going to become a Bob Anderson or a Bobby Knight. I also credit [former Botkins superintendent] Jim Degen who was willing to take a chance on me right out of college and hired me as a JV coach and then as the varsity coach the very next year. He had a lot of faith in me and I had a lot of chats with him about kids and problems. I'm not sure I would have been able to handle some of those early situations without a mentor."

Rogers wanted to become a coach, so he went to college and began to work on his degree in education. As the years passed, teaching became his first interest, but the desire to coach was still strong.

"Back in those days, you didn't find many coaches who weren't teachers. If you wanted to become a coach, you were going to become a teacher. I think having coaches who are not teachers is needed today. The commitment that sports has become as a twelve-month job is hard. You don't see the thrity-five-year coaches who are teachers anymore."

Rogers developed his own coaching style by staying true to some basic beliefs about kids, management, and personal values.

"At Botkins, we had an unwritten rule that you didn't cut kids. There were kids I wanted to cut because of attitude, but I couldn't. It was an obstacle I fought. At times, I think, you need to cut kids. If you don't, they think it's an automatic ride. Some kids will go out just because their friends are on the team or there is some prestige involved. I believe kids need to work to get that job.

"I was fortunate to work under two superintendents who let me make the decisions. I was allowed to decide how things were run. Discipline was up to me or my coaching staff. Over the years, I've been fortunate to have some great athletes. I've had the all-time leading career scorer [at Botkins] in Bob Burden. I've coached most of the thousand-point players during my career, and those kids were team-oriented. Bob Burden, even though he was the leading scorer, was a most unselfish player.

"I was strict on kids not drinking or smoking, but it was a constant battle in Shelby County. They knew where I stood. I remember Bob Anderson saying, 'If you're going to do it, you'd better go deep, deep, deep into the woods. If I catch you or hear about it, it isn't going to be good.' I took that philosophy from him. You can't stop it, but kids need to know you won't tolerate it. I also wanted kids to become good people as well as good players, so one of the most important parts of the job was being a good role model.

"It wasn't much of a decision for me to come back to the area, having graduated from Anna and then Wright State.

I married somebody from
Botkins. Loyalty is very
important to me, not that I
haven't looked other places
throughout my career, but
this place has been good for
me and my kids. I'm probably
one of the few coaches who
have coached a varsity sport
three different times, and I
felt fortunate each time I was
allowed to do that. Each time
I got out, there was a reason,
but I'm fortunate they hired
me three times here."

Rogers coached the varsity girls team for ten years after he
left boys basketball in 1995, but even today, his mind isn't very
far from the game.

"One of the things I miss is the clinics and camps. I went to
many clinics where I made some very good friends. Bobby Knight
and Rick Pitino had three-day clinics that were instrumental in
helping me become a good coach. Back in the early 1980s, you
didn't have the team camps you have today. If a kid wanted to go
to an individual camp, that's what you did. A lot of my knowledge
came from things I picked up at clinics and camps."

Rogers put that knowledge to use in 1994, the first year of his
second stint as head coach, and came away with a trip to the state
tournament. Getting to state was an emotional event beyond the
tournament itself. Rogers had come back to coach because the
position had been left vacant after Bill Elsass left Botkins and
took the head coaching position at Upper Scioto Valley.

"The biggest game of my career was the regional final against
Minster in 1994. Besides the obvious reason of winning the game
and going to the state tournament, I thought it was a big game in
that I had been Bill's JV coach before, and even though I wanted
the job, I thought I was almost in a no-win situation. Those kids
grew up expecting to go to state, and the community thought it

was their time to shine. They had been to the regional finals a couple of times; a year or two previously they had upset Loramie who was undefeated at the time, and they'd had a great career. Knowing the expectations those kids had, knowing what the community wanted, and having been beaten by Minster in the regular season, it was the biggest game, not only in my career, but in the kids' career, and probably in Botkins history. I felt like I was in a tough situation because some people and kids wanted Bill Elsass, and I knew their expectations of getting to state. We got there and didn't win it, but I felt people thought those kids were going to get there no matter who was coaching them. I talked to Jerry Harmon about the year he went to state, and he said it was one of the toughest years of his life. I'd have to put my year going to state right up there, too. Getting these kids to where they needed to get was very tough. That game allowed all those things to happen. If we'd lost that game, I'm not sure what that would have been like. That would have been tough on me, tough on the kids, and tough on a lot of people. That game defined Botkins."

Had Rogers moved ahead one game after beating Minster and won that state semi-final match-up against Worthington Christian, in the state final he would have faced eventual state champion Upper Scioto Valley with Bill Elsass as the coach.

"At that time, only Jackson Center and Loramie had taken teams to the state tournament before. The competition that year was so good. Jackson Center had an excellent team and Loramie was Loramie. Anna wasn't great but they were so competitive. Russia had an excellent team. We didn't even win the Shelby County title that year, which tells you a little bit about the competition we had.

"That state team, when they were playing well, was almost like a machine. I don't think I've seen a high school team run the floor as well as that team. The Minster game was a little slower, and we still scored sixty points or so. The game before, we had beaten Twin Valley South in the regional semi-final. We had scrimmaged them before the season and they beat us. We thought we were going to have our hands full, but we didn't. We ran the floor; we shot the ball. This was their sixth or seventh game on UD's floor, but we just annihilated them because we just did nothing wrong. Their best player was averaging twenty-five points a game and we held him to twelve or fifteen. The final score was eighty-something to forty-something, and in a regional semi-final, you just don't see that very often. That's the best game those kids ever played. This played a big part in our upcoming game. We knew Minster was going to be one of our toughest games of the year and Twin Valley South gave us a lot of confidence going into that regional final.

"The most exciting game of my career was the state semi-final game. I had many people come up to me and tell me it was the most exciting game they had seen at St. John Arena. That was one of the last years they played the tournament there. They played the state tournament at Dayton [in 1986 and 1987]. How would you like to go to state and play at the University Dayton Arena? It just isn't the same.

"Our state semi-final game was tied 42-42 at half time and that was a humongous number of points. That year we ran the ball up and down the court so well that it was one of our biggest strengths. Spectators got tired of watching all the up and down. Worthington Christian had eleven threes in that game and I think we had eight or nine. That was a fun game to watch. I thought we got beat by a very good team that shot very well that day. That game taught me how important scouting is. I was a big believer in scouting. I was one of those coaches who was always somewhere watching a game. We had two tapes on Worthington Christian and one of my junior high coaches had gone to see them play one game that year. They had upset a couple of teams to get to state, so they weren't the team you would think would possibly be there. Seeing those kids play live, though, taught me that tapes lie. Tapes don't show how good kids are or how fast they are. I don't think we underestimated them, but we sure did not see the team we faced that day on the tapes. We couldn't see how good their point guard was on the tape. That game taught me you have to be prepared and do your work scouting. I wish I could have seen them live or maybe called people to get a little more than what we had."

Early games as well as state appearances in a coach's career often serve as lessons in the school of hard knocks. Rogers had an especially instructive game in his first coaching experience in the early 1980s.

"It was maybe 1983 and we were playing Jackson Center who had a very good team that year. It was one of the biggest possible upsets I'd been a part of up to that point, and we were up eighteen sometime in the fourth quarter. Basically, we let it slip away and Scott Doseck beat us at the last second on a one-handed runner. I remember how devastated I was to lose that game. It taught me that a game is never over until it's over. Jerry Harmon understood how much that game hurt me. Here was the rival team whose coach told me we played a great game, that winning isn't everything, and that this game should go a long way to help us get better. That's tough to understand as a coach or player. It taught me that some games you get hurt and some games, like that regional final, make it enjoyable. He and Fred Nuss [Houston coach] really took me under their wing. It's one of the reasons why coaching in Shelby County is so special. The coaches are ready to help you at any time."

Rogers found that even with good teams, there are aspects of the game that are difficult to teach.

"I've always considered myself an offensive [oriented] coach, so defense was a constant battle. I loved coaching the offensive part of it. I loved running the floor, so I never was one of those coaches who played man-to-man and nothing else. I usually made our defense better by pressing a lot. Our defense was always better because of our pressing.

"We had so many highs and lows that year, from losing early to Jackson Center to an injury to our point guard, forcing him out a lot of the season. At the end of the season, we had lost two games in a three-game stretch. We were down and tired and mentally fatigued. We brought in a motivational speaker, Bruce Boguski, who worked with the team and coaches. He spent nearly the whole day with us and at the end said that we were all a mental mess, but after that session, we didn't lose a game until the state game. I credit a lot of our success in the tournament to what he did for our mental state. He made us believe in ourselves and each other. He did it in a way that allowed us to relax and be confident. Then, the two phrases I used were, 'Expect to Win' and 'Never Be Satisfied.' The mental part of the game of basketball is just as important, if not more important, than the skills."

Rogers wrestled with the mental part of coaching and the toll it can take on an individual. Having made the decision to leave varsity basketball coaching three times – twice with boys and once with girls, he knows the reasons that coaches want or need to leave the game.

"The first time I left varsity coaching was after two seasons when we had won eleven or twelve games and then those were followed by a season that we won only four games. I really felt burned out. I put too much of my time into my coaching. It was affecting my teaching. It was affecting my family. It was affecting my kids. I felt like Botkins needed to go in a different direction. I got out my second time for a career change. I wanted to become the athletic director at Botkins and we had an unwritten rule that you couldn't coach a varsity sport and be the AD. The only way I had a chance to get that job was to get out of coaching. The third time I decided to retire, I wanted to watch my daughter play basketball when she went off to college. I wanted to be able to follow her. These are three reasons coaches get out of it, but I'm sure there are other pressures. When you don't win, it becomes a burden for you and a burden for the kids. Sometimes a fresh approach is needed. The first time I got out, I thought I was doing what was expected of me, but it was time to get somebody else in here, a little fresh blood, and get some excitement back in it. Winning is so important, and when you get a losing season, it gets tough.

"For me, the commitment is tough, too. As a kid, I loved going to open gym, but the summers are almost as competitive now as the season is. Those games mean absolutely nothing, but coaches want to keep up with the Joneses. I went from loving taking the kids to camp to thinking I was doing too much with them. I could see them bogging down and not enjoying it.
"Someday, I'd like to see [the state] open it up and allow you to do whatever you want whenever you want, just because there are coaches that take advantage of the ten-day rule. You can't say today, 'Kids, enjoy your summer and I'll see you when the school year starts.' It's gotten to the point where it affects the kids and you're fighting coaches from other sports. Kids are pulled in so

many different ways in the summer. I went to a clinic and got an outline for the season which showed me what to do the next day after a game, how many times down the floor for kids in practice, and how much time should be spent on the court. I was never like that. Practice was two hours and I ran the kids. That clinic changed my philosophy. I was careful to cut back on time. Later in the season, we'd only have hour practices. And I just wish I'd known that back when I coached the first time. It helped me think of the kids and the other things they have in their lives. Having my own kids and watching my daughter after practices and seeing how fatigued she was and how she was staying up late getting her homework done helped me see the kids' point of view. It's too bad coaches can't see that early in their career. It helped me be a better coach. Also, I became a referee later in life, so if I could go back, I would treat referees better and I would treat my players better."

"The biggest reward of my coaching career is not being able to say I went to state. This might be a contradiction, but coaching the girls in the regional finals was so fun. We weren't expected to do much, but to win the Shelby County Athletic League title is tough and it's special. When you aren't expected to do much, and you do, it makes it much more fun. Being able to coach my daughter was the biggest reward for me. I spent my whole life coaching other kids which took away from my family life. I didn't get a chance to see every game my son played because I didn't coach him. Being able to say that I could help my own daughter was important. Future coaches should make sure family comes first because I made those mistakes that family didn't come first. They should enjoy the time they coach, but they don't want to look back and say they messed up because they took time away from what should come first. I felt that basketball kept me from advancing in my career, but something, though, kept me going back again and again. I'm not sure, even today, that I could rule out doing it again sometime.

"Other coaches understand that. It's a lonely career. I can't explain how tough it is to face losing a big game, going through a tough season, experiencing things that don't go your way. I can't explain what coaches go through. It's tough on the family, too. If you're winning, it's better. If you're losing, it can be worse. It's tough to get a loss out of my mind and focus on my family. It cost me some good family time in my life with the emphasis I put on coaching. Some of my best friends are coaches, so that's had the opposite effect. Without coaches, I wouldn't have the friends I have today."

Game day didn't have enough time in it for Rogers.

"The game was on my mind the whole day. I'd go to bed the night before and couldn't sleep, thinking about the game and if I'd done everything I needed to do. On my teaching days, I would watch tapes every spare minute to come up with one more edge. I was fairly superstitious and nervous. Game day was fun but fairly nerve-wracking for me. I couldn't wait to get to the game. I had a routine after my teaching day of coming home and taking a nap. I couldn't eat too much. If we got on a roll, I'd eat a certain food or wear the same thing. The coaches had black jackets with the Botkins Trojans emblem. Every tournament game we played, I wore that coat. We were confident we were going to play two games at state and I didn't want to wear the jacket twice in a row, so I wore a Botkins sweater. I guess I can put that partially to blame. After that, we got everyone rings for going to state, so I wore that ring on game days. If I didn't wear it, it seemed like things didn't turn out so well. I did little things like that, but the purpose was about the mental aspect – to have anything that made me comfortable.

"Before the game, I would go over the game plan and discuss our strategies. As a younger coach, I was more upbeat in the pre-game, and it was all the rah-rah stuff. Later, I learned that I should try to keep the emotions at an even level so kids didn't spend too much of their emotion before the game. Boguski taught us how to focus on our confidence to get things done. If I went back to coaching, I would focus on that mental part. At half-time, it all depended on what happened in the first half. At the state game, we spent half-time trying to get one of our players back in the game mentally. He was not happy. I think he thought we should have been going to him a little more often. He was frustrated that the other team was scoring so much. We needed to get him focused. We set up the first two plays of the second half to go to him just to get his confidence back. We knew we had to have him to win the game. It worked, too. He scored a couple of times and got back in it. You are constantly making adjustments at half-time. It's important to have the mental aspect because you are always fighting kids' emotions. It's good to meet with the other coaches before you walk in the locker room at half-time to decide what needs to be done. A coach needs to say as little as possible in the post-game and try to get everybody out on a positive note. The best post-game talks came the next day at practice."

Rogers cautions new coaches to be ready to put in a lot of time and have a willingness to do the work that must be done with every team.

"I've seen coaches come and go who didn't do a lot in the summer and even though it wasn't work I enjoyed, I had to do it. Coaches are confident people. Their conduct and the way they handle things shows what kind of a coach they are. Coaches need to be hard workers. They need to show a desire to learn by going to clinics and workshops. They have to be willing to put the time in. I can't say one-hundred percent that my background, playing the game and being around the game, allowed me to be a good coach. I'm not saying you have to be a great player in your high school days or your college days, but you have to have that special competitiveness to be good."

Rogers has coached successful teams, both boys and girls, so he has often thought about what it takes to be successful.

"Successful teams have expectations, and if they use expectations in the right way it can be a powerful tool to get them where they want to go. Successful teams have confidence that their expectations will take them in that direction. On that state team in 1994, we had a lot of different personalities. They were a tough group to coach, but they were a close group. When you have a long stretch of four years going deep through the tournament, it can be stressful. People want a lot of your time. You better have people you can rely on, lean on and understand what you're going through. As good as you are, though, you have to have some luck. In the state year, we barely got the number one seed. We could kind of determine our brackets and who we played down the road, which was important to our run. We got Jason Wendel back at tournament time from his earlier injury, so you have to be good, but you have to have luck and skill, too."

"Basketball in the 1990s was number one. We didn't have football in these small schools. I used to wonder what made Loramie so good, and I always came back to the idea that they have athletes growing up and marrying athletes and they stay in the area. I think that's one of the things Botkins is fighting right now. We're having our better athletes move away and go to New Knoxville or Anna. When I had second-generation kids of parents who played that were good, I knew it. I could get things out of them. Today, you need parents who value athletics. This location has a lot of parents who think athletics is important and they push their kids to do the best they can. You have to do it at a very young age. Parent commitment leads to kid commitment. Anytime you have a team like that state team, you have parents who have invested a lot of time into their kids' athletic careers. It's not easy to be a parent. A coach needs to understand parents and know they want what is best for their kids just as you want what's best for your team. Not all parents are like that. There are some that you just can't deal with. A coach needs parents on his side to push their kids to be the best they can be. Also, the coaches in this area grew up in this kind of atmosphere. Growing up in Shelby County, being part of a state tournament, and winning a Shelby County Athletic League title, I know how special it is to be part of that. I'm not sure a person coming from Wapak or Sidney would understand what I'm talking about."

The people in Shelby, Auglaize, and Mercer counties understand how important basketball is to the small communities here. It's the reason for many of the long-standing rivalries that have developed among them.

"Our biggest rival was Anna. We were always 'the school up north' to them. Anna's Bob Anderson made it sort of an Ohio State and Michigan rivalry. He kind of wanted that, being an Ohio State grad and seeing how important it is to have rivalries. I think he treated it right. He was always respectful of any Shelby County League team. At one time Loramie was the team we knew we had to beat to get where we wanted to be, but Anna is definitely a special one for us. We have so many families that are related and both communities have long-time fans like Ronnie Dunn at Anna or the Finkenbine brothers here. The first year of my coaching career, I was the JV coach and we went to Anna, and as an Anna graduate, it was very important to me. My brother was a varsity player at Anna and it was a physical game that was back and forth with little skirmishes on the floor. After the game, I had a man attack me and hit me from behind. I was close to Bob Anderson at the time. He shielded me and got me away from him. I can't even remember who won the game or whether he thought I was a traitor or what. That's taking it too far, but it shows how special it is because it means a lot to people."

Rogers has experienced being ahead in a game, but he has also known what it is like to be behind late in the game.

"With the three-point shot, you don't want to give up too early. Going back to that game against Jackson when we were up eighteen in the fourth quarter and then got beat, you don't give up until the game is over. I remember playing Houston and Fred Nuss was coaching. They had a nice team. We were a little over .500, and we were up eleven points or so late in the game. I was still coaching away. I looked down at Fred who was waving a white handkerchief. I had to sit down and relax. You do know when it's over, but you don't want the kids to know you've given up.

"I think you just know when it's time to get other kids in the game. I never wanted to embarrass another team and you sure don't want to get embarrassed yourself. However, when I coached girls, it seemed that anytime we took the press off, we became a very mediocre team, allowing other teams to come back on us. I think it's one of those coaching qualities that you do know when the game is over or when you need to sub. When we were behind, we pressed more. We tried to keep the game up-tempo, but when we played Loramie-type teams, they wanted us to play at their tempo which was a little slower and making a certain number of passes before they scored. I felt that if we controlled the tempo, we had a pretty good chance of winning the game. The losses we had that year – Knoxville, Minster, Loramie and Anna – were all teams that shut down our up-tempo game. We worked every day on being the best up-tempo team we could become. We worked at getting the ball across the floor in a certain number of seconds. People sometimes think those coaches aren't as good a planner as Bobby Knight, but up-tempo coaches do the same thing in a different way. We didn't like to slow things down, and we had a hard time doing it. That team hated running something like the flex. When we were ahead and we needed to slow down, we'd take the press off, back it up a little bit, or not trap so much. We had difficulty taking time off the clock."

Rogers planned his years of coaching around trying to find the best competition in the off-season.

"I really didn't like open gyms. I was always looking for other schools who invited our players in to play so that we could face competition. You're trying to get your team to have the best competition. My bottom five players from that state team could have been competitive in another league. Our practices were so competitive because we were so deep. We had great practices and that was one of the reasons our team was as good as they were as long as they were. They all had competition for their jobs.

"I went through many different philosophies with practice. We would spend time in stretching and getting ready for practice. We would break our practices into offensive work, defensive work, and special team work. I copied Kentucky when I went to Rick Pitino's academy. I wasn't big into five minutes for this drill or that one. We'd have blocks of time and try to get as much done as we could. In my earlier career, I did a minute-by-minute schedule, but after going to Kentucky and seeing that, we thought that was the greatest thing since sliced bread. I wasn't restricted by a time schedule. If I had something written down for five minutes and we didn't get it, I felt like I could spend a little more time to work on it. If it's important, let's not drop it because a horn blows."

Anyone who visited The Kitchen wondered how players could practice on the black tile floor in Botkins' old gym.

"We had one of the biggest advantages on that tile floor. I remember playing Anna when they were state–ranked. They had the Fogt boys and were one of the best teams in the area. We were up eight or nine points with four minutes left and they called the game because it was like an ice rink. The gym was so hot and sweaty and the floor was slick, so we suspended the game and came back Monday night to play three minutes or so. Bob Anderson said they held a practice in our gym before the game. They got on the bus an hour earlier than usual and came up here to be on the floor to get used to it. I'm sure people hated to come to Botkins.

"Anytime you are winning, fans are so important, too. The difference is night and day between knowing you'd be playing in front of big crowds as opposed to times when you were only playing with a few people in the stands. It isn't going to make your team good or bad, but it can be advantageous to have a fan following like good teams have."

Rogers relied on people behind the scenes for the success of his program, and he believes this is another reason so many schools in this area have their own strong programs.

"Booster groups can be a big help as long as they are there for the positive part of it and don't think they are bigger than what they are supposed to be. I've worked with boosters who raise money to help kids and they are needed, but you have to control them. Every school needs individuals like Anna's Jack Billing who did so much to build both their boys and girls teams. He had kids playing ball, so he would take all those kids to team camps when they were very young. I credit Don Mack in our girls program. He would do anything I wanted him to do, whether it was scouting or anything else. One year, we had a girls game with Miami East and we packed our new gym when that was unheard of with girls. Both of us were ranked in the top five in the state. I sent him to scout a Twin Valley South game because we could potentially be playing them in the tournament. He didn't say anything, but he still lets me know how mad he was that I sent him to a terrible game while we were playing the biggest game of our career. I really think you have to have special people do the things other people don't see. In terms of my assistants, the more experience I had, the more trust I had in them. I let my coaches take care of certain parts of practice, so I could sit back and watch. I had good assistants to handle that. When we went to state, we had a new coaching staff. My assistant was a non-teaching person and the JV coach was Brett Meyer. Sometimes when you have non-teachers, it's difficult to meet with them during the day. Loyalty is a big part of being a staff member. If you had someone who backed you, not necessarily agreed with you because you want coaches to give you advice, and you can keep that staff together, it's better for your program."

The three-point shot was a big change in the game and it was a big change for Rogers' teams as well.

"In my second stint, we had the three-point shot, but the first four years, we didn't. We played in that old gym and I can remember kids from Botkins and from other schools who took shots that were way beyond where the three-point line is now. The three-point shot has made games so you are never out of it if you have good three-point shooters. You have to spend time in practices now shooting the three and guarding against it. One of the stats we kept track of was what our three-point percentage was and what the opposition's was. It was important that we won that stat every game. We felt that one of the reasons we lost that state semi-final game was that they beat us in that category.

"That game happened so quickly. I called Jerry Harmon and asked him a question. I knew what answer I was going to get and I didn't want to hear it. I asked him what he would do differently if he could go back to 1985 and do it again. He tried to talk me out of taking the team down early to spend the night. Kids should stay in the same routine that got them there. You just don't have the control when kids aren't going home to sleep in their own beds. I felt the kids had earned that opportunity and that was one of the rewards. We played Thursday night, so it didn't matter as it turned out. We had a pep rally and a send-off. I remember leaving and one of my coaches had forgotten something at his house at Anna, so we swung by his house and changed our route to Columbus because of it. We missed going through Jackson Center who had a big banner out for us. I'm sorry we missed that. It would have been special for them and for us to see that. It was hectic trying to organize everything in a very short period. You have to plan where to eat and when to get to the gym for the late game. You try to keep it similar to their routine, but it happened so quickly I didn't get a chance to savor that experience of playing at St. John Arena that every coach dreams of. It was a tough situation in a way. I kind of wanted to play Bill's Upper Scioto Valley team because I think our kids would have responded in a way that could have been a good motivation. At the same time, a part of me said it was good it didn't happen. It probably worked out for the best.

"Something I was not ready for was the state media coverage. I always like dealing with Ken Barhorst at the *Sidney Daily News* who does a good job of reporting on Shelby County teams because he understands Shelby County coaches. When we played Minster at UD, there were a couple of scuffles and after the game the Dayton media were badgering me about the personalities on my basketball team. This team had the reputation of being cocky and brash. I'd spent the year trying to get them not to do things that weren't good for the team, and then I spent that whole media time defending them and getting the media to understand how that was a reason why they were so good. I thought I did pretty well at trying to curb that and make it positive."

Teams that get the opportunity to go to Columbus usually have a few people with the qualities Rogers identifies as those necessary to become an outstanding player.

"What I always wanted was somebody who loved the game and who would do anything to play. The years that I didn't have good teams, the players often complained about practices or about going to shoot-outs. A school like Botkins maybe only gets a good team like that state team once in a lifetime. Most of the players during those years we were good had those qualities I mentioned. They loved the game and they played all the time. It's all they played. It was hard to get them out of the gym rather than, with others, getting them into the gym. Bob Burden fit this to a T. He was not the most talented kid in town, but he worked so hard. He loved the game. He played it from the time he got up until the time he went to bed. Without his work ethic, he would have been an average player. You need the Bob Burdens who will score twenty-five points per game. I had kids like Jason Wendel and Josh Steinke who won MVP awards throughout their years in high school. I like to say I had five kids who were all equal and a different kid is high scorer every night, but that doesn't happen very often. All my successful teams had overachievers because they had the work ethic that caused their teammates to follow along.

"Kids, then, have to be put under pressure, and it's important that a coach role model how to do it. The state team had to live under the expectations and the stress, so they became very good at managing pressure. Every day of their basketball career was pressure. Being involved with big games was an experience that taught kids more how to handle pressure than a coach could. You can set up situations in practice, but it isn't the same. Leadership is something else. Leaders are born. You learn to become a leader through your whole life. Burden was a leader, but some kids don't want to be leaders. I don't think you can teach that. Players who are lucky enough to be part of a good team find that the experience helps them later in life. If you have kids who don't want to be pushed competitively, they won't allow themselves to be pushed."

Rogers gave a playbook for summer workouts to his players. Any drill that had a time limit and a goal was important. One of my favorites was an X-out drill where you start at the free-throw line at the right elbow and you go in and make a right-handed lay-up. Then you go to the left elbow and go right back in and make a left-handed lay-up. You try to do as many as you can in thirty seconds. A player like Bob Burden wanted to break the record every single time he tried it. I had all kind of scoring drills, just because I had that offensive-oriented mind-set. I had a fifty-five-second drill with a rebounder and a passer and they tried to see how many three-point shots they could make in fifty-five seconds. It was a war. Kids wanted to beat the record or be the best on the team. It's tough to get kids to practice as hard as they can at all times, but if you get drills that push kids and they don't know it, they'll improve.

"I thought that getting some of my good players to play in college was very important, but other coaches don't think it's their responsibility. Guys have to be pretty good to get a scholarship at those bigger schools, but it's a little easier with girls. A coach has a responsibility to do everything possible to help them play at the next level."

Rogers is content with the way the game is played now but the game has been changed in the way officials are hired.

"Back in the old days, we all had an athletic director who hired the officials and that's where I think the term 'homer' arose. Now we have assigners. It is good and bad both ways. Assigners are good, but sometimes we get officials who aren't from this area who don't understand the Shelby County way of playing basketball. You're fighting one group who lets you play and another that doesn't. Officials can control the outcome of the game. As I got older, I think that helped me understand how important it is to treat an official with respect. You aren't helping yourself when you treat an official poorly, the way some coaches do.

"The best change in the game now, is no change. At the time I wasn't sure I liked the change to a three-point shot, but it helped my philosophy turn into an up-tempo game with a lot of three-point shots. Right now, we have a good thing going and I don't think they should mess with it."

Chapter  Eight

AL SUMMERS

ST. HENRY HIGH SCHOOL

2000 STATE FINALS

*"The greatest opponent players have is anything
inside them that keeps them from playing up to their potential."*

A
l Summers' first big influence in basketball was the high
school coach at Celina when Summers was a student there,
but Summers never played for him. Dean White, who
coached Celina to the state tournament in 1972, sparked a deep
love of the game in the teenager who served as the team manager.
Summers was destined to coach for nearly thirty years but spent
just one as head basketball coach – the 1999-2000 year when St.
Henry played Fort Jennings in the state finals.

"I played junior high basketball, but in my eighth grade class of
172 kids, I was the smallest of all. When I got to high school, my
playing days were over. The coach was Dean White. I was his stat
guy and team manager and jack-of-all-trades. I just did whatever he
needed done. I went to practice every day and was at all the games.
Then when I went to Bowling Green, I played intramural basketball.
The secretary at our dorm was the wife of the basketball coach, Bob
Conibear, so I hung around him a lot. I knew I wanted to coach but
at the time, football was my favorite. I went to college in chemical
engineering, but I realized that was not going to interest me, so I
switched over to education without knowing if I would be able to
coach or not. Luckily, my first job was at St. Henry where they were
willing to take a chance on me, a guy who hadn't been a college
player. In the 1970s you would be amazed at how many schools
were demanding college playing experience to be a coach. I got into

junior high basketball and it
soon became apparent that
basketball is what I wanted to
do. Then Fran Guilbault was a
big influence because he was
the head coach at St. Henry
when I started as seventh
grade coach.   When Jim
Niekamp went to Coldwater
to coach, Fran came out to
the field where I was coaching

baseball and said, 'Well, the JV job is open if you want it.' And that
was in 1980. So I was Fran's JV coach for nineteen years. When
Fran retired, I got the varsity job."

Summers was prepared for that position, not only having studied
under his long-time mentor, Fran Guilbault, but also because he had
observed other coaches who gave him all the ideas he needed to
equip himself for the eventual head coaching position.

"Once I began coaching, there were three guys who had a
tremendous influence on my actual career and coaching strategies.
One was Bob Knight, who probably influenced every coach in
that era in one way or another. If you take his teaching strategies
and philosophy, that's good. If you take his coaching style and
you're coaching younger players, that may not be so good. Another
coach that influenced me was Rick Majerus. I worked a big-man
camp with him until he left Milwaukee, and I used to go out to
Utah and work his camp when he took the job at the University
of Utah.   Another person was Bernie Balikian, the coach at
Mt. Vernon Nazarene in the late 1980s. A friend of mine told
me about Bernie and his style of play. Bernie was playing this
wide-open offense that focused on the three-point shot. He was
playing a pressure-switching man-to-man that was forty minutes
of pure hell for the other team. He was pressing, switching every
screen, and just getting in your face, so I decided I had to see his
team play. That style of play then became my mantra. The year I
coached St. Henry's varsity and we went to the state tournament,
that's all we played."

Summers began his career at St. Henry coaching the junior high boys. He began to develop the foundation of his core principles of coaching.

"All my principles make sense if you take into account my background. I believe that you have to be yourself. The minute you try to emulate someone else, you're in for failure. What works for one person doesn't necessarily work in another context. The smart coaches are like the smart teachers. They take bits and pieces of this philosophy and that philosophy, but they mold it into their own personality. I also never called a kid by his last name. It seemed so degrading. It created a level of the boss and the little peons. I only called a kid by his nickname if he liked it.

"Then you have to teach what they need to know. You have to figure out what the individuals on your team need and teach that stuff. Don't waste time with a drill that looks pretty or sounds good unless it's something they need to know. Too, you can't be inflexible. The more rules you have, the more trouble you get into. You have to enforce it. There are seventy to eighty kids, boys and girls, in a grade, so you have to play with the kids you have. You can't say, 'This is my style, and this is the way we're going to play every year.' You can go many years without kids who can play that style. In big schools, you might be able to find the kids who can play your style, but in a small school, you have to go with what you have."

For Summers, games came in two varieties. There were games his team should win and games that were toss-ups.

"You have to make sure you win the games you should. You'll win your share of games that are toss-ups, so you have to communicate that to your kids. Too many coaches don't have conversations with kids.

"In my entire career of coaching at all levels, I only went into one game thinking, 'We don't have a prayer,' and guess what? We didn't have a prayer. I was coaching the JV team and we were playing Elida, a Division I school. Fran was having trouble with his guards at the varsity level, so he told me on game day that he was taking one of my JV guards. They beat us by twenty, but it wasn't as close as the score indicated. If you are fortunate to coach at a school like St. Henry, you very seldom will go into a game thinking you don't have a chance. That's one of the real positives of coaching at a school like St. Henry. Kids feel it, and you win several games a year that you probably shouldn't have won. Kids believe that they are going to win. You'll play teams who don't believe they're going to win because they are playing St. Henry. And they don't. After the game we can sit and talk about why we won when the other team had us by six, and I think it's because the other team thinks they aren't supposed to win and our kids think they are.

"I used everything I could get my hands on to learn about coaching. I had subscriptions to *Scholastic Coach* and *Athletic Journal*. When I first started coaching there weren't any videos. I bought books with sometimes only one thing in it that helped me, but it was worth the price of the book. It's the same thing with clinics. If you got two things out of a clinic to improve your program, it was worth it. Later in my career, I used Bernie Balikian's video on pressure-switching man-to-man. Here's how we teach it; here's what it looks like in a game. Pete Newell was the U.S. Olympic coach a few times and he had a big-man training video. Pete Carril had a video on the Princeton offense. It was fascinating watching those kids with no scholarships and none of them quit and none of them had the great athletic talent that other schools had. Time after time they took those athletic teams to school with that offense and just being patient and wearing them down."

As with many other coaches in the area, Summers decided to coach here because it was close to home. He interviewed as far away as St. Louis but the opening at St. Henry allowed him to begin coaching right away. His college training was with high school students but he took the middle school science teaching position and never left that age level. He coached 28 years but only served as head coach one year, the year St. Henry made it to the final game of the state tournament.

"In January of my only year as varsity coach, I was sitting in the doctor's office because I'd had episodes of atrial fibrillation and had coached an entire game during one of those episodes. The doctor told me I had to get out of coaching because the problem was stress-related. The only surgery they had was to insert a pacemaker. He offered me some experimental surgery that didn't need to be done immediately. I had some time to think and decided that I needed to end my coaching, but I didn't tell anyone. Then, I thought of the team and how we were on a roll. We got rolling in tournament and I couldn't say anything then. I told only my superintendent. So that was the story of my one year of success. In early 2005 I had a procedure done that didn't require a pacemaker. I haven't had a problem since."

While he was managing his health, he experienced two unforgettable games that stand out in a year of memorable contests.

"Our state semi-final game was against Worthington Christian. They were on a thirty-seven-game win streak. Worthington Christian had won the previous year's state championship by beating Fort Recovery, so they hadn't lost a game in two years. They also had a couple of players who were going on to play college basketball. In the third quarter Ryan Post, our leading scorer, came out with an injured hand. They had Ohio State trainers there who took him off the court. We had been up thirteen at half, but the whole complexion of the game changed without him. And it wasn't his scoring; it was his personality and leadership. The score margin kept getting smaller and smaller until it came down to a last-second shot. Worthington Christian put it up and it circled the rim. I got up and began to walk down to congratulate their coach because I saw the ball go in, but as the buzzer rang, it circled around and popped out. We had won the game by one point.

"At least as big a game was the first game of the season when we played Wapak at home. We didn't have a kid over 6'2". They had lost in the first round of the tournament the previous year, and they graduated all their talent. We had put in this open-post offense with five guys on the perimeter. We also were using the Bernie Balikian defense. The advantage is that these kids had been running this defense with me for two years on the JV team. They believed in it. Joe Niekamp had come from Celina to be my assistant coach that year, and Joe is a traditionalist. He would say to me in private, 'I don't know about this.' With this new system, which nobody had seen because it was the first game of the season, we had no idea what was going to happen, but we just overwhelmed them. Joe came into the coaches' office after the game and he said, 'This stuff just may work.' Having Joe buy into that was as critical as having the players buy into it. A coach can coach anything in practice, but if he really buys into it, he'll coach it with all his heart. We played Parkway the next night in our first league game. They had three super players that were getting all the press. They came in loaded for bear and we beat them by twenty. After that weekend, everybody knew that these guys were the real deal and what we were running was the real deal. We finished 18-2 in the regular season and played Fort Jennings in the state finals."

These games were not his most exciting games, however.

"We had seven seniors and a junior, who in a close game, were our eight main players. In other games everybody got to play. In each of those eight-man games, a different player was our leading scorer on any given night. It wasn't the same one or two. Joe and I would sit around and wonder what it would be like if they were all hitting on the same night. When we played Upper Scioto Valley in the districts, they came out in a triangle-and-two, and they were playing man-to-man on the two kids who had been the best shooters on the one night they scouted us. But those two weren't our best overall shooters. They were leaving our best shooters open. Our leftie, Neil Schmitz, shot an air ball the first time down the floor because he was so wide open with nobody guarding him. After that, he made seven three-pointers in the first quarter. I looked down at their coach and wondered when they were going to guard him. At the end of the half we had fourteen three-pointers. At the end of the third quarter, we had twenty-five. I had to tell the kids no more three-pointers. The next day I started getting calls from all over the Midwest. A guy from the Indianapolis Star told me that was the second highest number of three-pointers ever scored by a high school team. I had no idea, and I'm glad I didn't. I might have been tempted to go for it.

"In the mid-1990s, I was coaching JV. The varsity game against Delphos was on TV-44. Joel Broering was a sophomore on the JV team, and in that previous summer, he had been diagnosed with leukemia, so he didn't play his sophomore year, but he stayed around with the team. We were playing Delphos and it was the last game Joel would attend before he went to the hospital for his bone marrow transplant, so I called Randy Ayers, Ohio State's coach, and got a ball signed by all the Ohio State players. My two sophomore captains were going to present the ball at the end of the JV game. At the end of the third quarter of that game, we were down seventeen, and I told the kids at the quarter break that we weren't going to give up hustling and trying. We were going to go down with pride. We outscored them 22-4 in the fourth quarter and won by one point. It was the most amazing thing I ever saw in my life. The game was finished, but the best part wasn't over yet. I knew how crushed their coach would be – being up by seventeen and losing by one. I told him his team didn't have to stay for the presentation ceremony if they wanted to go to the locker room, but both the Delphos JV and varsity players were on the court for Joel and even though the JV had gotten beat in a rather shattering way, every single one of those players came over and shook Joel's hand. There wasn't a dry eye in the house. That was my most exciting game, and it was a JV game."

Summers learned many lessons in 28 years of coaching. He held onto his belief that players should practice the correct form every day until it was second nature, and if some continued to make the same fundamental mistake over and over, it was a cardinal sin.

"We were playing at New Knoxville. It was a game that even if you thought you could win, but you were playing at their place, all bets were off. We were playing this game in a stretch of five games in nine days. I took one kid out of the game and berated him rather sternly. Later, one of the coaches told me the kid was going to quit. I was thinking of how well we were doing and we had some big games ahead. No one in his right mind would want to quit. Fifteen years earlier, I probably would have said, 'If he doesn't want to be a part of it, screw it.' Instead, I brought the player in and asked him what I could do to get him back in the game. We walked out of that office with an agreement. The next night at practice, he came in and was totally dedicated and with it. I knew that everything was right with the world and I had done the right thing. That game taught me that I had learned a lot."

Summers has no regrets from his year of coaching and told the media that very thing after the state finals when Fort Jennings beat St. Henry for the title.

"However, if I had realized that Fort Jennings had two kids doing all the scoring, we would have played a triangle-and-two that fourth quarter. I didn't realize that until I looked at the scorebook after the game.

"We had a lot of games where the plan was working. We played Fort Recovery in January and we knew if they had to guard our open post man-to-man, they were screwed because they didn't have five kids to match up with us. Our point guard was our least prolific three-point shooter, so they backed off him and he started launching over the top of them and making his shots. Early second quarter they went zone and the lead was six points. Normally we loved zone because we played open-post. We made a couple of trips and we didn't do so well. I called a time-out and said, 'We're ahead and we should never let the team that's behind dictate how the game is going to be played. We don't want to play against the zone and we're not going to. We're going to make them play man-to-man.' We went to our four corners with the point guard just across half court in the middle. They were still in the zone. In this part of the country, you don't hold the ball. You just don't. People get violent if you hold the ball, but we held the ball. They stayed in their zone. We held the ball. They stayed in their zone. The Fort Recovery fans were starting to hoot and holler and we were just staying there. Our fans soon started clapping. We ate up over six minutes and the noise in the gym was deafening. Our fans don't like that style of basketball, but if it made the Fort Recovery fans mad, it was fine with them. At the end of the quarter, they came out of their zone. We made three shots and were up by twelve. And that was in the first half. They came out from half and started the third quarter in that zone. We held the ball. Of course, they came out of the zone right away and we ended up winning by about twenty-five. The lesson is that you don't let the losing team decide how the game is going to be played.

"Then Loramie came in and they went zone in the second quarter. We wanted to play them man-to-man, so guess what we did? We ate about four minutes off the clock. Then they came out man-to-man and we ended up winning."

Summers found that for his players, offense was troublesome to learn because basketball is a game of getting and having the ball.

"Good offense is difficult to teach. It's so alien to the kids. Good offense is getting kids open and playing well without the ball. AAU ball in the summer makes it worse and worse. The state should say if kids are going to play competitively in the summer, they should be with their own group and learn the skills. Do away with that ten-day coaching limit. That rule was set up for a good purpose, but it pushed kids to AAU where you can't have more than a few of your own players on the team."

Anyone who is thinking of a career in coaching should consider how to manage the years ahead.

"New coaches should understand that being true to yourself is the most important thing. You have to look at yourself in the mirror every day. Patience, internal drive, and a distinctive view of the big picture are the three qualities a coach needs to be successful. Why am I coaching? What do I want to get out of my participation? How long do I expect to be in it? What new coaches should also realize is that losing, or if your kids aren't doing the kinds of things you've been working on, is something only understood by other coaches. At the end of a career, the key is going out on top. Bob Arnzen of Delphos St. John was a great example of that. Everybody thought Arnzen was out to break Paul Walker's 695 total wins record, but when he was about thirty away, he retired. Arnzen was one of the most intelligent coaches I ever knew."

Parents with the wrong attitude make coaching more difficult.

"Parents who think their kid is way better than the kid really is, have the wrong attitude. The majority of parents at St. Henry were very realistic, but if they aren't realistic, that can be the worst nightmare. Bobby Knight once said about parents, 'You ought to put them on a desert island and check on them once a year to see if they have food and water.' The other problem is the prevalence of alcohol and the parents who say, 'I'm so glad my son is playing basketball because now he has to follow training rules.' A mother and father can't enforce rules for their own sixteen-year-old? It's really bad in this area. If a kid is playing on a high school team, it's against the law in the state of Ohio to drink. So why should it be the school's responsibility to police it? And the schools only police it on the athletes. Some schools only have rules in-season. Any athlete representing St. Henry should be under those rules all year. Our rules say that a kid who gets caught drinking in-season sits out twenty percent of the games. An athlete out of season has nothing to lose. So parents, or fans, with bad attitudes make us spend an inordinate amount of time dealing with that stuff.

"The parents' role is to provide positive support and most of our parents always have. Even though there are those problems, the biggest reward of coaching is seeing kids be successful with their lives."

Besides the issues coaches deal with, there are the mechanics and the logistics of getting the job done. From practices to planning a season, organization is the key. Eventually, it all boils down to game day.

"Our typical games were Friday and Saturday. I couldn't think about it on Friday until the last couple of hours because kids were in school and I was teaching. My mindset was that I, as a coach, had to remind them before the game of the essential points, and it couldn't be a whole lot of things. I also had to help them get to a frame of mind where those obstacles that prevented them from performing to their optimum were minimized and they could go out and play. The greatest opponent players have is anything inside them that keeps them from playing up to their potential. Saturdays were better because we had a little extra preparation time. We'd bring them in around noon and they'd shoot a little, but then we'd have a walk-through for all the opponent's inbounds plays and all their main offenses and their main defenses. We had two or three key things and we tried to help them be in the frame of mind to give it everything they had when they went out on the floor and to leave it all there.

"The pre-game talk is to remind them of two or three particular key things for that game and remind them of the big goal for the team. Each game plays a part in that goal. If you have to fire them up in the pre-game talk, then you have a major problem. When I got the job at the end of the tournament the previous year, I had the juniors come to my house to write down general goals for the next year. Through the season, then, one game couldn't ruin the goal.

"The post-game talk is a time not to say too much. If you do, you'll watch the tapes and find out you were wrong. Then you have to go back to the team and apologize, so just wrap-up and keep it simple. The most important post-game talk is if they happen to get beat. There are coaches who don't say anything, but if you don't, the message you send is, 'I don't care about you.' After a loss, you go back to the big picture.

"Half-time is all gut level. Sometimes, you raise hell with them. Sometimes, you pat them on the back. Sometimes, it's instructive. If you feel like the effort wasn't there, then it's a whole different approach. You have to look at what you can do better. Half time is a great time to change momentum and wrestle it away from them. If you come out strong in that third quarter, half-time can be the best thing that happens in a game. If we go in with the momentum, half-time can be a negative thing. The first few minutes of the third quarter are critical in determining if you are going to keep the momentum or not."

All this can take a toll on the people who decide to pursue coaching, and it can affect those they love.

"I had eight friends in college who became coaches. In ten years, I was the only one still married. Because of the time, the emotion, and the commitment, coaching takes a toll. I was fortunate to marry a woman who was very understanding. Those were the days before cell phones. We'd have dinner at 6:30 and I'd show up at 10:00. Everybody involved has to understand. When I gave up coaching everything but basketball, and I was down to one sport, I realized what a good father I could be. I also realized what a good teacher I could be."

Successful teams are a combination of many qualities. Summers believes it all starts with talent.

"A successful team has talent, a willingness to put the team first, an effort to put in hard work, and an agreed-upon team goal. After having lived near Columbus the past four years, I can definitively say what makes this part of the country uniquely successful in producing good teams and players. It is small towns, close-knit communities where you can develop an identity, and a good gene pool, which always helps. We have a lot of Hoying genes running around, and we have a lot of Post genes running around.

"When you get to regional and state, you're playing against pretty good teams who are seasoned like you are and who have probably the same big-picture goal you have, and they've been working on it all along. It comes down to who is the smartest when you play a regional or state game. We had an antidote for everything the other team did, but we didn't have an antidote for our own stupidity. If you're going to win regional or state, there's going to come a time when you better take care of the ball and be able to make your free throws. Your plan all season is to get in situations where that has to happen.

"We were in the state semi-final against Worthington Christian and we were up one, holding the ball. There were fifteen seconds to go when we got fouled. That game should have been ours as soon as they fouled us because we were so good at making those free throws, but our player missed the front end and we had to scramble to win."

"When we were ahead, we knew we were going to go four-corner, we just didn't know when. It's a gut feeling and it's by the seat of your pants. Sometimes, it's with four minutes to go. Sometimes, it's later. When I went to Fish-Mo's after the game, they all wanted to talk about it. If you won, you sat up front with the old guys. If you didn't play well or lost, you'd go to the back with the young guys, because they would pick you up. Someone would ask me, 'At 4:10 in the third quarter, why did you call that time-out?' They would analyze and even take notes. Seriously, I had to tell them that it's a seat of the pants situation."

Over the years, the success these teams experienced didn't keep them from having some main rivals who tried to thwart that success.

"Marion Local, Coldwater, and Ft. Recovery were big rivals due to the closeness of distance. Everybody in St. Henry is related to or knows everyone in those communities. So if you lose, you have to go to family reunions where it is embarrassing for some people."

Knowing that his rivals would be prepared gave Summers the reinforcement necessary to run a program that would prepare his team.

"We had to make the best use of our ten days in the summer that we could. Our team reached consensus in the late spring on their priorities for the year, so we went to a local camp for a few days that was really a practice. We taught them what they needed to know. You can't wait until winter to help a kid with his shot technique. You have to teach that in the summer and they have to work on it all summer so it comes naturally. The other five days we went to a team camp where we played the best teams from Memphis [Tennessee] to Marion Local. We played better competition than we were going to see all year long, and we learned from it. That set the tone. In a small school our basketball players have to be key players on the football team and they have to be key players on the baseball team. So we didn't see most of our kids, starting in July and going through October or November. Your good athletes will come from football ready to go. We had open gyms in the fall, but not many kids were there. I'd rather have that problem than have such bad athletes that they aren't good in football and then they aren't good in basketball, either.

"Our practices were organized down to the minute. Each practice has to be designed for the team you have. And you always do defense last. Do defense when they are tired so you make sure they are still working hard."

Summers liked preparing his players to play at home because he felt there was a home court advantage at St. Henry.

"We had a home-court advantage until we built a bigger gym. Coldwater did for awhile until they built their big gym. Marion did for awhile before they built their big gym. I don't think in the MAC there is an advantage like it used to be in the small gyms when the fans sat right on top of the floor and it was rabid. You would go into Coldwater and Marion and those were scary places to play. When teams came into our old gym, I'm sure they thought that was a scary place to play. When we built the new gym we put in the yellow lights and we'd have teams show up an hour early to get used to them."

Going to those gyms to scout was a regular event for Summers who didn't trust anyone else to do the job the way he did it.

"Also we only had a JV coach and we didn't practice together. During games I'd sit with the JV coach in his games and he'd sit with me during my games. The JV coach fed the varsity coach information. What I wanted from an assistant was to keep me up to date on the data. Who has fouls? How many time outs? Who's doing the scoring? I wanted Joe to watch their defense and give me ideas on adjustments. Then we had a freshman coach and I asked him to watch their offense. You can get involved in a game and not be thinking in that regard."

In those years at home or on the road he saw big changes in basketball. It was the advent of the three-point line and the defined area of the coaching box.

"The three-point line in high school is a bit short. A good shooter, boy or girl, has no problem making shots from there. The coaching box is the most stupid thing they've ever done. They were saying they wanted to find ways to restrain coaches. They don't do it in football or in baseball. They were saying they didn't trust basketball coaches and they needed to restrain them. The biggest way to straighten out the game of basketball, whether it is bad behavior by coaches or bad behavior by athletes, is the official. You don't need a coaching box. If a coach is doing something he shouldn't be, you T him up. There's no other sport that the ref can control the entire flow of the game like basketball. The flow can be smooth or all cut up and depends on how the ref calls the game. All refs need to get rid of that stuff about letting players decide the game at the end. If it's a foul in the first half, it's a foul in the second half. It's ridiculous."

Summers respected all coaches but feared none.

"The guy who knew the most about how to get the most out of a game that he could was Bob Arnzen. He was crafty, in a good way."

The pacing of the game is something Summers has lived, as well.

"If you are ahead in a game, you want to shorten the game and do everything you can to make the time go faster. You don't want to stop the game with fouls or throwing the ball out of bounds. You don't want to give them a chance to catch their breath. When you are behind, you want to add to it.

"One of the best things I did was send a letter to parents inviting them to a practice. We tried to get one parent from each family to come. We handed out a sheet that had our entire practice on it. It contained the drills and explanations of each thing we did. At the end, after the players left the floor, they had an opportunity to ask questions. The more they understood about what we were doing and why, the less we had parents come in with questions during the rest of the season."

Summers had gone to the state tournament when St. Henry made its 1979 appearance, but he didn't sit with the team. He sat one row behind the bench.

"I soaked everything in. Then in 1991, I was Fran's assistant and it was totally different. You don't take it in. You are focused on the game. Then when we were there, I had to force myself to look up. When the game is going on, you don't see the people. You don't hear the people. You are totally focused on the game you are trying to win. It's totally different as a coach. It gets more focused the higher up you are. When you are a head coach, you are totally focused on the game. I think the kids were the same way. They walked out on the court and it was like, 'Oh, man,' but then it's totally different in the huddle. They were completely focused on the game."

In the 2000 tournament, Summers coached many excellent players who made the most of their potential.

"I think if I'm an average player, I can be a good player if I make the most of my talent. Some years we've had players who weren't very good, but they worked so hard, I wanted to find a place for them. If you find a place for them and they are smart enough not to do anything they can't do, it's a good situation. Then there is the player who has the talent who makes the most of his talent. That's the best of both worlds. The most frustrating is the talented player who doesn't understand about making the most of his potential. I'd rather have a bad player who gets the most out of his talent than to have a problem player who doesn't know how to do it.

"It's a shame that every coach and every player can't get to the state tournament at least once. I have friends who are good coaches, but they don't get the talent. I've known coaches who have coached for thirty years and never even won a district championship. Then I have the opportunity to coach in a place where you feel like every single year you have a chance to go a long way. That's what this part of Ohio is all about. The coaches in Marion Local feel that way. The coaches at Coldwater feel that way. The coaches at Versailles feel that way. You go to games here and the gyms are packed.

"I've coached over five hundred different kids but Pat Droesch is one I remember who played JV for me and I knew when he was a sophomore that he was going to play varsity and I had to have him ready. He was talented and a bit soft when he first came out. I worked him and worked him. He went through three pairs of shoes. He said even in college he didn't go through as many pairs of shoes.

He worked so hard and became dedicated. In a JV game at home against Minster, somebody tried to throw him a long pass. It was too far and he went for it, swatting the ball back in, but going head-first into a concrete wall at full tilt. It sounded like a rifle shot. The game stopped, the squad transported him, and the final analysis was that he had a concussion with no lasting injuries. He had a really supportive dad and a caring mom, but after consulting the doctors they left the decision to play up to him. He wanted to play, so his mom asked, 'What will you do tonight if the same situation comes up?' And he said, 'I'll go for it again.'

"Another player was Randy Hemmelgarn who played in the late 1990s and ended up playing football for the University of Dayton. As a high school freshman, he was so interested with the prospect of playing on the JV basketball team the next year that he shot hundreds of shots in his driveway every single day all summer long. He was one of the best shooters I ever coached.

"Neil Schmitz was uncanny in his ability to play the game. If you watched him in practice, you wondered if he could play that hard every minute. My Lord, did he play hard every minute. We were playing Worthington Christian in the tournament and they had a player who had at least four inches on Neil and who was headed to play for the University of Dayton. He was driving in on the right baseline and he went up in this sky-ing lay-up and Neil came across from the other side to stuff him. Neil stuffed him so hard that the kid kind of crumpled up on the floor."

"We teach kids pressure in practice by putting six on five so that the pressure they had in practice was greater than what they would have in a game. For free throws, we'd put everyone on the endline. I'd call one kid out, and it was always a different kid, to shoot a free throw. If he made it, the team didn't run, if he made the first but missed the second, we'd run a certain number of sprints. If he missed the front end, they would run a lot of sprints. To me, that's more pressure than a game if your whole team has to run if you miss your shot. It got to the point when they would groan when you'd call a certain name because they just had the feeling. That puts additional pressure on you if you're walking out there and the team is groaning. Anytime you can outman them in practice or make the whole team run for a guy not making free throws, it puts additional pressure on them. No matter what you do in practice, though, it's always a little different in a game.

"You also give kids opportunities to be leaders, but if they don't have a competitive drive, they aren't going to get it. We did take-the-charge drills all the time because if they don't take a few in practices they don't know what it feels like. It was controlled, but we always told them that once you take the charge, you don't want to stay down. There are lots of players stomping around and you don't want to get stomped on.

"Other drills that are big impact are form-shooting, which is done early so they can work on it all summer long, and four-on-four shell drills you can work on every day."

At the end of their high school careers, some players Summers coached decided to play at the college level.

"I don't think the coach has a responsibility to help kids get to the college level. You have to be careful with that one because if it means I have to highlight a player so that he will get to play in college, you can do that to the detriment of the team, and you've done a big disservice, You set goals for the team, and if you see kids who could play on the college level, you should work to help them with those opportunities, but if that ever becomes the major goal above the team doing well, you're in a bad spot."

One of the additional elements a coach handles is the media and the dispensing of information to groups outside the team and their parents.

"When you coach at St. Henry the media coverage is small time. It's the [Celina] *Daily Standard*. If you play Sidney Lehman, you might get the *Sidney Daily News*. If you play Minster, you might get covered by the *Minster Post*. It was never a major thing. Bob Schroluke was a reporter for the *Daily Standard* many years ago. Jack Albers would remember him. Fran would remember him. He came to the practices when I was in high school and he was the guy every sports writer should be like. He got to know the kids and he never said a negative word about a coach or a team or a player. When he got there on Friday night, he knew what you were trying to accomplish. He was the best thing that ever happened to Mercer

County high school sports coverage and it's a shame we ever lost him. When it's small-time stuff you have to be so careful about what you say, and you read the article the next day and you wonder how they ever got that. You don't want to talk about individual players and single them out because you don't want to look at the stats and find out you were wrong.

"The most frustrating thing is to play a game and they don't cover it. Then they call you and want to know about it. If you don't care about it enough to send anybody, why should I take my time to tell you about it? Then when you get to the final game of the state tournament, the media controls the momentum. Up until the state championship game, any game that is broadcast has the time-outs when they are called. They are all one minute long. Quarter breaks are one minute long. When you get to the championship game, every time out is two minutes. The quarter break is two minutes. If there are no time-outs called in a quarter, they will call a media time-out on a dead ball halfway through the quarter. So, I'm a coach and my team has played twenty-six games with one-minute time outs and no media time-outs. So there we were in the state championship game. We wanted to wear teams down. At the time out there was too much time. Who does that favor? If they said whenever the media is there, we're going to do this, okay, but to change the game for the media is bad."

Through the entire run in one magical year of varsity coaching Summers credits his booster group and a supportive administration.

"Overall, coaching is like teaching. The more the public knows about what you do and why you do it, the fewer problems you are going to have."

Chapter  Nine

PAUL BREMIGAN

RUSSIA HIGH SCHOOL

2002 STATE FINALS

*"Everybody thinks he's a three-point shooter,
and in this game there are a lot of three-point
shooters but not a lot of three-point makers."*

For a man whose first love in sports is golf, Paul Bremigan has made plenty of room in his life for basketball. His first teaching and coaching job out of Otterbein College was in 1979 at Russia, and that's where he has spent his career.

"I grew up around a lot of sports. My dad was a football coach for thirty-six years, so it's kind of been in my blood. I played basketball and golf every day in the summer. In college, I was the student assistant for the basketball team. I grew into it and then when I came to Russia, I was the freshman and JV coach for five years. I sat on the [varsity] bench and coached some fifty games a year, so when you're exposed to two hundred and fifty games over five years, you learn a lot. Once I got the varsity job, I thought I had a good base for starting.

"My father coached football and track and I kind of took basketball on like he took on football. I learned a lot from him as far as preparation and getting ready for teams, even though in football, you have seven days to get ready, but in basketball you sometimes have less than twenty-four hours. It was essentially the same, though. You're watching film and breaking things down. That's the way I am and that's the way he was.

"My mother always supported me throughout my coaching career, and my wife, who is from Fort Loramie, has helped my

coaching record. I met her in 1990, and my coaching record has been a lot better since I've been married than it was when I was single. She's had something to do with that, I'm sure."

As is true with many coaches, Bremigan was a fan of Bobby Knight and John Wooden, but unlike some others, Bremigan had to figure out the game on his own without a mentor.

"I was always a big fan of Bobby Knight. He revolutionized the game. I'm not crazy about all the things he did, but as far as a basketball mind, I thought he was outstanding at his clinics. I wasn't blessed to fall in under someone who was an established head coach and learn from him, so I had to fly by the seat of my pants and learn from my mistakes. Some coaches are able to be a JV coach for eight or nine years under a Fran Guilbault or a Dan Hegemier where you are learning from one of the masters and you're there at practice every day. Basically, you just steal from other people, use their stuff, and call it different things. We've all taken something from everybody. Dan Hegemier is a good friend of mine and we've traded stuff. We've taken an out-of-bounds play from Mike Lee. That's all part of coaching, taking other people's ideas and tweaking them.

"If I hadn't been a coach, I might have been a golf professional or maybe a state highway patrolman. I used to work at Arrowhead golf course in Minster and I loved hanging around the pro shop and talking to people. I like to drive and I think that being a patrolman would be like education. No one day is like the next. It's not like working in a factory where you are doing the same thing."

Although Bremigan doesn't have many rules for his team, his requirements for developing his players are stringent.

"We want to play hard and make sure we defend. We want to be unselfish. We have to rebound, and we have to be tough. It's very simple. I'm not big into rules. The more rules you have, the harder it is for kids to keep track of what rule belongs where. When we start the season, we tell the parents we have six rules and that's it. Sometimes, I'll combine rules, but on offense and defense I'm not big into listing twenty-five and then [during play] shouting, 'Remember rule twenty-four.' Too many rules inhibit the way they need to play. Our athletic code counts as one rule.

"We pride ourselves on wanting to play hard all the time. It's pretty much our number one theme. Everyone says it but I think

only coaches realize how hard it is to get kids to play hard all the time. You can't do that with twenty games. It's like asking somebody to go out and run their fastest mile every day. It just doesn't happen."

Bremigan has found video to be his most helpful resource, but he drove out to Kansas once for an up-close look at the University of Kansas program.

"I'm a video addict. I tape things all the time. I tape to scout. I tape to watch things. In the past five or six years, I've become a big Kansas fan because of the coach at Kansas [Bill Self]. We run a lot of stuff that he came up with. I tape all their games, and it just so happens they won the national championship this year. Three of us decided on a Tuesday to drive out there for a clinic in the fall a few years ago. We took off on a

Thursday, stayed in St. Louis, drove the rest of the way to Kansas and only were in Lawrence fifty-four hours.

"I'll watch all these tapes at maybe ten or eleven o'clock at night. I stay up until one or so, and a lot of times on Friday and Saturday nights, I can't go to bed until I've watched the game that we played. It's kind of a closure thing. A lot of times I'll watch our game and then a tape from the team we're playing next.

"You can get overwhelmed with all the resources out there. I remember when I was a young coach, I wanted to do everything. I wanted ten defenses and a hundred out-of-bounds plays. Kids can't absorb all that and be able to play the game. You have to focus on one or two things and tweak it to fit your personality."

Russia was Bremigan's first job and he now considers the village his home. When he first came to the area, he quickly realized how competitive the people were.

"I like it here. I've lived here longer than I've lived anywhere else in my life. I interviewed at a couple of places all over the state a few years into my JV coaching career. I came in second, third, or fourth, and when you come in second in a job search, you might as well have come in sixtieth. I got the varsity coaching job here, and after a couple of good years, we struggled for awhile. That was back when Fort Loramie was very, very good and Jackson Center was very, very good. They were battling it out for the league, and I was in a learning phase. We've had a lot of success lately, though.

"The competition is huge. In the Shelby County [Athletic] League, you have to be pretty good or you're just going to get whupped. We play a double round-robin, so you know the good coaches in the league are going to make you change something the second time they play you, and that's what makes the double round-robin so neat. Then you throw in your non-league teams from the MAC schools. We play Marion [Local], [New] Bremen, Minster, and Versailles on our non-league schedule and that's a neat atmosphere for the kids to play in. You don't want to get your brains beat in, year in, year out to the point where it's hurting your program, but we went through a stretch of four years where we thought, 'Yeah, we can play with St. Henry.' Twenty years in a row? I don't know. For the most part it was very competitive. The atmosphere over there is outstanding and the atmosphere in our gym is outstanding. I think the lack of football in Shelby County makes us a little more competitive in basketball. When Anna and Fort Loramie started football, there was a little bit of a transition there, but now they're getting back. Unfortunately."

Bremigan has coached several games that have remained clear and vivid in his memory. They span much of his career with a tournament game in 1986, a district championship game in 1995, a league championship in 2001, and the biggest game for him, the state semi-finals against Mowrystown Whiteoak in 2002.

"My favorite game was when we played Whiteoak in the state semi-finals. We were down eleven in the second half and came back to win by seven or eight. We played just outstanding. In the fans' eyes, the biggest game was probably the Southeastern game in the regional final when they were number one in the state.

"We beat Fort Loramie in 1986 to go to the district tournament for the first time in a long time, and that was my second year coaching varsity. It showed the kids that it can be done because we had been to the sectional finals so many times and never got beyond that to UD Arena. That was the first. Then nine years later we beat Twin Valley South for our first-ever district championship in basketball. We went to Dayton, then, and won our semi-final game, but Springfield Catholic beat us in the regional finals with Jason Collier, a player who went on to play for Georgia Tech and then the Atlanta Hawks in the NBA.

"Those games unfortunately were nine years apart and since 1995 we've had, I think, only one losing season. In 1999 we won our first league championship. It wasn't really an individual game to describe, per se, but that group had a lot to say about what we did in the league. Since 1999, we've won six league championships.

"I had the coolest weekend in 2001 when we had to beat Botkins here to win the league. Botkins was in second place and we were in first place and it was just a war. We beat them, but then we had to turn around on Saturday night and play Marion Local who was ranked number one in the state, and we beat them. That really stands out, even though it's hard to pin down one game with so many games that mean a lot to me.

"Now, the most exciting game was the Southeastern game at Millett Hall at Miami University in 2002 because we knew what was on the line. We played really, really well. We made nineteen of nineteen foul shots. In the fourth quarter we were up ten or twelve. It was one of those feelings that I knew in the last two minutes we were going to win. I remember their coach with about a minute to go, motioning for a substitution. It was a fourteen point game. He said, 'I want to sub,' and I said, 'You first,' because I've had kids on the bench sub in and suddenly, there's a six-point swing in the game."

Bremigan has worked through learning how to keep kids in a game, but the results haven't always been the most enjoyable moments for fans.

"We went to Minster one year after getting beat up the night before. One of the players had an ankle injury and another one was sick. I had three really good guards, so we slowed the game down and held the ball the last six minutes of the third quarter for one shot. Minster stood in a zone. I looked at Minster at the time and some of the people were kind of irate, but we have a hard time holding it that long, too. It's something you have to teach the kids to buy into. If you have one kid that doesn't believe that's what you have to do to win, he's going to kill you. Mike [Lee] sat over there and I just sat over here and we ended up scoring at the end of the quarter. They ended up beating us by two or three and the final score was something like twenty-nine to twenty-six. I learned from that, and Mike understood, it was the only way we were going to have a chance to win.

"We did the same thing earlier in the year with Versailles who was number two in the state. We were patient and we beat them fifty-one to forty-nine in overtime. You learn to do things whether people like it or not to give kids an honest chance to win or compete. I don't say the word 'winning' very much during the year. I say, 'If we're going to be successful' or 'If we're going to compete.' That way, if we play the number one team in the state and we get beat by six or eight points, I feel like we might not have won, but we were successful in the things that we did. If you talk about winning, you put too much pressure on kids. Then again, you can beat a team by ten points and just stink it up. They can say, 'Well, Coach talked about winning and we won,' but sometimes the coach isn't very happy with that win. Sometimes I catch myself, but I try not to talk about winning too much."

Bremigan thinks of his state final game against Delphos St. John as a big lesson in momentum. The fourth quarter found the Raiders swimming upstream against the Delphos current.

"Things happened in the fourth quarter of that state final that I'm not sure we could have changed, but we might have been able to affect the outcome. They came out and really, really played well, and we didn't play so well. We lost a seven-point lead going into the fourth quarter. We ended up losing because we gave up thirty-three points in that quarter, which might still be a state record, but I don't know if that's the kind of record you want to have. They came down the floor and hit two or three three-pointers. We missed some foul shots. They made some foul shots. We turned the ball over, and they went on a roll from a seven-minute mark to the four-minute mark. For a team that's trying to win, that's the best time to go on a roll.

"My favorite game to coach was the state semi-final against Whiteoak. We were in unfamiliar territory and we were playing a team we had very little information on. It just so happened we had four scouting reports on three out of four teams we might possibly have played, but the team that came out of the regional was that fourth team with only one scouting report, Mowrystown Whiteoak. We hopped in our car and drove to Lancaster to get a tape, and we sent our secretary, who was going to Sandusky anyway, to stop at Sandusky St. Marys to pick up a tape for us. We had other guys helping us scout. Sometimes when you're in the tournament and you get that far, other coaches in the county will help us with that. We've done that for people, too. It was neat for our kids to come out in the second half after being down eleven. Here was little old Russia in this big arena and people thought we were going to gag it away, but we didn't.

"At the time we were about the fifth-smallest school in the state and it's always kind of neat for the press when small schools get to play the *Hoosiers* [movie] card. The local press focus a lot on kids. The state media focused on our town and how small we were. They didn't want to talk to us about our team as much as they did the size of our town and how you pronounce it Roo-she and not Rush-a. They got a kick out of that. Ken Barhorst has done a great job along with one of our grads Matt Zircher. I don't degrade the team or players in the press. If I'm angry at the end of the game, I'll take maybe ten or fifteen minutes instead of letting them strike while the iron is hot. We ran into a problem a few years ago when a reporter in Dayton wanted to drag some kids through the mud and I wouldn't do it. He got mad at me, but you have to watch that. There are certain guys you trust and others you have to just give the standard, 'One game at a time' deal. We can liven it up a little with Ken on Thursday night. Sometimes, with certain guys, you just have to make sure you say it's off the record and sometimes you have to know what's fair game, because they can make you or break you.

"They also treated us like kings at the Schottenstein Center. We had our host assigned to us, and we saw LeBron James play in the game before us both times. Our locker room was just down the hall from his and the kids thought that was pretty cool. Our host showed us Ohio State's locker room, and the kids got to go out on the floor and shoot. Even our own sons got to shoot out there. The reporters who didn't have anything to do between games were feeding them balls to shoot constantly.

"We were pretty disappointed that we didn't finish it out in the final game, but kids bounce back better than adults. By the time we got to Bellefontaine on the way home, they were talking and laughing. We stopped at a gas station because the kids were kind of hungry, and we bought about a hundred dollars worth of candy and junk food. I knew they were going to have food for us in Russia when we got back, so we didn't want to feed them too much.

"We prepare our kids in a certain way. I like practice and I like coaching in practice. Some coaches hate practices, but I'm the exact opposite. I practice up to the game. Some coaches are very good game coaches and make a lot of adjustments, but I don't make a whole lot of adjustments. The kids play and the assistant coaches help me out a whole lot. The way we played against Southeastern in the regional finals was about as good as a Russia team can play. They were the number one team in the state and were undefeated.

With that much atmosphere and that much pressure, our kids responded well.

"The year the team won the district in 1995 was a good game against Twin Valley South. Our kids played very well that night. In 2001 we came back and beat Marion Local, and the game against Loramie in 1986 and the Southeastern regional game in 2002 are games when the kids played great. Those were situations the kids had never been in before."

The hardest part of the game for Bremigan to teach is shot selection because he finds that kids overestimate their abilities on the perimeter.

"It's hard for kids to understand what shot to take and what shot the coach doesn't want him to take. Everybody thinks he's a three-point shooter, and in this game there are a lot of three-point shooters but not a lot of three-point makers. I tell the kids that when they are open, it isn't a green light for everybody to shoot a three-pointer, and I say, 'You're open, but there's a reason why you're open and the reason is that people don't think you can shoot. Sometimes you have to be blunt and tell them they have to make a shot in practice before they can shoot it in a game. Kids think that if they made one once a few days before, they can make that shot in a game. You can get them to do anything you want, but sometimes in a pressure situation, they want to show Mom, Dad, Grandpa, and Grandma that they can shoot and that's hard to fight. Kids shoot differently every day. You have to be positive with them, but you also have to tell them it isn't the shot we want in particular situations. I don't want them shooting a three-pointer if we're up three with thirty seconds to go. They have a hard time understanding that sometimes.

"They also have a hard time understanding the team concept and the importance of communicating. Some teams are very good at communicating and other teams just won't talk to each other."

These difficulties don't cause a coach to abandon the cause, however. Bremigan believes it's time for a coach to call it quits when it isn't fun anymore.

"If it isn't fun for the coach and the players, you have to make a decision, but you can't do that within a month after the season when everybody is tired. You have to let it process a little bit. If you aren't ready to go at the end of May and start camps, I would imagine that's when it is, even though I haven't gotten there yet.

"Parental influence is a concern. You say something and you know Mom and Dad are saying something different at the dinner table. You fight that battle all year. It's the parents' role to be supportive of their son, whether he is playing a lot or whether he isn't, whether he's winning or whether he isn't. I don't think a parent should be a sounding board for what I'm doing wrong. It puts the player in a bad spot. I've had parents rant and rave at me. It comes with the territory. I'll sit and talk as long as they want but once they start talking about other people, that's when the conversation ends. I'll talk about their son and their son only. Playing time is usually the biggest complaint.

"Another problem is kids that don't have the work ethic academically and athletically. There is no switching the ethic on and off. I keep tabs on that at school. It isn't an eligibility issue; it's a concentration issue. There have been times where I've taken kids out of conditioning or out of practice and sent them to my coach's office. Early in my career, I took the whole team, and instead of conditioning, we had study tables. But they didn't get out of conditioning. We had study tables for two hours and then we had conditioning following that. They thought they were going to get out of conditioning, but they didn't."

Those situations don't deter Bremigan from enjoying the rewards that come with the job. The happiest moments for him are experiencing the memorable moments with the players.

"Seeing kids work together and creating good memories is important. I see ex-players, and they say, 'Remember when you told us this,' or 'Remember when you said that.' I don't remember all those things, but it means a lot to me that they sit around their dorm rooms or at parties and talk about the good memories of playing, whether they went 15–5 or 5–15.

"I'm also appreciative of our boosters. The kids do everything they ask because they've done so much for us. The boys help change the gym over from our practice to being ready to host a girls game on the same night. I also have a good relationship with our administration and community. If they want me to talk to their groups, I try to do that as much as I can."

New coaches can expect the same rewards if they approach their work with a basic understanding of what it takes to get to that point.

"When I was a JV coach, I went to every clinic I could find and wrote down as much as I could. If you can learn under a coach that's been in it a long time that's good, but it doesn't always work out that way. There aren't too many coaches who have been in it a long time anymore. It isn't as prestigious a job as it once was, I guess. I watch teams all the time. I still scout and go to clinics. Good coaches are constantly learning. If you aren't winning, don't let it get to you. Everybody loves you when you win, but you have to understand that in the fans' eyes, when you win it's the kids and when you lose it's the coach. That's the way it has always been and that's the way it always will be. I've had a lot of support at Russia and the people have been great to me.

"My scouts, Brad Francis, Doug Foster, and Dave Borchers, are very good, too, because they've been doing it a long time. A lot of times when we're together scouting tournament teams we'll sit together but far enough apart that we don't talk to each other so that if you say something, the other person doesn't write down what you said. If we're playing a league team in tournament, we'll have ten scouting reports on them. We'll make out a shot chart where every kid shoots from and you can see some tendencies there. One kid a few years ago shot sixty-something percent from the right side of the floor. He only shot twelve percent from the left side, so we told our kids to guard him on the right side and let him shoot from the left. The first time down the floor, the kid shot from the left and made it. Our kid guarding him looked over at us [questioningly], and I looked at the coaches and asked, 'Does that shot surprise you?' It turned out that the kid was two for three from the right side and one for nine from the left, so it panned out, but we laugh about that one. In league and district voting at the end of the year, most people are going to vote for the kids they see the most. Maybe it isn't the best way to do it, but we scout so much we see lots of teams outside our area, so scouting helps us make those decisions, too."

"My junior high and freshman coaches know that if the varsity is playing, they are scouting. We'll get together later that evening and talk about everything. My varsity assistant and JV coaches break down film of opponents and create scouting reports. My freshman coach keeps track of fouls and time-outs during a game. The other two coaches on the bench give me feedback all the time. I don't want yes-men. I respect their opinions. That's what I like. Having the same guys, like I've had the last five or six years, makes for a good coaching staff. You don't want to worry about a brand new coach and what he's teaching. Jerry Harmon had Don Thogmartin and Larry Andrews for so long. Dan Hegemier had his assistants a long time. Fran Guilbault had Al Summers for a long time. Roger [McEldowney] had his brother. Tony Rogers had Brett Meyer. Jack Albers had Bill Elking and Keith Westrick. All those coaches had the same guys for so long.

"Only those other coaches understand losing. When you aren't playing well and you can't get the most out of your players, it's a long season. When we get beat, I make sure I watch the sports scores on TV. At least I know fifty percent of the coaches feel as lousy as I do. That makes me feel a little bit better, knowing about three hundred head coaches feel as bad as I do. I usually watch the tape of the game we played that night and [the tape of the next team] even if we don't play until the next Friday. If I don't, I can't go to sleep. I watch it, take some notes, and then I can wash my hands of it. I can enjoy my Saturday and Sunday and worry about it Monday when we practice.

"Then on game day, I'm busy with teaching and guidance. The only thing different is that I go home after school. I don't eat anything until after the game. I eat lunch, but that's about it. I get back to school about an hour before the bus leaves or before the JV game starts to help get things ready. I try to stay the same during the day in case the kids are looking at me, wondering if I'm nervous. I still joke around with them and try to keep on being the same day after day. After we lose, I tell them that the sun is going to come up in the morning. I'm not always like that inside, but I try to hide it as much as possible.

"The pre-game talk focuses on two or three key points we need to be successful. We try to relate what we're doing to everyday life. The things like behavior and sportsmanship are emphasized. We keep things pretty simple. At halftime the coaching staff talks. I have three other coaches on the bench, so we have these different perspectives. Three of my coaches played for me, so they know what I expect. We go into the locker room and talk to them and keep it simple. We try to stay positive and make certain, just like in the pregame, that the last thing we say is positive.

"After a win, we talk about what we still need to work on. We emphasize what we did well. We usually don't talk about the next team we play. We talk about curfew, making good decisions, and they know what I'm talking about when I say that.

"After a loss, we have to make sure we control our emotions before we go into the locker room. In football you can rant and rave and by the next week when they play, they've forgotten about it, but in basketball, if you rant and rave on Friday night, you might have to play in less than twenty-four hours and it can have an impact on them. So it's the same point as the sun coming up tomorrow."

The family has to understand the time and the demands on a coach. Bremigan incorporates his family as much as possible.

"Your wife has to know that on the weekends, if you aren't playing, you're scouting. We usually have a night during the week when we go out to eat. My two sons think it's pretty cool. They've been in the gym a long time. I've never made them, but they come along when they want to. They've always been my ball boys, my stats, and my video guys. Socially, we hang around with the coaching staff and their families. After the game, we're in one of our basements and we have a good time. If I quit coaching I'll miss those nights after a game more than anything because we have a lot of laughs.

"The things I don't like very much are open gyms, evaluating referees, and doing statistics. I have kids who do the stats right there at the game. I keep it simple for them. I give them a shot chart and I want rebounds and turnovers. All the other stuff is blocked shots and assists. Those sheets need to be re-done because they aren't very accurate, so I do those when I watch the tape.

"To be successful, you need to be personable and be honest. You have to have the ability to find out what motivates each individual player. You have to find what buttons to push on each kid because everybody is different. You have to have knowledge of the game and be able to handle a lot of situations in and out of the gym. You have to be politically correct and tactful with parents. You have to find what works for you, but some people have a system and they get their brains beat out night after night because they become close-minded and don't want to change. You can't be afraid to change something. If things aren't going well, and I don't mean just two games, sometimes you have to move some things around. Every team I've had has been like a puzzle, and you have to put the pieces in the right place to get it to work. To force a piece in there, to force a kid to play a spot that he can't play, is usually not going to work. That's the way I approach it at the beginning of the season to figure out where a kid can play and where he goes in the puzzle, but you have to realize that sometimes the puzzle isn't going to be very good."

Successful coaches look for the components of a successful team which generally begins with recognizing talent.

"Talent and competition among players are two important elements. I've had kids in some classes who knew they were going to play because there were only two of them, so they didn't practice between their junior and senior years. They just knew they were going to play because no one was there pushing them for a spot. That hasn't been the case lately because we've had success and a lot of kids want to play. Having a coaching staff that's been with me a long time helps a lot. They know what to expect. You have to be sure your coaching staff is doing the right things and ours is pretty solid.

"Our two leagues with the MAC and the Shelby County [Athletic] League playing each other is a lot of fun for people to watch. It's the competition, the rivalry, the state championships and the success we've had. It's very competitive. Fort Loramie and Anna picked up football lately and are having success, particularly with Anna playing in the MAC. It gives a renewed respect to us that we're not afraid to go over and play St. Henry in basketball. I've had some St. Henry fans tell me they enjoy it, and even though they might not want to admit it, I think in the past ten years or so, they see Shelby County in a little different light than they saw us before. That's good that there's a lot of competition in the area.

"Fort Loramie is still our biggest rival and I don't see that changing anytime soon. The history goes back to the Germans in Fort Loramie and of course, we're French. They called Russia the frogs and Loramie the cabbage-heads. From what I understand, they used to throw cabbages on the floor. I think somebody threw a cabbage right past [Fort Loramie coach] George Hamlin's ear the first or second year I was here. And then the next year, they brought some frogs and put them out on the floor. That's been a big rivalry game for us, and I think it always will be. The Versailles game is always a big rivalry for us, too, just because of how close they are."

Bremigan has reflected on his team's state tournament appearance and has found that the elements to get to that level are as much psychological as they are athletic. He knows that a key factor, though, is luck.

"You have to have very good talent that believes in itself. You have to be able to handle pressure, and at tournament time, a lot of it is luck. If there is a team you see that could possibly give you problems matching up, it's big if they get beat before you play them. Minster played Southeastern and beat them in the regional semi-finals. My assistants wanted Minster, but I wanted Southeastern. We had beaten Minster earlier in the season, but I told them I'd rather go against a team that was unbeaten and we matched up pretty well than to play a school with so many family connections. Whenever you go against kids who have a parent from your own community, they just kill you. You can always count on a kid who makes two points in every other game going off for about fifteen if his mom or dad graduated from your school. We always joke about it when a kid like that makes a shot. 'You know why he made that? His mom is from Russia.' Southeastern ended up winning, though, and our kids had the mindset that they had to play really well to beat the number one team in the state, instead of thinking they had already beaten Minster and they could do it again. Luck has a lot to do with it in a tournament run, along with not having to play the teams you don't want. You also have to play more good quarters than bad ones. One bad quarter can cost you a tournament game. You have to be really, really consistent in what you do."

Making decisions during the game from a vantage point on the bench can be risky. Bremigan has found that sometimes what looks to be a very good situation can be treacherous.

"I never want to sub too early. My assistants are always telling me, 'Come on, Paul. You're up fifteen with two minutes to go.' I've been burned. You don't want to ever put kids in with three minutes to go and you have to take them out and put your starters back in. That's something you might have to do, but it would be hard on the kids to come out. When you prepare for a game, you feel as though certain things have to happen for you to win. If they don't happen you lose. Some of the hardest games to coach are when you jump out to a big lead in the first quarter and now you're trying to hold that fifteen to seventeen point lead against a good team all the way through. Those are about the most gut-wrenching games to play because you know the team you're playing isn't fifteen points worse than you.

"When you're ahead in a game, you have to stay aggressive. You can't get complacent or the other team will sense that and it sets you up for them to make a comeback. When you're behind, you can't try to get it all back in one trip down the floor. A kid will try to come down and make a twenty-point shot, a hero shot. You have to give them goals in time-outs and at halftime. I might say, if we're down twelve at the half, 'Let's try to get it down to six by the end of the quarter.' Sometimes, we're down by four at the end of the quarter and then we're better than where we wanted to be. Sometimes, we're down eight or ten, and then I'll say, 'Let's try to get it down to six by the five-minute mark.' I try to break it down into increments so the lead doesn't seem so ominous. We were down against Yellow Springs in the district final by twenty-three points at half. We ended up getting beat by three, but we had a last-second shot to tie. We kind of did that. Yellow Springs got complacent, but we just didn't have enough to get over the hump. We'd spent so much energy coming back, and one of the tendencies is to relax because you finally caught up, but that gives the other team a chance again."

"The pacing of a game comes down to what you've prepared for during the week and what you think can work based on what you've seen in practice. You can sometimes take advantage of individual match-ups. Sometimes we'll play a lot of zone late in the game to let the other team pass the ball a few times more and burn the clock on their end, rather than play man-to-man and you're fouling and stopping the clock for foul shots We've had a lot of success with the four-corner, delay game. We've had good guards who can handle and take care of the ball, and we have good foul-shooters, so kids have a lot of confidence in that. We've been able to win a lot of games like that. Other teams can also have kids who are getting a little tired and you can push it up the floor against them, or maybe they don't have a lot of ball-handlers in the game. The personnel they have in the game versus the personnel you have in a game can make you change [the pacing] more than anything."

Even though basketball players are working on their game all year, Bremigan plans plenty of breaks for his team.

"We start with conditioning in October five weeks before the first practice. I took it from Jerry Harmon to do one day the first week, two days the second week and so forth. I did it that way when he first told me that and I've been doing it that way ever since. At the halfway mark in the season, we always cut our practices from two hours to an hour and a half to save their legs. Then we always give them Sundays and Mondays off after a two-game weekend. We aren't allowed to practice on Sundays here, anyway. Then after the season, we'll start open gyms from mid-May to late July. Then we have camps in June and July with a summer league in June. We're pretty busy in June and July. We don't go to any team camps. We stay here and do what we need to do so when November hits, we pretty much know what we want to do.

"Practices are planned to the minute, but nothing is longer than ten minutes. If you don't plan to the minute, you can spend a lot of time on one thing. Usually we spend forty percent of the time on defense, forty percent on offense, and twenty percent on special situations and free throws. I run off my practice plan and give it to my coaches that day. We try to keep things moving. We don't scrimmage much in practice. We work constantly on fundamentals.

"We do a lot of drills others do. We start with a combination of ball-handling drills that I got from the coach at Memphis. You have to do everything right to get out of the drill. You have to make the lay-up, you can't drop the pass, you can't travel, so it's called Perfection because you have to be perfect in everything you do right off the bat. That starts practice with the mindset that we're going to do things right. Most of the time, it takes us six or seven minutes to get through it. Then we go into a five on zero fast break where they have to sub and know what happens when a certain person comes into the game. Who plays what spot? Johnny comes in and you're a post player. Billy comes in and you're a guard. We do those to communicate and we do those two every day. We do shell drills for defense and we try not to do the same drills day after day so it isn't monotonous for them. We always have the same principles of defense and the same principles of offense. It's just a different way of teaching it."

Visiting some schools for a tough game has posed a challenge for Bremigan's teams.

"Fort Loramie, in their old gym, would jam-pack that place. They'd give you a corner and that was it. It was wall-to-wall people. I like to think now that people don't like to come into our gym to play. We have two student sections. Our high school kids are on one end and the elementary kids are on the other with parents sitting right in the middle on the other side. It's tough to play at Fairlawn and Anna where it gets loud. The old gyms were hard to play in, too. The fans aren't right on top of you in the new gyms. It was tough back then. It was exciting, but I can't say I really liked it. I'd rather be in my own gym."

The changes Bremigan has seen over the years also include the three-point line and the physical change in the athletes.

"There is more physical play today. Athletes are bigger, stronger, and faster. It's harder for officials to control and it's just going to get more and more physical. I think you're going to see more technology for athletes to do that.

"A good player is not only athletic, he's coachable and aggressive. He's a hard worker and he can play a variety of positions. That's very valuable to us in a small school. I always tell kids if they can play more than one spot, it improves their chances of playing. When you are playing a team like Versailles, they have a hundred more boys than you do. They have a lot bigger talent pool. Two years ago we had some really athletic kids who could really press and run and get after it all the time, so we pressed a lot. That worked for that group, but it might not work for this group. I don't think you can get a coach in here who says, 'This is my system and this is the way we're going to play all the time, no matter if I have five clods who can't get up and down the floor. We're going to press all the time.' Well, that doesn't make sense. A coach has to be flexible with what personnel he has. We don't make drastic changes where we change everything, but five or six years ago we began to get some size coming through and we had some really nice post players which we continue to have, so we're keeping that kind of offense, but there for awhile we had five guards on the floor, so we ran a completely different offense.

"We always look to score on a fast break, no matter what type of personnel we have. That puts pressure on the defense. Shot selection plays a role in there and some coaches don't like to do that because it gives the kids too much control. They like to walk up and down and call a play. I've been blessed with some athletic kids who can fast break. If they are less athletic you're less likely to let them run and give them that freedom. You control them a little more.

"You have to put kids under pressure in practice during free throws. When they are shooting free throws, they always have pressure on them. They always have to run if they don't make a certain number. There is always a consequence. In special situations we have pressure, too. Some players handle pressure easily. Others don't. Those kids usually don't play. I tell them that if they can't make more than fifty percent of their free throws, they won't play late in the game. I can't afford to take a chance on them.

"We give ownership of the team to them early in the year. I'll pick a couple of seniors to organize the summer league. I give them a list of kids to call and they have to make sure they have eight players and they know where they are going. When we vote on captains, I get on them pretty hard for other kids' mistakes. If a sophomore makes a wrong move in an out-of-bounds play, I'll get on the captain and tell him he needs to do a better job of explaining to sophomores how to run the play. The sophomore sees me getting on a senior for his mistake and knows I'm taking it easy on him because he is a sophomore. He then pays attention because a senior is probably mad at him. The seniors know they have to take some leadership to avoid that. Little things like that help build leadership. Some kids just have an innate ability to lead. Some kids just try to be popular.

I try to tell them when they vote for captain that you don't have to be popular to be a leader because sometimes it becomes a popularity contest. We have to work on that some.

"The best way to build a competitive drive is competition in practice. The bench also is a great motivator. Bobby Knight said that there is no greater motivation than when that rear end hits the bench. I'm a firm believer in that because nobody likes to sit. If they don't do things up to your expectations, they sit. Somebody else goes in and gets another chance. Those two things are important in teaching kids to compete. If they don't want to play, they don't want to play."

Some players not only want to play in high school, but they have aspirations to play in college. Bremigan serves as a mediator.

"Colleges send information letters that we send back out. If you think you have someone who can play then you send tapes to coaches and colleges. To have a college coach walk in your door doesn't happen very often at a school like Russia, but usually coaches find you before you find them. A good tournament run has a lot to do with it. That's where they see you, but if a kid wants me to send a tape somewhere, I'll be more than happy to do it."

Bremigan emphasizes the role of the fan as being "loud and proud." It's an advantage in a gym to have enthusiastic fans.

"They have to yell and scream. Our elementary kids started another student section and they just have a ball. Sometimes I'll be watching the game video and I'll just laugh. A group of dads sit with them and teach them a few cheers, not the cheerleaders' cheers, but the "air ball" type cheers. We had a dad put rocks in about fifty pop containers and he handed them out to all these little kids. It was so loud it was just annoying. We felt like we were at a European soccer match or something. It was a one-time deal after the administration got ahold of that. That was enough. Brad Francis, our athletic director, ordered T-shirts for almost nothing and he worked it so that a family could buy five of them for twenty bucks, and so they just buy them like crazy. Every now and then we'll have a Gold Rush game when everyone is supposed to wear gold. He does a good job of creating school spirit. He gets out the old uniforms and at pep rallies he tosses them out to the kids.

"Our fans sit mostly on the other side, and there's a reason for that. There's more seating over there, and I'd rather have the opposing fans yelling behind me. I only see them twice a year. I see our fans all the time."

Bremigan sees some situations in games that give him pause to think in some ways about the direction basketball is headed.

"The officials are necessary for the game, but I'm not a fan of the three-man crew. It's made officiating more complex than it needs to be. If we're going to a three-man, why not just go to a four-man and divide the court into four equal parts and each official is responsible for everything in his corner, just like Four-Square. Some people get all ticked off when I say that. We had a two-man crew at Versailles a couple of years ago and it was one of the best-officiated games.

"It was decided to go to a three-man crew because of the three-point line. It was explained to me that there is a part of the court around the three-point line that can't be seen by two people, but with these three-man crews we've had more physical play. They don't call three-seconds. If they called that rule, it would get the offensive player out of the paint more and there wouldn't be as much congestion and physical play. The three-point line is a dunk for guards, so now you have to go out and guard those guys who are shooting. If somebody shoots forty percent from the three-point line, it's the equivalent of shooting sixty percent from the two-point line, so you have to get out there and guard him. One official said he wasn't going to call three seconds, so I asked him to tell me what other rules we weren't going to play by that night so I could tell my kids. Let's just rip that page out of the book and move on. Traditionally, we're not very big, so we don't want their big man in there getting offensive rebounds all the time, so we harp on that call. The officials tell us that when we had our big guy in there a few years ago, that we didn't say anything about the three-second call. They were right. Of course we didn't.

"I think the three-point line has been good for the game. It has spread play out. I thought it was pretty cool when you could go into the lane on the release of the foul shot because you could come up with rebounding plays. They cancelled that a few years ago, but I still have my plays in case they come back to that.

"The worst rule change was the coach's box, and you have to sit down for the rest of the game after a technical. I can't sit down to coach. I've never been able to do that. These restrain the coach and the officials are too worried about the coach. They should be watching the game. It's all a sportsmanship issue.

"I always wanted to make the opposing team's coaching box three feet shorter than mine so that when Matt Meyer or Dan Hegemier came in, they'd look down and see that my coaching box was bigger than theirs. My athletic director won't let me do it."

Chapter  Ten

KEITH WESTRICK

MARIA STEIN MARION LOCAL HIGH SCHOOL

2004 STATE FINALS
2003 STATE CHAMPION

"Fans will accept mistakes,
but they will never, ever accept lack of effort.
And that's the one thing you can always give."

Keith Westrick was in his second year of teaching at Marion Local and his first year of coaching eighth grade basketball when head coach Jack Albers took the high school boys to the state tournament in 1984. The influence of that year was important to building Westrick's already considerable love of the game.

"He [Albers] was passionate about the game. He'd always spend time with you. Even when you were sitting on the bench with him, he'd say, 'I want to know things. If you have suggestions, throw them out there.' He'd be in the middle of the most intense situation and you'd throw out a suggestion, thinking it would go in one ear and out the other, or it might just bounce off of him, but he always heard everything you said. A lot of times he'd say, 'I don't want to do that now.' He was definitely focused on basketball and the rest of the world didn't even exist."

Westrick was hired at Marion Local to coach football, which he did for 23 years, but he also spent the winters coaching eighth grade, freshman, or JV basketball, depending on the year and the needs of the program, until he replaced Albers as head coach in 1996. In that time, he soaked up knowledge from the two men he credits with teaching him the details of the game – Albers and JV coach Bill Elking.

As head coach, Westrick has taken teams to the state tournament twice, winning it all on one of those occasions. It is an accomplishment very few coaches can claim.

"I never fully understood why I love basketball as much as I do. When I was younger, I put a court up in our barn and just played constantly. We had a basket on the outside of the barn, too, and in the winter I'd put gloves on and dribble in the snow. We'd play for hours. Then I put the court in upstairs with the wood planks on the floor and I had to learn to dribble where the solid boards were and avoid the loose ones. A lot of times, as a kid, I played imaginary games. I watched my Alma Mater, which is Ada High School, back in the early 1960s. I thought tournament action was the greatest thing there ever was. Back then the gyms were small, hot, and sweaty, and it was crazy with people on top of each other. To me, that's the fun of basketball. The bigger gyms are nice for the fans, but some of the best memories are in the little cracker boxes where you couldn't even hear yourself think."

As Westrick grew, he discovered he had more success in football and track than he did as a basketball athlete, but basketball was his greatest love.

"I remember calling the coach on snow days wanting to know if we were going to have practice. The coach would say yes, but only if I wanted to call the rest of the team. So I did, and then I would drive the tractor four miles or so to town.

"I went to Ohio Northern University to play football but not basketball. That was short-lived, though. In high school, sports are the thing, but in college it made more sense to get a job and make some money. I got a job at Ford and the paychecks looked awful good. I finished my college career working and going to school. However,

I never finished my student teaching. In 1980 Ford started laying people off. If that had never hit, I might have been a thirty-year Ford man.

"I did my student teaching in the fall and before I was finished, I got a job at Logan Elm High School, just to the east of Circleville. I was one year there. Then a friend of mine who was at Marion Local left to go to Parkway, but he saw my name on a list from Ohio Northern and told the administration that he knew me. I got an interview, wanted to be back closer to home, and decided to take the job. I've never regretted one time my decision to go into education."

It was at Marion Local, as well, that he met another big influence on his game. Bill Elking was the JV coach who took time to describe and explain the Marion Local style of basketball.

"I still have some notes from him," Westrick admits.

It was during these years that the basic principles of the game became clear to him as a coach.

"You have to be prepared and you need to have a list of fundamentals that your team needs to accomplish in order to be successful. You need to keep track of those fundamentals and be sure that you touch on them on a regular basis. At some point in the season, you can lose a game because you didn't do this or that, and you haven't practiced the fundamentals. You should touch on those at least every two weeks. We don't want to get into a ball game faced with something we haven't emphasized. Regardless of how things are going at any one time, you have to make sure you hit your basic fundamentals and skills equally.

"You have to demand that kids play hard in practice and they play hard in a game. I've always told my players that fans will accept mistakes, but they'll never, ever accept lack of effort. And that's the one thing you can always give. The game of basketball has been described before as a chain of mistakes, and the team that makes fewer of them is the team that's going to win. The parents that are driving there, the aunts and uncles, the fans that are coming there, sometimes through adverse weather, want to see kids who are busting their tail.

"Kids have to know you're prepared. They have to know you put in more time than they do. You have to have knowledge of your opponent and you better be one-hundred percent sold on everything you want to do. It's not experimental."

Westrick bolstered his skills by watching videos of college coaches, particularly Gary Williams and his discussion of the flex offense, and by attending clinics.

"A lot of times you'll go to the state clinic and listen to speaker after speaker and you take notes on everybody, but you might only get one or two things from that whole clinic. Maybe it's just a couple of drills or maybe it's something that you think would really work well with what your team is attempting to do. If you try to do everything from a clinic, it'll be a mess. See what fits in your program, believe in it, and coach it."

Westrick has unlimited confidence in the small schools of west central Ohio and the people who live in the region.

"More than anything else, if you go back into the 1970s when the state wanted to consolidate schools, they thought bigger was better, the little schools were outdated, and you couldn't function that way. They started consolidating schools, but the little schools were kicking their butt on proficiency scores. It's not so much schools or the philosophy of how you go about it; it's the product that's coming to the schools. You have families, good family values, and kids who aren't afraid to work. You have a community that values that athletic competition."

Although Westrick has appeared in two state tournaments, the most exciting game for him was the one that landed him in Columbus in 2003, the year he eventually won it all. It was the regional final against Fort Loramie when the Redskins were led by Jordan Pleiman, who later played Division I basketball at Wright State University.

"Pleiman was a junior and we had two very nice teams going head to head and two nice communities down at Miami University. The seating there is a little off the floor, so you don't have that small gym feeling anymore. We were down, I think five points, going into the fourth quarter and our guys were determined. They started the season determined and they had goals they wanted to accomplish. When they put the time and effort into it, and they paid the price, they just believed they were going to get it done.

"A few years back, there was another game when were down four points with 3.4 seconds to go, and I remember one of my players later said, 'I still thought we were going to win that game.' That's the kind of belief these kids have. They weren't going to accept it.

"Fort Loramie was the same way. Jason Shatto was the coach. He was a great guy. We competed head to head and they came up a little on the short end, but he came over to our locker room and congratulated us. We were ready to get on the bus and he came back over and wished us luck at state. That's a wonderful feeling when you walk out of a competition like that, knowing you're going to state.

"Another big game was the state semi-final in 2004 when we played Sebring McKinley. We had gone all the way to state in football that year, which made it a shortened season, and we had a struggle with focus and the physical nature of the game. We had lost everybody from the 2003 team so this was a completely new group of all JV players who were coming up. To get back there again and get back to the finals was big. We lost to Holgate in the finals and it was probably for that reason – the physical nature of the game, but just playing at the Schott is an incredible experience. Our state final game in 2003 against Convoy Crestview still holds the record for the biggest attendance at a [Division IV] game there."

What Westrick has learned from this experience has more to do with his players than the game itself.

In 2003, we had two losses in the league and Coldwater had two losses in the league. Delphos came to our gym with one loss in the league. It was a TV-44 game and it was sold out, maybe a little bit plus. The next thing I knew, we were down 23-9. Those kids kept their composure. They kept doing the things they knew they needed to do to be successful. Sometimes kids surprise you. They stepped up and won that game, along with a share of the MAC title. On the other side of that, the years you have the better team, the superior team, and you just can't buy a basket are frustrating times. They just take years off your life."

"We played a game down at Miami against Bethel who went on to win the state that year in 2001. They had the Southwest player of the year, Matt Witt. We had the game won. We had a three-point lead and the possession out of bounds. Most of our out-of-bounds plays are designed to attack the basket. So here we were with thirty seconds to go, we had the lead, and we had the ball out of bounds under the basket. The play I called was designed to score. We didn't have the 'Let's get it inbounds and hold the ball' mentality. Our planned shot got blocked. We thought we were going to the line, but they didn't call it a shooting foul. They called it a block out of bounds. They got the ball, went down and hit a three, and the game went into overtime.

"The game is played at such a speed that at those times the coach has to have confidence in what he's doing and the players have to have confidence in what they're doing. You make a decision in a split second and you have to live with that decision. If a kid makes a bad pass in a press offense for example, he doesn't go back after a ball game and beat himself up for it, and I don't think a coach can go back and beat himself up, either. You made that decision in the heat of the battle. It's the way you've played all year, so you go with it. That's something I've thought about a lot over the years and wondered what would have happened if we'd run a play in that Bethel game or maybe just gotten the ball in bounds or maybe if we'd made them foul us. But the referees at that time didn't seem willing to call the foul.

"Officials just need to make sure that they're controlling the game from the start all the way through and they need to be consistent. Sometimes you'll see games that will get very, very rough, and they try to reel things back in. It's their job at the very start of the game to make it obvious to the coaches that this is the way it's going to be called and this is the way it's going to stay. It's not going to be a foul outside but not a foul underneath. They need to be consistent and they need to understand that the players put an awful lot of time and preparation into that game, and they are there as an agent for the kids to compete on a level playing field. Officials generally love coming to Marion Local. They love the atmosphere as much as the players and the coaches do. They like the crowd involvement and the intensity of the players. Most of the officials are past athletes and they just enjoy that."

Teaching the game isn't easy, and sometimes the most difficult elements for players to grasp are the most obvious parts of the game.

"It shouldn't be difficult for players, but learning to run an offense is tough. Sometimes it's hard for them to see the momentum of the game. We talk about it all the time. Kids want to run. They want a fast-paced game. Our philosophy is that it has its place. When the momentum is in our favor, that's when we want to push it, make quicker shots, and run our transition because things are going our way, and the other team is back on their heels. When you can score in bunches, it's a coach's nightmare to have the other team keep coming at you and coming at you. When things are going their way that's when you want to make sure you get the high-percentage shot. We always talk about the momentum. If you have it in your favor, push it. Maybe shoot a little more, and if you've just knocked down a three, take the next three. But if they've just scored a couple of threes and you've kicked the ball up into the stands, now it's time to slow it down and take the momentum out of their hands and make sure you get to score. Some kids do it well, but unfortunately, you have to have five kids who do.

"One year, we were in the sectional finals. We were up four points with a minute to go and one of the seniors pulled up and shot a dead-corner three. On the tape, yes, his guy did back off of him and he drained it, so then we were up seven, but if he had missed it, it could have gone the other way and they could go down and score, then it would be a one-point game, and why? Those things drive you crazy as a coach.

"We went to Delphos a year or two ago, and we ran an inbounds play that has four options to it. The kids didn't carry it out. And someone asked me later if that's why we took a time out – to draw that up? No, not at all. They're kids and they do crazy things. What they do reflects on you, though, and that's why I have a head full of gray hair.

"The number one thing kids need to understand is the team concept. They need to know what we want to accomplish in terms of long-term goals and short-term goals, and how we're going to get there. Then they need to do the things necessary: practice hard, compete in practice, do what the coaches are telling you to do, and don't overstep your role. They have to think unselfishly and they have to think that this team will function best if we all do the things necessary to achieve this goal. Some of those goals will have to be individual: How am I going to make this team better? How can I become a better penetrator? I need to work, I need to concentrate, and I need to look at situations where I can make this team better, and when I do penetrate, why am I doing it? Because I'm a great pull-up jumper or because we're going to pull some people in and kick it out to our three-shooters out there?

"We really try to incorporate everyone's full game, but at mid-season we try to concentrate on individual strengths. Am I a perimeter shooter? Am I a penetrator? Do I need to stop short and shoot the pull-up jumper? A team has to understand what their goals are and how they're going to accomplish them. An individual has to understand his role on the team and what his goals are going to be and how his success is going to help the team. It doesn't do any good for a kid to score twenty-four points a night when he's giving up twenty-three because he doesn't want to play defense. He's hurting the team with that mentality. The obstacle to success is people not willing to play for the team."

A coach is the first person willing to sacrifice for the team, but Westrick believes that when the drive to do that begins to fade, it's time to get out of the ranks.

"Everybody tells me I'll know when it's time to get out of it. They say it will be time to stop coaching when I go to an open gym and I don't enjoy watching it anymore, or I go to a summer shoot-out and I don't want to be there, or I'm going to team camps in June and I've lost the desire to do it. It will eat away at me and bother me. I won't enjoy it anymore."

Although he hasn't lost the drive, Westrick still endures some of the unpleasant chores of coaching.

"Game preparation is tough. We're a little different from some teams in that we are playing every Friday, every Saturday, possibly a Tuesday in there, and throw in a Monday because we've had no preseason. [Marion Local athletes often compete in the football playoffs in the late fall.] We have four practices and we're playing the first game. You lose all your early fundamentals. You also lose time in the middle of the season to actually improve. A lot of people might have a Friday night game and not play until the next Friday, or they might have a double weekend and then another single weekend. We play on a Friday, and say we have a lackluster performance or just lose. I'll go home and watch that game late Friday night. Then I'll start watching the team we play on Saturday. I'll get up Saturday morning and I'll finish that tape. We'll meet with the team after that, so we don't get a whole lot of time to review what happened on a given night because we're preparing for the very next team. Condensed seasons with a lack of time for fundamentals and shortened time between games are the things that drive me crazy.

"Another problem is competition for athletes. These guys are playing Acme baseball several nights a week, and I'm asking them to be at open gyms a couple of nights a week plus morning workouts. The football coach wants them there four mornings, so we're constantly pulling these kids in all directions. We try not to get ridiculous, though, especially in the summer. We have morning workouts, open gym, and team camp, but the kids need a little summertime, too. A lot of parents love their kids being busy, though, rather than having them out there with too much time on their hands. Last year we won the state in football and I had my parents' meeting and talked to them about only being able to practice four days and then having our opening game. We wanted to get these kids some rest and have some time to enjoy their championship. One of the mothers said, 'When are we going to do that?' And I had to say, 'I don't know.'"

"Another problem is gym schedules. In a small school that has one gym, it's incredible. It could be post-season volleyball, elementary musicals, a financial aid meeting, drama club since we have no theater, or grandparents' day. All these things limit gym time."

Westrick stays with the game because the rewards outweigh the negatives and the satisfaction supersedes the disappointments.

"When the players themselves buy into your system and become coaches on the floor, and they are giving other players the advice that's consistent with what you would give, or you have a body of guys who are all thinking alike and beginning to coach one another, that's fun. You don't have individuals that bicker and they've bought into what Marion Local basketball is going to do and how we're going to be successful."

He encourages new coaches to focus on balance in this business.

"Future coaches have to have a passion for it or they won't go into it, but they have to make sure they can keep their teaching, family and basketball activities balanced. They can't shortchange one area in order to be successful in another area. And when they figure that out, they can call me and tell me how to do it.

"I was fortunate. My son played at the lower levels and my daughter was an athletic trainer so I always had time with them. The one who got the short end of the stick was my wife. Whenever something would come up, I'd have to be somewhere else. Coaching is hard on the family. I've had this discussion first with my wife and then with my kids. My kids will tell you I'm not the same person during the season that I am at other times. I laugh at that, but they insist it's true. One story that comes to mind is when I came home from a bad practice. I made some kind of statement about the practice and my daughter who was a sophomore or junior in high school said, 'Dad, not everybody is as focused as you are. They have other things in their lives besides basketball.' I bit her nose off and she stomped out of the room. My wife came in and said to me, 'That's uncalled for.' Well, I was in a bad mood to begin with, so I snapped at her and out the door she went for a walk. I had cleared the house out in thirty seconds. It puts a strain on the entire family. They want you to win as much as you do, and they can't do anything about it except be supportive. They feel the pressure when the community is getting on you. They sense it. It's very hard on a family. Basketball, then, is your social life. A lot of it is that you don't have time to go to this or that function. Your activities with your friends get minimized because you're putting everything into basketball. You have to put it aside for awhile, but you don't. You just keep hammering away at it.

"The loneliest part of coaching is when you have to come home from a devastating loss and you're searching for advice or answers. On Friday night after a road trip, it might be midnight before I get to it, but I'll sit down and watch the game. You know where the responsibility lies and you have to get it corrected. The first step of that is understanding what we need to do. Sometimes it's obvious and sometimes it isn't so obvious. Usually, it's just me and the remote control figuring out what we're going to do when I'm searching for answers by the next morning so we know how to correct the problem. The loneliest times are when you are struggling and the pressure to be successful is mounting on you and you have to turn things around as quickly as possible."

Game days are good days for Westrick. It's a time to be certain that the preparations are complete and his head is clear.

"Typically, the week of a Friday game let's say, I get out all the information we have on our opponent. We scout an awful lot. We might have four or five scouting reports on a team. I also have a couple tapes. I make sure I get all that consolidated, and I look at the tapes as much as is humanly possible so as not to have any surprises. I do that early enough in the week to talk about it in practice and get it ingrained in the kids. I do that as early as possible. Once I talk to the team for the last time, let's say it's a Thursday night, and we've handed out the scouting reports and we've talked about the personnel on the other team – their tendencies as individuals and as a unit, then Thursday night is my most peaceful night of the week. I've looked at the tapes on Monday, Tuesday, and Wednesday. I watch tape at lunch time on a regular basis. I think we're prepared, so Thursday is a night to let my head clear and then we're ready to play. Sure, there's nervousness, even when you think you're the better team. There's always a little bit of anxiety about how you'll come out and how you'll handle their pressure. There's always a certain amount of nervousness, but there's no reason to fear anybody, and really no reason to be nervous before a ball game. If you've prepared as hard as you could and you go out there and play the best possible game you can on the floor, that's your responsibility to your teammates and your fans to be as prepared as possible and play as hard as you can, and then hope the results are the correct ones.

"I'll go into the locker room before the game, knowing we've talked about each individual person on the scouting report. The kids will be stretching and I'll review the report. Oftentimes, they're getting ready to go and you just hit the high points of the scouting report to bring up their strengths and their weaknesses. The purpose is to be positive about the things you're going to do and what you need to do to be successful.

"At halftime, it's always different given the situation. As I walk to the locker room, I try to think of the whole two quarters as opposed to the last three minutes. A lot of times somebody just stole the ball and knocked down a three, slopping it in just before halftime. You can spend all your time ranting and raving about that three when your team hasn't been boxing out for a quarter and a half. We like to bring the stats into the locker room and look at them prior to talking to the kids. You see things like maybe they scored six baskets inside the paint or they scored three times on second chance baskets or they scored too many times against our half-court defense or it's all been transition because we've thrown the ball away. Try to figure out what you're doing well and what you aren't doing well and correct it. A lot of it is sometimes giving it back to the kids. As a coach, you can assume certain things are happening and get on somebody's case, but I've had kids step up to the chalkboard and say, 'No, that's not what they're doing. He's setting a screen here and he's coming over the top of it and it makes it almost impossible for me to get over it.' A lot of times it's how we are doing, which evolves into an X's and O's type thing, and then how we are going to solve it. Then we head back out.

"The post-game talk varies a lot also. You can be very pleased with their effort in a big win and you can be pleased in how they competed in a loss. A lot of people say the best time to chew them out is after a win. Sometimes you can win ugly and that's the time to jump all over them. You have to know your personnel and what they react to and how they are challenged. If they aren't putting the effort out, they have to be confronted one way or the other. Typically, kids play hard and put the effort into it. If they aren't being successful, in the post game, sometimes you lay it right in their laps and say this is why we aren't being successful. Sometimes, you are very vocal after a game, but sometimes you only nurture the thought to execute better."

That ability, to know when to push and when to pull is a quality that grows within a coach. Westrick believes that reading personalities, to determine what response from the coach is necessary, is a requirement of the job.

"Coaches have to have a strong work ethic and put the time in. Show your athletes it means a lot to you. You aren't going to cut corners and you aren't going to assume it comes easily. You leave no stone unturned and you can expect them to do the same. Whether it be morning workouts, open gym, a shoot-out, or summer leagues, they need to know you're gong to be there on time and be enthusiastic during that time. Personally, one of the best things a coach can be is someone who can really read personalities. Sometimes you can read a real quiet kid as not buying in to what you are saying or being a bit stand-offish. You need to understand what's going to motivate him. Is this the kind of kid who needs me to be a teacher or is he going to be motivated in a more vocal way? Some kids, you raise your voice to them and they get a little bit irritated and they go right out there and play harder. If you raise your voice to other kids, they back down. A coach has to understand the personality of the player and know the best way to get him to think your way."

Once a person decides to coach, he must consider the qualities necessary for a team's success. Westrick found he had the makings of a solid group who became state contenders and, in 2003, state champions.

"It goes without saying that you need natural athletic ability, but it must be instilled in them to utilize that ability God gave them to be successful at the highest level possible. The thing I remember about the 2003 team is that they lost in the football playoffs and they seemed to have a purpose right from day one. They had a taste of having a very nice team and getting defeated in football. They just knew what they wanted to accomplish. I think it was team focus and what the group wanted more than what any coach instilled in them. They had played together since seventh, eighth, and ninth grade and they knew they had a nucleus, so they wanted to go get it done. They had a commonness of purpose.

"Sometimes you see teams that get split up a little bit. Someone plays with the older guys as a sophomore, but then in a couple of years, his teammates catch up and they start playing well again. There is no doubt that they play football and baseball together, and since they are in athletics, they kind of hang out together. I don't think there is any doubt that plays into it."

"Without a doubt, desire is one thing, but you have to put the time in. They have to pay the price. They come to everything the coach organizes, but they also get together at the park and play. For example, [Tony] Meyer from New Knoxville shot sixty percent from the three-point line. That doesn't just happen. He put a ton of time in. It's the off-season commitment."

"To win a regional or state championship isn't too much different from what we do all year. Once you play twenty games in a season, you go through the sectionals, and you go through the districts, you've already played some of your toughest games because you're playing people from you own area. It's one game at a time. You're playing Dayton Jefferson, so you have your scouting reports, you have your information, you're prepared, and you play. You don't even think about the regional finals until you stop for a minute and think, 'Hey, we're in the regional finals.' Then you make preparations for that. You've made some connections around the state. You talk to some coaches. You have some tapes lined up. You've got to do that. You have people scout those games. You're thinking ahead, but your team isn't. There have been very few teams I've coached when I haven't thought that we can do it one game at a time. A couple of years ago, we played New Knoxville in the district finals. They were the team everybody talked about all year. Suddenly, we thought that if we could win that game, we could be playing at Miami again. It's always one step at a time and the levels will take care of themselves."

Westrick credits the support from the families and the community for the strong tradition at Marion Local. That support is often matched in nearby communities, fostering rivalries that cross over from basketball to football and vice versa. Westrick identifies the school's biggest rival as Coldwater because of the head-to-head competition in football, but for many years New Bremen was the team to beat. However, New Knoxville has the biggest home court advantage in Westrick's experience.

"It's a tough place to play. People are right there on the court. The second biggest home court advantage is Delphos St. John.

We always talk about going to play at the Vatican when we go there. The advent of all these newer gymnasiums has taken away the personality of some of the gyms. You can go play anyone with the two thousand seat gyms, and they all have the wide aisles and the fans are sitting away off the floor, but when you're over at New Knoxville the fans have, at least in the past, been right behind our bench. I remember Bill Elking talking about a guy who had his program rolled up and he was hitting him in the head the whole time he was trying to coach. Or they're leaning in to see what you're doing in the huddle. I dread going to new Knoxville more than anyplace else. I like playing at St. Henry, Coldwater, New Bremen and Minster. I like Loramie's gym, but I'm not real crazy about Anna's gym. It's got a little bit of that closeness."

There comes a time in many games when a coach has to decide when the game is over, even if there is time left on the clock.

"I really don't think we ever give up or we ever say, 'This is it. We won.' Basketball is so funny. You can be up by six points with thirty seconds to go, but then someone knocks down a couple of threes and you're in overtime. Sometimes it is frustrating when you try to play and you're not getting it done. You're not executing and all of a sudden you're down and you just realize your level of play isn't going to change. Some nights just aren't your night. You can play your butt off and not be able to throw it in the ocean. Sometimes there is no rhyme or reason. We might shoot twenty percent all night and it doesn't change. A lot of times that's what you look at after the game. We keep a possession chart so we look back through there and see how many shots we got off and what kind of shots they were or how many times we turned the ball over. If maybe you got eight shots off and they were the shots you were looking for but you didn't make them, what do you do? And then sometimes the score is insurmountable and you sub in to take the pressure off the starters if we're losing, or let the bench enjoy it if we're winning."

Practices in the Marion Local gym are very structured. Conditioning is vital to the program, as well.

"We start our practice with a two-man shooting drill, very briefly. Then we get together and stretch, and during that time we address anything we need to talk about. It might be organizational things or something we're going to do in practice or something we did in the last ball game, but it only lasts five minutes. Then we go into some pretty high-level drills that typically are full-court passing and shooting type competitive drills. It's almost a conditioning time. It might be running your fast break in a continuous drill. That's for ball-handling, aerobics, and shooting skills. It always ends up in a conditioning drill to get them sucking wind hard. All this is in the first half hour of practice. The reason we do that is because that's the way the game is played. Now you have an hour and a half left of practice. The legs are a little weary and you're a little tired. You don't play the game fresh. You play with a little bit of fatigue, so that's the way we expect them to go through the rest of practice. And from there, we work on what we need to work on that given night. It might be a half-court offense against a half-court defense we're going to see, or it could be some full-court press stuff. Most of it is going to be situations and typically it's varsity against varsity kids. The JV team practices on another court, but if we need a spark, we'll get together and play varsity against JV, just to get some new people to go against. It's usually all game situations. If we're going to go up and down, it will be at the end of practice. We might put two minutes on the clock and you're down eight points, or maybe it's out-of-bounds plays or last-second, quick-hitter type plays at the end of practice, and then we'll have ten or fifteen minutes of conditioning at the very end of our two-hour practice."

Besides physical preparation, the team needs to know the opponent. The way to do that is to have scouts who know what information the coach needs. Scouting hasn't changed much over the years – every team has always needed to know the adversary – but some of the information collected has changed.

"We all scout, but probably my best scout is Dan Koenig, our eighth grade coach. He will do whatever we ask. He's a great man to have on our staff. Mark Ronnebaum, our seventh grade coach, helped me with varsity and freshmen over the years, just loves basketball, and is very passionate about it. We have a JV coach and a freshman coach who spend time with their teams, but on game nights we try to help each other. The freshman coach keeps a chart so we can keep track of fouls and other information. The duty of the coach who isn't coaching at that time is to watch the floor so we have as many eyes as possible on what's happening out there. We have real good continuity throughout the levels. We do the same thing all the way through. When the other coaches are spending time with their teams, they are helping develop the higher level programs. We all scout for the varsity games and I scout for the JV, too.

"Good coaches have to love the game and be willing to put the time in and be unselfish. We are all out for the good of the kids. We're willing to go to clinics and share knowledge. Probably a big thing is agreement on philosophies and agreement on your system of coaching. If a coach doesn't like the offense you are running, it's going to be counterproductive. We sit down during the summer and hash things out and discuss all these things."

"The physical nature of the game has changed. It's a lot rougher inside. Things that used to be fouls aren't fouls any longer. Out on the perimeter, you'll see hand-checking on the dribbler, steering the dribbler with the hand. Some referees will say you can't put a hand on the dribbler and other referees will let you put a hand right on his hip and steer him all over. In tough games it's almost ridiculous. How do you shoot a shot when you're getting pounded on all the time? Also, there used to be a lot of officials that would interact with the coaches. They would talk and explain things to the coaches. Now it's become a lot more impersonal. Now they're doing things to discourage any interchange between the coach and official. I appreciate some of the officials that will actually talk to you during the game and just explain situations during the game. There used to be better interactions."

Westrick has great respect for the coaches he faces on game nights.

"There are no bad coaches in the area, but you have to respect the experience of a Dan Hegemier at New Knoxville. Every team you play, the coaches are going to have them well-prepared. There are very few times I go into a game thinking the coach won't have his team ready. It's not a thought that crosses my mind.

"In those games, if you're behind, you're obviously more apt to try some different things. Maybe you'll change defense or full-court pressure and try to change the flow of the ball game. If you're behind, it's because the momentum has been all their way. If you're ahead, you don't want to get passive, but you do want to get intelligent. If things are going your way, keep pushing it. Keep running the floor, keep attacking. If you have a twelve point lead and you feel the momentum shift, then you have to get smart enough to say we're going to slow it down a little bit. We aren't going to feed their momentum. If they hit a three and you come down and take a quick shot yourself and then they hit another three and you come down and take another quick shot, you're just feeding the momentum they have. When you're in the lead that's when you need to sense the momentum. When you are trailing you have to try to figure out how to change that momentum by maybe trying to get them playing a little bit faster than they want to or to get them to do things they don't want to do.

"The pacing of the game goes back to what you want to teach a kid. A few years ago we played Lima Senior. They pressed us and gave up some lay-ups and they didn't care. They won with eighty or more possessions, so we knew we were going to run like crazy, but they were athletic enough that it was to their advantage. We've had teams that pressed us, and we didn't want that pace so you almost pass up a shot out of your press offense to set up your half-court offense and slow things down a little bit. That's a very hard thing for a kid to do – not attack in his press offense when the other team is pressing you. We have to take a time-out and ask when the last time we ran a half-court offense was. We've taken six shots off our press offense and we're not scoring, so now we need to pass that up and run for a little while. This comes down to discipline and intelligence. This was the Holgate thing. They beat us in the state final in 2004 because they are the most deliberate team on the face of the earth. They'll pass the ball fifteen or twenty times and if they don't get the shot they want or the kid they want to shoot doesn't have the ball, they won't take it. They will ball-fake-pass, ball-fake-pass. It's over and over and over. They win games 29-28 or 31-30. They might be 17-15 in the fourth quarter and the philosophy there is that they'll never be out of a ball game. They are always within striking distance that way. Some people say they won't watch basketball if they have to watch that every week. Holgate wins, so they do. We ordinary people just go with the momentum."

Marion Local was able to gather the momentum that carried them to the state tournament in 2003 and again in 2004. Westrick's reflections on those games begin with the enormous amount of activity surrounding those weekends.

"One of the things that amaze me is that it's extremely hectic. I talked to some people before we went down and the people who had been there before said it would be extremely hectic but that I should try to enjoy it. I remember trying to prepare for that next game, but at the state level that all goes out the window. Nothing is normal anymore. You're worried about bus trips, room assignments, meals, travel, a place for practice, and everything else. It's amazing the amount of stuff you're dealing with that has nothing to do with being successful in basketball. We just took the coaching staff and started delegating certain things. Dan Koenig got the money for all the meals, and he was in charge of making sure we had somewhere to go eat. I didn't want any money. I didn't want to deal with any money or that type of thing. You have to delegate because you're trying to get all your information together, trying to work your practices in, and dealing with pep assemblies, send-off, getting out of school, and making up the school day. The further you go along, the more people become involved, and a lot of the time is being taken away from the things you really want to be doing as a coach.

"Once you get past all that other stuff and you get out there on the court, it is really phenomenal. It was an experience I wish all coaches could have. There are tons and tons of great coaches in the state of Ohio that never get a chance to play in a state game, and sometimes it's just a great team who had a bad shooting night and they didn't make it there. Or it's some guy who coached his whole life and really deserved it. It's fickle. Some great coaches never got the opportunity, and they really should have.

"Just to be down there and get a chance to win it, cutting down the net, the final buzzer, and watching the kids do their happy dances and hug each other along with the cheerleaders and the fans is a neat experience.

"I thought in 2004, since we had won it before, it might be less hectic, but it didn't seem to be any less hectic at all. When we beat Elyria in the state semi-finals in 2003, right away I was in the press room and talking to everyone. My team had been showered and was on their way to the bus and I hadn't even had a chance to see them. It's neat in one way, but you just get shuffled back and forth, here and there, asked questions, and in a very small way you can see what some of these athletes at a big time school have to put up with on a regular basis. The state tournament is an experience like no other. Everything gets put on hold. Everything is basketball. You get a chance to win that state title. One of the realizations is that you come back and on Monday you're back to your normal job. You work so hard to get that championship, but it points out that even though that was a great priority and accomplishment, the rest of your life goes on right away. That's the neat thing about a loss, too. The sun is going to come up and life is going to go on just like before. You have to keep moving on, too.

"The loss was like any loss in tournament. You get yourself the opportunity to win, to get your players in position to possibly win a state championship, and then after you lose, you do the same old stuff. You second guess, you watch, and you replay. It shouldn't minimize the accomplishment. Those kids, even though it was a Holgate-style, deliberate ball game, put every ounce of effort into that thing. If you can walk off that floor, or walk out of the locker room at the end of a game or a season, you make sure you can hold your head up high and say, 'I did everything I possible could.' If you second-guess or think you could have put more effort into it, it all comes down to having to answer to yourself. If I, as a coach, can look in the mirror at the end of the season and say I did everything with my God-given abilities to do what I needed to do, then I can feel happy. You have to do the same thing as an athlete."

Players can help themselves move closer to those opportunities by exhibiting and internalizing some basic qualities necessary to become excellent as an athlete and as a member of a team. Westrick's first demand of a player is that he must be coachable.

"A player must put the time in to make himself a complete player so he has no limitations. He's able to dribble with both hands. He's a good shooter. He's put the time in to developing his skills. If he hasn't developed his skills, he's behind the eight ball right from the start. The number one thing, after that then, is to be coachable. If that coach is telling you that you need to do this or that, he's not giving you bad information or leading you in the wrong way. Other good qualities include being a positive leader with his teammates, being as hard a worker as is humanly possible and being willing to put in extra time when necessary. Being a leader off the court is necessary, too.

"To play at Marion Local, a player has to be aggressive because we play a match-up zone defense. In order for it to work we emphasize aggressiveness. We need a player to attack and execute the offense. We want to attack, but not to the point of turning the ball over. We are going to make sure we get the offensive flow of the game we're looking for. We have continuity throughout the program, so all the players grow up realizing that if they don't play the defense hard, we're not going to be successful. We value our possessions, so the players learn that they have to play that style.

"As far as pressure goes, our kids are involved in a lot of different sports. We've been in the playoffs a lot in football, basketball, baseball, and track. We try to run some drills so they have to make shots or the whole team runs. We try to put people on the line and then tell them they can't steer the situation, so they have to think of the positives. Think about the reward. Don't think about the negative. Don't think, 'What if I miss?' Think a positive thought before you shoot a free throw. We tell kids to step up there, be confident, and knock it down.

"When we get our captains, I bring them in and tell them that they have just accepted more responsibility than they've ever had before. They will see things and know things on this team that I'll never know. They will handle some things on this team that I'll never know. They will know when someone is disgruntled or doing some things off the court they shouldn't be, so they'll need to repair it, and I'll never know. They are the first level of stopping or repairing it before it comes to me. If they can't repair it, they need to bring it to me, and that's a tough thing for a kid to do. Some players will and some won't, but you try to put leadership in their lap. Some handle it well, and some never become good leaders.

All they want to do is yell at somebody else. When I see that going on, I have to pull them aside and tell them that isn't leadership. We tell them leadership is their responsibility and they have to do something with it. They can't walk out of my office thinking they'll be a good captain; they have to work at being a good captain.

"Competitive drive can be developed to some degree. We try to encourage older kids to come back for our open gyms. If you have only high school kids, the play stays at a certain level, but if you get someone who has graduated to come in and play, the high school kids go at them a whole lot harder. I like to see the older kids come to the open gyms.

"In practice, we make things a competition, such as blue team against the gold team and we're playing to three. I've had teams be too competitive and they just beat the hell out of each other. We've had a kid go to the hospital with stitches. It's like a war zone sometimes. At other times you have teams that are too nice."

Players can also make big gains in their personal game through the drills Westrick uses in practice. The coach carefully selects drills tailored to the individual skills he needs his players to develop.

"We do a lot of shooting drills, but they are short and brief. Our shooting drills are typically a competition. If you just shoot for ten minutes, the next thing you know, the shot forms are going to hell or the intensity is not there. If you aren't going to shoot like you shoot in a game, there isn't a point to it. Get a lot of shots off in a short time, putting the intensity into it that you have in a game.

"We do a lot of post moves. You have to teach kids what to do when the defense is [in a certain position]. You give them the four options and then let them go at it as hard as possible, and we try to make those competitive, too. We try to take situations we aren't doing well and put them into practice. Maybe it's a penetration dribble. We'll give the ball to the guy and tell him he has two dribbles and you have to penetrate down and get a shot off. Now they aren't out front dribbling around and playing one-on-one. They have two dribbles to get a shot off. We'll do a two-on-two. We'll punch down in and if the help doesn't come, you take your pull-up jumper and if it does come, you kick it out and your teammate has a shot. We try to put them in situations where they're reading defenses. Where the defense is, dictates what you do. In other words, we do game simulations and reading defenses. We also play match-up defense so we break down situations for each position in our defense. We have drills just for the guards, just for the big man, just for the forwards. We can work on what to do when the ball is passed to the corner, what to do if it skips to the other side and what to do if the zone shifts. Then we can look at one player in isolation."

Sometimes players want to play at the college level and Westrick is willing to serve as a facilitator when needed.

"If I know I have a player who wants to play at the college level, I print up a sheet with his stats, along with a picture, his forty time, his vertical leap, strengths, weaknesses, aspirations, and interests in college. When I get a letter of interest from a college, I'll take the sheet, stuff it in an envelope and away it goes. Sometimes, I'll ask that player where he wants to go, and I'll make contact with the college. Sometimes, I just send letters to a certain list of people who might be interested in this player. Other times, kids only want to play at a couple of places, so it varies quite a bit. Unfortunately, it occurs at a time when you are very, very busy. A lot of the college stuff is being done at the AAU level. It's when the college coaches have a lot of time. They see more kids there than during the high school season because their seasons are going on at the same time. During the season, an Ohio Northern person might get down to see your player twice, but during AAU there are twenty different kids they have information on."

Westrick also takes the extra time to prepare a sheet entitled "The Coach's Corner" for the program at each home basketball game. The information on the page includes a brief overview of the opponent's strengths and possible strategies. It also provides an overview of the previous game or week and the impact of the result on the season. It's an extra way to communicate with the fans and make the game even more meaningful and understandable.

"You know parents are going to be supportive of their sons and daughters. You want them to be positive even if they don't always feel that way. I encourage parents to come in if they want to talk, but right after the game isn't the time to do that. Some parents won't keep quiet and they'll say whatever they want to the kids, which puts those kids on an island. In this area, as competitive as it is, to think that everybody's going to be happy all the time is a pipe dream. Being negative to a player or an official during a contest doesn't do anything for the game. People who go to the game and support the team with all their heart and try to stay upbeat are positive for the program. Anything negative only slows the team's progress."

Westrick has been in the coaching ranks long enough to see change in the game and its rules. He has some hopes for the future of the game as well.

"I'd like to see them move the free throw line up and don't put somebody on that low block. The advantage is almost to the offensive team on a free throw. They took people out of the lane a couple of years ago to clean it up, but they actually made it worse. The one thing we see that is interpreted differently all the time is the hop move where a guy dribbles up and swings the ball over the top and then comes down with both feet planted. Some referees will give you a long dissertation on if he moves step, step, hop, it's actually a travel. I don't think you get the same interpretation at any given time whether that is a travel or not. It's a very effective move, but if you can use it half the season and then at the end of the season it's being called a travel and he's doing it exactly the same, it's frustrating."

"The professionalism of the people in our area, though, is amazing. The coaches in our league and in District 8 handle the voting well. I've never seen any ganging up on somebody else. They are professional about it. Our boosters do a great job and do what they can for you. Our administration has always been very supportive. They realize what I need to get done, they know their duties, and they keep everything balanced."

Chapter  Eleven

JOE NIEKAMP

ST. HENRY HIGH SCHOOL

2004 STATE CHAMPION

"I'll never neglect to tell the kids to play until they hear the buzzer. Any little hesitation can mean the difference between winning and losing."

As a high school coach, the biggest reward for Joe Niekamp is to see kids develop, mature, and become successful adults. No doubt, there was a coach or two in Niekamp's youth in St. Henry who felt the same way about him. It's a cycle that started generations ago in this Mercer County village and Niekamp is one of a long line of athletes and coaches who grew up in St. Henry expecting each succeeding generation to find success by developing the personal qualities that emerge from hard work and competition.

"I grew up in a family of nine boys, and I was the second youngest, so seeing my older brothers play basketball was something I enjoyed doing. I remember being pretty young and sitting around the kitchen table on Saturday mornings. It was kind of like a round table with all the older brothers going through the events of the game the night before. We were all involved in all kinds of sports. We poured the patch of cement in our backyard and put a hoop up when I was really young, and we used it all the time. We came home from games, and we'd shovel the snow off of it so we could play. In these communities, you just kind of grow up with it. The parents have a passion for athletics and it's something you just pick up.

"Also, to this day, I have a tremendous amount of respect for Fran Guilbault. He built the basketball program here at St. Henry. That kind of success and the number of wins he had is just really, really rare. I give Fran a lot of credit. He really loved offensive basketball and he let his teams play. He didn't put a lot of restrictions on them. It provided a lot of enjoyment for the fans and for the players and was a good environment to be around.

"I played basketball for Darrell Hedric at Miami University and Darrell was friends with Bobby Knight. Darrell was a defensive-minded guy and still to this day there are a lot of things that he used to say about the game of basketball that ring true. One of those was, 'Quickness is a state of mind.' It really is. It's not necessarily about the person who can run the fastest. It's the person who is mentally in tune with what's going on. It's being mentally alert and ready to go. His defensive terminology was tops. He had a good team concept. It wasn't about how quick or how athletic you were, but if you played team defense and worked together that way you could be successful. If somebody broke down and let his man get around him, you had to be in position to help out. It was fun playing and I learned a lot from him.

"My brother Ron, who played at Miami and has coached at Parkway, Ottawa-Glandorf, Lima Senior and the University of Findlay, has had so much success and he's been really open and helpful, so I've picked up things from him. He's a great resource to have. Those three guys have had the most influence on me."

Niekamp teaches sixth-grade math at St. Henry. He can't imagine being anywhere else but in the classroom.

"Teaching is something I really enjoy more and more each year. To be a teacher at any of the schools in this area, you have to consider yourself pretty fortunate. You're in a good situation with a lot of support and kids who are eager to learn. It's a good place to be a teacher.

"Having grown up in this town and gone to school here, I knew what kind of community it was, so it was a natural progression for me to take the opportunities when they came up and come back here.

"You have to keep in mind that you are in this business for the kids and you have to keep them first in your priorities and do what's right. Sometimes things will come up and you're going to have to bend a little bit to be sure you do right by them, whether it's for school-related activities or family."

Niekamp keeps on top of his own coaching education by using resources from Bobby Knight and the Championship Productions, Inc. videos. He obtained University of Kansas Coach Bill Self's high-low offense tapes. He attended many clinics and ordered the clinic notebooks from clinics around the nation.

"There are so many clinic notes on the Internet that you probably don't have to order them anymore. I've seen a lot of the Memphis dribble-drive motion offense because they've had so much success. It's kind of a new thing so it's splashed all over the Internet."

Niekamp spent two years as a varsity coach at Vanlue and two years at Carey before he returned to St. Henry as JV coach for one year under Al Summers when the Redskins made it to the final game of the state tournament. In 2000, he assumed the duties of the head coach at St. Henry and in 2004 returned to Columbus to capture the state title for the fourth time in the school's history.

"After one year as a JV coach, it was kind of a surprise getting this job, but on the other hand, my sons were getting of the age to play and the thought of being involved in helping them and their friends made me think that maybe I ought to be the one in the gym and make it available for them and do everything I can to help these guys have the opportunity to become successful trying to be the players they would like to be. That part of it has been a lot of fun and it has been really good.

"My first year here we made it to the final game of the tournament and it was a wonderful experience. It was a lot of fun. I picked up some good things from Al, too. We just grab all the information we can from other people. That's what coaches do. There are very few people who do their own stuff. Most of us just learn from other people."

In his second year at St. Henry, Niekamp became the head coach, leading the Redskins to a state championship within a few years.

"Nothing can compare to that 2004 game when we won the state with that kind of atmosphere and being in the Schott with the community and kids. As fate would have it, we played Versailles in that final game and they had beaten us at their place earlier in the season. They finished the regular season 20-0 with mostly seniors. We started a sophomore and a couple juniors and only lost by a point or two at their place late in the season. One of their leading scorers was out but they managed to get through the regionals and their first tournament game at state without him, even though they probably weren't as formidable a team at that point. There's nothing you can do about that, though. When Al was the head coach, Ryan Post broke his hand in the semi-finals, which was a quirk that year, too.

"Some people would say that the most exciting game in St. Henry history would be when Minster beat us 101-100 on our floor way back when I was in high school in maybe 1975. There was a lot of outstanding basketball between us. I still remember that game. We were winning by one in overtime and the clock was running out. They took a shot and missed and for one second, I thought way in the back of my mind, 'The buzzer is going to ring,' but it didn't and one of their players went over my back – it wasn't a foul – and tipped it in. I'll never neglect to tell the kids to play until they hear the buzzer. Any little hesitation can mean the difference between winning and losing."

Niekamp has weathered some difficult games and decisions. He knows what can get in the way of success.

"The year after 2004 we had some pretty good players back and we only lost a couple games. We played Archbold in the district and it was one of those games when all our starters picked up two fouls in the first half. We had gotten out to a really nice lead, so I sat them down. Then Archbold went on a run and took the lead by halftime, and we just never got back on top. We were fighting that uphill battle all the way. I wish that I would have let them roll. If you play them, they might pick up that third foul and then they're going to sit anyhow. That changed the complexion of the game and that's one of those things you'd like to have back, so Archbold went on to beat us and win the state.

"Developing a nice shooting stroke can be a difficult thing to do. Setting effective, hard legal picks is a difficult thing to get kids to do, too. It's hard to say that it's only one thing that gets in the way of success because being in a league that's highly competitive you sometimes see a team style of play that can be an obstacle. Sometimes, it's a certain individual player's skills or abilities and sometimes it's your own mind that gets in the way. League games help you work through those things, and everybody's league is tough like that because you are playing people who know you the best.

"It's difficult, too, for kids who play three sports to hone their skills anymore with everything that's required. I feel that we're pulling these kids in too many directions. I'd rather have my kids busy, but I hope we don't get to the point where we're robbing them of their childhoods. We all want our players to do a lot of stuff. If you want to reach your potential you have to work at it, but if you are playing three sports, it's tough."

A few items on Niekamp's wish list are consistency in officiating, the traveling call, and the addition of a shot clock.

"Something else that has always bothered me is the traveling call. It's really difficult to be consistent with that. High school also needs a shot clock. Coaches are going to coach to be successful. You wouldn't expect anything different. Sometimes, though, it seems as though we're playing a sophisticated game of keep away. I don't think that's fun for the fans or the players. A shot clock forces you to play the game. I don't think we're promoting our game as much as we could. If you look at all the years ago when colleges went to it, they wouldn't dream now of living without it. Defenses have gotten better and more athletic, so you have lower scoring games and I don't think people enjoy it. Now, it's not a panacea. It's not going to guarantee that all games will be high-scoring, but it's going to put us on a course where we're going to have to practice our offensive skills. It will take out the element of slowing the game down when you're an underdog. I don't think that's the kind of basketball people want to watch. My recommendation would be to put the lowest number of seconds possible on that clock. I've heard people say that a forty-five second clock would work. I don't think that's going to do it because that's down to everybody only getting a couple of possessions each quarter. If we want to promote high school basketball, we need to put these kids in a situation where they can score some points. I think it will lead to more opportunities, more skills, and more scholarships. There was a petition a few years ago to allow twenty-two games a season. I say get a shot a clock and play more basketball in the games we have."

Anyone interested in becoming a coach must keep kids first in every consideration. Niekamp also would encourage those new to a head coaching position to be ready to work.

"You have to keep in mind you are working with really young minds. Keep what's best for kids first. You have to be yourself and learn what works best for you. There are a lot of different ways to be successful. You're going to have to work really hard and it's going to take a lot of time. Just be prepared.

"You'll also have to go on some long scouting trips. I can remember being in Celina as a varsity assistant. The only chance we had to see Columbus Briggs, the team we were playing in the Holiday Tournament, was to drive down to Philo. To get there, you drive clear to Zanesville and go south. To make matters worse, we hit a nasty winter storm in Columbus on the way back. This year [2008] we drove to Elyria to see a Cleveland-area team we thought we might be playing if we made it out of the district tournament. When you have those opportunities you have to go take advantage of them. The worst thing is to get somewhere and find out the game was cancelled."

All the scouting and the preparation should be done by game day. Then, it's just checking the details.

"By Thursday, the hay is in the barn. I've been through the scouting report and I've watched film, and so I try to keep myself busy on game day. I make sure the scorebook is ready and double, triple check that. I make sure video equipment is ready. I get the towels and the things we need, but there isn't much more than that. Oh, we might get a tape on somebody late in the week, so I'll watch that, but we're usually finished by then. If we have a game on Saturday, we'll watch the tape after the game on Friday or maybe watch some tape with the team when they come in for shooting on Saturday morning before a game that night.

"I like to keep the pre-game talk succinct, just to remind them of the important things. Most of the things we've already talked about. I don't like to stand in front of them a long time, boring them. I tell the guys, 'If you are going to sit here and wait for me to motivate you before every game, and you need me to get you fired up, it's probably not going to happen.' We try to touch on the important things we've already identified, such as the key things the other team likes to do offensively or what they do defensively. We review what they're probably going to see. The past couple of years, we've been switching a lot of picks on defense and you don't stay with match-ups too long when you are switching defensively like that, so going over match-ups before the game isn't that big of an issue. I give them time to listen to their music or stretch or dribble the ball, all those things they like to do to.

"At halftime, I like kids to come in and have a few minutes on their own to get something to drink and get some towels. The most powerful things are the things they come up with themselves. Usually the coaches will take a few minutes in the office to see if we're on the same page or if there is something glaring we need to address. We compare what we've been thinking the first half. We always hope that halftime is ten minutes of clarity. Ranting and raving is usually rare because we like to talk to them about what we're seeing. We like to identify those things that will help them be more successful in the second half. If it's something that's killing us on the defensive end or if it's something that we aren't getting done on the offensive end, our kids always respond to that.

"The post-game talk is an honest wrap-up of the events we saw. Most of the time I try not to get too emotionally involved because then you go home and watch the tape and find out that everything wasn't quite the way it seemed. We hit on the things we think are real and we don't go overboard. These kids don't have a lot of free time, so they don't want to sit in the locker room listening to me for an hour. For some teams that might work fine, but our kids don't really respond to that. I don't like to overreact in a positive way after a game, and I don't like to overreact in a negative way after a game because sometimes it wasn't always what it seemed, or you say something you wish you hadn't said."

Being able to communicate at the right time in the right way with the players is one quality, among others, that Niekamp believes is important for a coach to be successful.

"You have to have some basketball knowledge, not that you have to have played the game, but you have to have that knowledge. You also have to be willing to put some time into it.

"You have a great chance to be successful if you have some skilled athletes. Kids have to be willing to put their egos aside and sacrifice for the good of the team. It's rare to see those problems here. Kids are willing to sacrifice their individuality for the good of the team. That's important.

"There is a tremendous love for the game in this area and when kids grow up, they see that, and they want to be a part of that. It's something they learn at home and they pick it up from their parents. We've had great support from the parents here. We've had nothing but the greatest help. They've done so much for our program. I don't know anywhere you can go where you have the kind of fan following we have."

Niekamp's three sons have been part of the game for many years, as well. His oldest, Ross, played on the 2004 state championship team and Mitch graduated in 2007. Spencer is a senior on his father's team this year [2008-2009] completing the group of sons who all played while their father was the head coach.

"At our home, it's been a family thing. We sit down and watch tape together and talk about teams. We've enjoyed it and it's been a fun thing and I'm lucky that my wife is a basketball fan, but she's had to take over the things I'm not around for. During the season, we really don't have time for a social life. It's pretty much playing games or scouting games. But what else is there to do in the wintertime? You might as well stay busy. I don't think basketball is any different from the other sports. People around here love them all. In the wintertime there really isn't that much going on, but you do have parents and kids who love the game. I like the saying, 'If you love your job, you'll never work a day in your life.' Our kids are doing what they love to do."

The teams Niekamp respects include all schools in the area.

"Right down there [east] is Marion Local. Right up there [north] is Coldwater. Right over there [west] is Fort Recovery. I don't know who our biggest rival is. Everybody in the league is a big rival. I don't think most of the people around here would pick one out, necessarily. What makes a good rivalry is the tremendous amount of respect you have for those people. You respect them so much that you want to do everything you can to be at your best. We have very close family relationships with all these towns. That respect comes from the marriages, our heritage, and our religion.

"Each year, the team that has the biggest home court advantage is the team that's the best. Right now [2008], it's New Knoxville, and they do have a tough place to play in. The best teams have the fired-up fans and their gym is full. They are all tough to play. Minster's old gym was a real tough gym to play in. The newer gyms have the fans away from the floor, and they aren't as homey as they used to be. We still have a nice balance here. Our gym holds about two thousand, but the fans are down there fairly close to floor. We can get a little home-court advantage out of that, I guess. As far as the coaches, we respect all but fear none."

Winning a state championship comes from having kids who want it and from staying in a routine that works for the program.

"It helps when you have kids who deep down in their heart and mind have decided it's what they really want to do. You treat these games exactly how you treat any other game. You have a certain routine and you have certain ways you want to be focused, certain ways you practice. You don't want to chuck everything out the window just because it's the big game and you want to try to do things differently. You want to keep your approach as normal and the same as you can. Kids will respond. You don't have to tell them it's the big game. They know. What's in their mind and what is in their heart will get you there. Kids around here want that and dream that and believe they can do that. There have been a lot of different championships in a lot of different sports around here, but I give Fran a lot of credit back in 1979 because they did it when nobody thought you could. To do something like that for the first time makes it special and everybody said, 'Wow. That was fun. Let's try to do that again.' You have a lot of coaches who have done a really good job here, but I don't think that's it. It's more about what's at home and what's in those hearts and minds. We were just the people who helped get them there. You have to depend on your kids to be hungry enough to go out there after it.

"The whole experience of the state tournament is such a blur. One thing I can remember for sure is hearing the final buzzer sound. I don't really remember a whole lot before that. You drive to Columbus ahead of time to go over all the rules and all the regulations ahead of time, but that doesn't anywhere cover it all because when you get there, you still end up talking to the OHSSA representatives about how things are done. They want to talk to you because they want someone in charge. Anywhere else you play in tournament you can't be on the court before the clock starts. In the Schott, you can. If you are there an hour before the game, you can go out and shoot for a half an hour. When you are playing in such a big place like that, it could make a little difference. So we hurried up and went out and shot. I don't think there is anything else to compare with seeing your school and your community and your players and your team have that much fun and that much enjoyment.

What could be better than that? That was pretty neat.

"There is nothing more fun in the tournament than going to talk to the [reporters]. When you win, you get to bring your players in there, and that is some of the most satisfying part of coaching since it's a nice reward for the kids. The players love that.

"It's the pinnacle of every coach's dream to get there, and to win is something no one can ever take away from you. No matter what, to have that and accomplish that, I'll be forever thankful for the kids that we had who were able to do that for the school. It's something that will live strongly forever as long as I'm around."

"In talking to people afterwards, I found that it's truly amazing what you can do when you work together. The parents teach the kids that stuff. Nobody cares who gets the credit because when you work hard together, you can do really good things. We've had so many good kids who have been successful in life afterwards. We're a small little part in helping them grow and develop. The things you experience in basketball are smaller microcosms of things that will hit you later. You get hit with adversity all the time and kids learn how to deal with that.

Since Niekamp has many of those hungry kids, he organizes his season and his practices to meet their needs and challenge them.

"After the no-contact period at the end of the season, we start open gyms and we're fortunate to have community members who are former players and they come back for open gyms. We've had college players who come back and play in the summer, so we have a competitive summer in those open gyms. I usually talk with seniors about when they can come in during the summer and lift and shoot. We go to team camps for our ten days in June. We go to shoot-outs and we've been to Capital and UD. That's been our routine. After Labor Day, the kids, who aren't in anything else, come in before the school day a few times a week. It's really hard to have a consistent open gym schedule in the fall because the other sports and activities are in the gym. We really don't have a conditioning program. I'd rather have them shooting and playing. We've never had a problem getting our kids in shape. They're active all year, and we just might be wearing them out if we bring them in to run. Most kids do weightlifting on their own and take the initiative to get stronger.

"On top of all that, you have kids playing wide open AAU stuff.

My son played about thirty games in the off-season this year. I've heard it said that in a lot of places, the AAU experience has overtaken the high school experience so that they really don't care about their high school. We don't have that here, but when you are traveling all around the country and getting shoes and staying in nice hotels, a lot of kids replace their high school with all that. We're fortunate that there is so much pride in their community and their school that we're still number one. I don't see that changing anytime soon. Those things are fun but they don't compare to being here on Friday night against a rival when the house is full. I realize there are a lot of negatives to AAU because of the coaching, but what we've had that's been a lot of fun is our kids making up teams with other kids around the area. I really like it because the parents spend time together and the kids get to know each other. The kids come to understand those people aren't the enemy. My kids have made so many good friendships with other kids, and it can be a good thing if it's worked out properly.

"In practice, we're going to shoot a lot every day. We work on shooting form and ball-handling every day. We'll do some break-down but not much because I'm the only coach there. We normally have a rhythm to our week and a rhythm to our practice. We try to stop and shoot some free throws while they are breathing hard throughout practice and then finish practice with free throws. We try to concentrate on keeping them active and keeping their hands on the basketball as much as possible, trying to do a lot of full-court work every day. At times, we scrimmage, but it's controlled. Everything is competitive. There is a winner and a loser for everything we do. Drills, warm-ups and lay-ups are all competitive to keep them concentrating. I do like to have a routine so the kids know what to expect, but it can't be too regimented. We change it up.

"We do form shooting every day to reinforce our kids' shooting touch. Fran did a drill that I still love to this day. It's called 'Give-and-Go.' It's a passing drill, a shooting drill, and kind of a rebounding drill and it's one of the best drills you can possibly do. From past experience, having done it myself, I really learned to know exactly where the ball is coming off the rim. You get to the point when you're the rebounder, before it hits the rim, you can jump up and tip it in because you know exactly where it's going to go. The big guys are working on their timing and their hands; the shooters are working on following their shots and relocating. It's a simple drill but it's really effective. St. Henry has been known for a long time to have good shooters and it's because kids grow up wanting to do that. They have a ball in their hands when they're young, and their parents know something about how to shoot, so they go out in the front yard and actually shoot. It's kind of environmental here, but another part is Fran's 'Give-and Go' drill that's been going on for about fifty years around here. Defensively, then, everyone is doing the shell drills. You can work on just about anything the other team is going to do."

Niekamp depends on his coaches for working with the players, assisting with games, and scouting.

"During the game, I'll talk with my assistants, and when we've come to the conclusion that there is no possible way the outcome could be reversed, whether we're ahead or behind, we want to have everyone get some playing time they don't always get. My nephew, Terry Niekamp, is the JV coach and my right-hand man. I trust his basketball knowledge one hundred percent. He's the guy who does the scouting. He and I do it. He can watch a game and pick up what's going on. He can watch a play and get it all. When he comes back with something, I trust it completely. I don't think I can say that about anybody else. That's why the two of us do it.

"Nowadays you get so much from other teams on video. You have to be willing to give if you want to receive, but now there is talk that the MAC might put all their games on the Internet. It would be a coaches' site, not for the public, but it would help with scouting purposes.

"Brad Evers, our freshman coach, watches the fouls during the game. That's about the only time I see those two guys because they teach at different schools. I have my practice time and they have theirs. This year [2008-2009] we're adding a varsity assistant, so we'll have to revisit those responsibilities during the game. We have a hard time scheduling the gym around other teams and coaches who don't teach here, but we know we have to be willing to work with others, so if it isn't working right, we're willing to change.

"A good coaching staff is one that communicates well and has been together. I was an assistant coach, and you don't want yes-men.

You want someone to tell you when they think you are wrong. Some of that comes with experience and knowing people well. I'm not going to get mad if somebody disagrees with me. I might not do what they say, but I appreciate the ability to go against the grain. We're fortunate because the coaches on our staff are in it for the right reasons. They keep the kids' interest first and they realize this isn't the end of the game for anybody. The coaches of the younger kids try to play a lot of kids and keep a lot of kids involved."

Niekamp has been with basketball long enough to see some changes in what takes place during a game.

"Defenses have gotten better. Kids are bigger, faster, and stronger. I coached in the North South All-Star Game and there was a guy from northeast Ohio who said to me, 'Down there, you guys are the western Europeans. You're huge. We're the eastern Europeans and if we get a big guy, it's rare.' It was funny, but it's probably true.

"The three-point line wasn't there when I played, but it is now. I think it's good. Some people don't like it, but I think you have to do some things to spread the court out and give these guys some room to operate. It forces them to play the perimeter a little bit more."

The tempo of the game is determined by the score, something that players need to understand.

"The kids have to mentally get to the point where they have to understand that if you have a ten-point lead with two minutes to go, that's a lot different than if you're down ten with two minutes to go. You can afford to be very, very patient when you are up ten. If you are patient, you're probably going to get fouled. If you are strong with the ball, you're going to get fouled and maybe get an opportunity for a lay-up to score. Mentally, there is a big difference in how kids have to think when they are on the floor whether you are ahead or behind, but that's what experience does for you. If you are down ten, you're going to have to be a little more aggressive defensively, but you really can't afford to go kamikaze and give them the easy ones. You have to do things out there that you are able to do in order to give yourself a chance.

"We had this come up several times in the past couple of years, maybe five or six times, when we've been up three with the clock running out and then people tied the game on us. We're getting to the point where we're just going to foul. We're giving up too many threes and then people tie the game on us. It's happened too many times. One game, somebody missed a three, but they had a wide-open shot. We decided we're just going to foul them in that situation and not give them the chance.

"One thing we have to be careful to do is not play ninety percent of the defense. Kids have a lot of confidence in their shot, but if they come down and maybe make one pass and shoot, and then the other team comes down the floor and is very methodical, you can get into this ninety-ten thing when you are playing defense ninety percent of the time and the other team is only playing it ten percent. You can't allow that. There are times when it's a tough, little balance to work through. You don't want kids out there wondering if they should shoot or not. You might have to play some possessions with a little bit of patience, but if a kid thinks he has a shot, I'm probably okay with that.

"You have to trust them. If you don't, and if they don't think you believe in them, they aren't going to be as good. I feel pretty comfortable that they are usually doing their best. What more can you do? It doesn't mean you are going to win them all, and it doesn't mean you are going to make them all. The mentality of it is special. I don't think people realize where you can go with your mind. It's all these thoughts of how to handle the end of the game and how to handle pressure. It's your ability to focus and live in the moment and your ability to focus on the task on hand that allows you to get rid of that anxiety. The mentality is a gigantic part of it. Somewhere, I heard somebody say, 'There is no time. It's only the perpetuation of now.' In basketball, it's really like that because there is a new play every second. In baseball, you have time between pitches, but in basketball, it's every second. You could write a whole book on the mentality of the game.

"There are so many different ways to be a good player. It's good if players are athletic. It's good if they're skilled. It's good to have mental toughness and to be unselfish. We've probably had more of a problem with players that are too unselfish than problems with players being selfish. We have guys who need to shoot more. Kids can bring certain little attributes that are amazing in what they can do for you. It might be defense. It might be rebounding. It might be passing. It might be the mental leadership.

"I try to be a forthright, honest, and open coach. I do not talk a lot, but the players know that when I say something, it's probably important. A few years ago we ran a high low offense to get it inside. We just change it up depending on our personnel. The past few years, we've been running open-post and trying to spread the floor and drive and shoot threes.

"A desire and an intensity of focus allow kids to play well under pressure. All coaches are looking for kids who have that leadership ability, and it's something you can see by the way other people treat them and by the way their peers treat them. Kids can lead in so many different ways. It's their team, after all. I'm going to try to give them all the tools and put them in a position to do all the things they can, but the really good teams are the ones that just take over. They know what they can do when they're out there. They won't turn their head and look at me for instructions on what to do. When you're in the big gyms or the big games, they can't hear a word I'm saying anyhow. There's something about leadership in kids who want to take over. They realize and want the responsibility. They don't have that fear of failure. Some kids have the ability to let a mistake roll off their back and others don't.

"Competitive drive is more of the same. It's just something that becomes evident. I don't give it to them. We could go out there, do hamburger drills, and beat the tar out of each other, but I don't think that would make my players more competitive. It just comes from wanting something badly, having that strong desire to play at a really high level, and being willing to sacrifice within the rules to do whatever it takes to get there. When you have players who have that, they really will stop at nothing, within the rules. We believe that if you have to cheat to win, it isn't worth it."

As part of his coaching responsibilities, Niekamp works to get players into colleges that express an interest in them.

"I follow up on any leads or a coach's inquiries. We send back any letters, and we email back and forth. I see coaches in the summertime and try to check back on those interests. I try to give them a realistic and honest opinion of our players, because you don't want to inflate your players' abilities. When they find out the real thing, pretty soon, they won't believe you. We've had several players go play and they've all done pretty well. We've been fortunate with that. I really think that if you're pretty good, the colleges will find you. I don't go beating down the doors of every college in Ohio. They will find the players.

"A couple of our kids played AAU ball in Indianapolis and Louisville during the college evaluation period. Colleges aren't allowed to talk to the kids, but they can evaluate them and there were hundreds there. The really big schools are following the big prospects, but then there are smaller schools that are looking at their needs, too."

Niekamp also has seen the effect of some of the changes in rules over the years.

"Changing the over-and-back call was really positive. It really cleared that up although I don't think the fans understand it. Maybe ten or fifteen years ago the call was changed to having to have both feet over plus be dribbling the ball over and then have anything go back before it can be over-and-back. It clears it up in the players' and coaches' mind and it's easier for the referees to call.

"The state always has points of emphasis and last year it was the illegal picks. I'm glad they do that because I always feel crazy teaching our guys to stand still when they set a screen, but other teams don't do that. I'm telling our kids how to do it right, but other teams are doing it illegally and getting away with it. It is hard to teach your kids how to do it legally and effectively, and it's hard for refs to call it consistently.

"The charge call is always a tough call, too. Palming the ball always was tough, as well, because it wasn't applied all the time. It's tough for kids to follow a rule when it seems to be applied at times, and at others, it isn't. I try to be positive and trust that the officials are doing the best they can. I let them do their job. No player has ever played the perfect game. No coach has ever coached the perfect game, and no ref is ever going to ref the perfect game. Their job is tough enough. Every night, they're going to go home and have half the people mad at them. I try to stay away from the negative stuff and I know some people don't like that when it's going crazy out there and I don't say much. I don't think it sets a good example, and it's not what high school sports are all about, so I try not to go negative on the referees.

"It's important to get along with people in sports and work together with people at your school who are involved with the other sports. We're all part of the same school and the same place. My sport isn't the most important although some people feel that way. It's impressive when people think that your sport is the most important, but we have to think of the kids here and do what's fair for everybody."

Chapter  Twelve

ROGER McELDOWNEY

VERSAILLES HIGH SCHOOL

2004 STATE FINALS

*"You can be the best coach in the world, but if you don't
have talented kids who are willing to work hard
and sacrifice for the team, it doesn't matter."*

The strength of west central Ohio basketball was never more evident than in the year 2004 when three teams from the Midwest Athletic Conference showed up at the state tournament. Marion Local fell one game short in the final Division IV game attempting to defend their state championship from the previous year, and St. Henry and Versailles met in the title game in Division III. It was the biggest game of Roger McEldowney's career as head coach of the Versailles Tigers and it was against a team in his own backyard.

"We played St. Henry here early in the season and beat them by one point on a last second shot by Joe Shardo. In the championship game, Joe had blown out his knee in the regionals, so we had to play without him. We knew we were fighting an uphill battle. Nonetheless, when you are playing for a state championship, you forget about those things and focus on the task at hand. You come into the arena and you watch your kids warm up. You're not really looking around and taking a whole lot in. It's kind of a shame because it is a great experience, but you are so focused the time you're in there, you could be playing on your own home court and it wouldn't be a whole lot different. After the game is over and maybe even when you come in, and you do look up and look around, that's when you realize, 'Hey, this is pretty neat.' The other thing when you reach the finals is the TV time-outs. They tell you there will be two-minute TV time-outs, but you're in your routine so you give your spiel, break your huddle, and the kids go out, but the ref says, 'No, you have another minute and a half.' We just stood around looking at each other. It's pretty neat to go back and watch it on tape and know that's our team.

"We had beaten Reading in the regional finals, but they had been the champions from the year before and had knocked us out of the regional then. We were favored in this game because we were undefeated. We had played them in the regular season and beaten them by twelve points or so. In that Reading game, the regional final we won to go to state, we were down eleven when Joe kind of got screened. They threw a skip pass, and as Joe went out to get his guy, he just dropped. I knew something wasn't good right away. The Nutter Center was packed and you could hear a pin drop. I went to check on him and he was in a lot of pain. It was pretty close to the half and we weren't sure if he could come back or not. It was amazing because I gathered up the team and told them we were going to have to play without him. We changed our philosophy a little bit to be more guard-oriented. We had Kyle Gehle and Ben Shappie who were just phenomenal athletes. I was shook. We were down eleven and the dream was starting to crumble a little bit. I looked at those guys and I could tell they weren't fazed. We went out and made a nice little run and cut it down to four just before the half. As it turned out, we didn't find out until half time that Joe wasn't going to be able to come back. I thought the team would be devastated, but they weren't. It was almost like they ran through the regular season and they finally had a challenge.

"I'll never forget the play we set up coming out to start the second half. It was for Gehle coming off the double screen on the back side, and Shappie was supposed to bring it off the screen and roll back side. Back side, triple stack, [Jerry] Harmon stuff. Shappie was supposed to get it over to Gehle on the back side. Shappie came off the screen, took about one dribble, and buried a three. The fans went nuts because he cut it to one. He looked over at me on the bench and cocked his head a little bit as if to say, 'Don't worry, Coach. We've got this.' I looked at my assistants and we were kind of laughing and saying, 'Look at this. He's in the biggest game of his life and he's just having a ball out there!' Then Gehle took over down the stretch. They couldn't guard him and

we were able to finish them off and go to state. That was fantastic. It was our vision. I remember getting the regional trophy. I went over to hug my wife and we teared up a little because we had spent seven years trying to convince people we could do this. I felt bad for Joe. He was devastated. He was a kid that worked at basketball his whole life and got to the pinnacle and wasn't able to play. I just felt sick for him. That next week we were practicing for the Bellaire semi-final game and his dad came in to tell us he couldn't play. I hugged him and told him how sorry I was. That was a tough family, and he just said, 'He'll be back.' And he was. He came back the next year and had a great senior season and went on to play in college."

McEldowney envisioned playing for Versailles, as most players in the area do, when he was quite young. And, as many fathers do, McEldowney's dad started him into the game early.

"He had me playing in the backyard or out in the driveway. When I was in the fifth and sixth grade, I participated in clinics. At the time, I just had a couple of sisters at home, so the thing about basketball was that I could go out in the driveway and work on it by myself. I didn't need anybody to participate with me. I was taken to some Versailles games at an early age and I had cut all the team pictures out of the program. I put them up on my bedroom wall. That was my goal, to play for the Tigers.

"My first real experience with basketball was with my high school basketball coach Dan Norris. He was a big believer in man-to-man pressure with help defense. He taught me that foundation. I met

Jerry Harmon, who had been the head coach at Jackson Center, while I was teaching there, and he taught me things about the approach to the game. He was the biggest influence on my coaching. Jerry would come to practices when I was coaching the girls team there, and he would speak to the team occasionally. I'd have him view some tapes and tell me what he thought. At Jackson Center we ran the plays that I got from him. We ran them here clear up until I got out of coaching. In fact, sometimes they are still being run here in our program and in our girls program. His influence has been tremendous, not only at Jackson Center where he was, but also here since I brought a lot of what I learned from there, and it kind of caught on."

As the principal at Versailles High School since 2004, McEldowney has had a career in teaching and administration that he has found to be rewarding. While he was a teacher at Jackson Center, he coached the girls basketball team to the Tigers' first state basketball championship in 1995. Nine years later, he made his first appearance at the boys tournament with another group of Tigers from Versailles.

"I just enjoy being with kids. My coaching developed my leadership, which helped me when I got into administration.

"I always tried to treat kids like I would want to be treated. As I got older and had kids myself, I always tried to treat kids the way I wanted my kids to be treated, basically just be fair and consistent and have compassion. You always have to place high expectations on your players. When I first came to Versailles to coach [1997-1998], they never thought about winning a state championship or getting to the state championship because that had never happened before. We tried to create a vision that it could happen my first year. We were 12-9 that year, and we were talking about trying to get to state. People thought I was nuts. You have to plant those seeds. Kids have to have a vision. High expectations are important.

"You have to focus on fundamentals. It comes down to keeping things simple and focusing on the fundamentals of the game. Coaching is teaching. Just like creating lesson plans, I created practice plans. We tried to teach certain things and assess them as we went along.

"The other thing I tried to do was to make sure I was prepared. I'd done my homework. I wanted to let kids know I was working just as hard, if not harder, than they were.

"If they gave a Ph.D. in basketball, I'd have it. I was a junkie. I have my own library at home. I studied tapes. I did a few clinics, but it was so hard to take notes. I would watch college basketball and high school basketball, and if I saw something I liked, I'd try to get a coaching video on it. When I was at Jackson Center, I took a lot of the Bob Huggins stuff, open-post offense, match-ups, and zone press. I'd see things I liked and I'd go out and learn as much as I could about it and then come back and teach it to my players. I have a lot from Jim O'Brien at Ohio State that we ran here at Versailles. As far as offense, I think we were one of few teams around here who ran that stuff. As far as X's and O's, Dean Smith was pretty good. Basketball philosophy was Bob Knight, without a doubt."

McEldowney came back to Versailles because it was where he grew up and he believes it's a great place to raise kids.

"You always think the grass might be greener somewhere else, but when you talk to people from those places, you find out they have the same problems you have. Versailles is pretty much a football school. I knew that when I came in here, but I chose to embrace it rather than compete with it. Sometimes that was difficult in the early part of my career here. Probably in my first year, we only had eight practices because they went late into the fall to the state championship. We were trying to compete with other schools that had five weeks and four or five games in before I had the whole squad. At the same time, I had athletes who knew how to win because they had experienced success. They were competitive, but we just started behind everybody and it made it difficult to catch up. That's why a lot of people told me I couldn't do it here. Fortunately, we had groups of athletes that didn't buy into that. The competitiveness in the fall carried over to the basketball team."

Versailles took that competitive spirit to the state tournament and was put to the test in the semi-final game against Bellaire which McEldowney describes as the most exciting game he coached.

"We didn't have a chance to celebrate the regional championship because the team we would play in the semi-finals was playing in Athens at 8 p.m. that night. As soon as we got done, we sent the team back with an assistant and four of us piled in a van and drove to Ohio University. We walked in and saw Aaron Agnew, one of Bellaire's

players, who was the biggest guy I've ever seen. He was about 6'10"
and probably three hundred pounds. He was huge, so I was thinking
he can't run and he doesn't have any hands. Well, he scored thirty-
six that night. He only missed one shot. They had a guard who was
a pretty good athlete, too. So the whole ride home was, 'Holy cow.
How are we going to stop 6'10"?' We really didn't know how, to be
honest. All week we just worked on collapsing on him. We didn't
have Shardo and I was resigning myself to thinking that the season
was great. We made it this far, but I really didn't know about Bellaire.
But after awhile we thought, 'Hey, we're going there and we're going
to try to win this.' We had some great players and some great back-up
players who hadn't had many opportunities during the season.

"So we went to the game. We started out with the philosophy of
collapsing on the Agnew kid but we'd get kind of confused, though,
because we were double-teaming him. We came up with some early
shots against him, but midway through the first quarter we decided
that we couldn't guard everybody, so we went to a triangle-and-two
defense on the guard and Agnew, keeping everybody else in the paint.
We weren't going to guard anybody else. Normally that doesn't work
very well, but the pressure of playing in a state game or whatever
caused them to have trouble making shots. So we were able to stay
pretty close to them and were able to kind of take Agnew out of the
game a little bit.

"Agnew guarded Paul Borchers, the player we put in for Shardo,
but the thing we noticed when we scouted was that Agnew wasn't
a very good defensive player. He could guard the post, but he never
really came out of the paint. So we would screen so he had to come
out and guard people. He wasn't able to do that. Borchers scored,
I think, eighteen points, probably the most he had all season. He
was a role player for us, and without a doubt, he played the greatest
game of his career up to that point. He knocked down big shots for
us. There was a time in the third quarter when Gehle picked up his
fourth foul and we were down a few. I looked at our coaches and
said, 'What do we do? Shardo is out. Gehle, our leading scorer is
out. This does not look good at all.' Shappie just really stepped it up
and kind of went nuts for an entire quarter to keep us in the game,
hitting threes and just playing like a warrior until Gehle could get
back in the game.

"The reason it was one of the most exciting games is that we were down three with maybe twelve seconds to go. Their guard was shooting two free throws. He missed both. We came down the court and got it into Gehle's hands. He came off a high screen and just buried it at the buzzer which sent us into overtime. We fought the whole game. We fought foul trouble. We fought not having Joe. To throw one in at the buzzer to send it into overtime was big. Overtime was a battle. Shappie hit a big three to give us kind of a cushion so we were able to hold them off. It was the most improbable thing with what we were up against and how our kids kept battling, Borchers stepped up. Shappie stepped up. I was probably the most excited I've ever been coming off the court because I knew we got away with one and that put us in the state championship game."

Not all games resulted in such a rush of feeling. McEldowney remembers some games early on that gave him a chance to re-think the endgame and the decisions made in an instant during the game.

"Early on in my career, I thought we had a couple of games tucked away in the fourth quarter. I found out early that you don't heave a big sigh of relief on the sidelines until it's over. Some people came back on us. My first year, we went 12-9 and lost four or five of those games when we were ahead in the fourth quarter. The kids didn't have the system down yet, and they didn't know how to finish off a game. It taught me that we had to keep going to the end and we had to practice those endgame situations."

"We needed a three at the buzzer during the regional semi-final in 2003 against Cincinnati Reading, the eventual state champions that year. They were on Gehle relentlessly all night. I wish we would have gotten him the shot at the end of the game.

"On the other hand, we played Greeneview in the district finals in 2004. Their coach did his homework. He was on top of his game. So the week before we played them we made a few adjustments knowing they knew what was coming. We turned those adjustments into at least a dozen points because they were playing against what they thought was coming and we gave them a little bit of something different. That really gave our team an advantage."

Teachers know that some concepts are more difficult to teach than others. For McEldowney, the hardest thing for his players to grasp was the zone offense.

"Man to man you can maneuver. You can get people shots and you can create situations, but in a zone, players have to read where the defense is on the floor a little bit more, and it's hard to simulate that in practice. It's harder to develop that in a player because it's a repetition thing."

"Coaching girls helped me become a much better coach because you have to break things down. When I was coaching girls, it seemed like I could control the game so much more. You have to let guys play a little bit. That was hard to make the transition from coaching girls to coaching guys. I came in and my team kind of looked like robots out there. We were good at running our stuff, but as soon as people took us out of what we were trying to do, we didn't know how to play. That's easier to do with guys than girls. It's hard to find girls teams who can take you out of what you're trying to run. The good teams can do it, but there are very few of them. In guys, a lot of teams can pressure you, and your offense has to put it on the floor and take it to the basket to make a play. There's more of that in guys than in girls. You can scrimmage and tell exactly what will happen and what it will look like with girls, but with guys it's not always that way. They have to play. That's changing. Girls basketball has changed a lot since I got out of coaching. Back then all you had to do was press the other team and force them left for them to dribble it out of bounds. It's not that way anymore."

Teachers also know that outside factors can influence what does or does not happen in the classroom. McEldowney faced those issues in coaching, as well.

"The year we went to the state and won the state in football, those guys took a week off and they came in and we had to play at Delphos St. John the first game of the year. We had a lot of people back from the year before, so they knew our stuff; they just weren't in shape. We got a double overtime win there and our kids were so exhausted they could hardly walk off the floor. It's a tribute to how competitive they were. I knew when we won at the Vatican [the gym at Delphos St. John] we were going to be pretty good because you don't win there very often. There are negatives to starting the season late and behind everyone, but you get so many positives along with it. You can't teach success. They learn it by having it.

"Summer in Versailles is football and baseball. I had the gym open the days kids weren't in a league just to get them in to work on getting better. My first year coaching here I was still teaching in Jackson Center. The first day after football we were supposed to have our first practice. There was a concert scheduled in the gym. Here we were, having waited four weeks to get into the gym and we couldn't have practice. I talked to Jerry [Harmon, who was the superintendent at Jackson Center], and he got me the gym over there, so I put the kids on the bus and took them to Jackson Center for our first practice. I'll never forget that. We always managed to work around the gym. We even practiced at Edison, too."

"We always talked about focus. I used to have them hold a ruler and try to balance it on a finger. When they looked at their finger, they couldn't do it. When they changed their focus and looked at the top, everybody could do it. By changing focus you are able to be successful. During the game all kinds of things are going on. You have your dad telling you how to play, you have your girlfriend, your coach is yelling at you, and you just have a lot of distractions. Basketball is a game of fundamentals that can change pretty quickly. You're on offense, then they get the ball and you're on defense. We break down fundamentals in practice. When we deny the wing, everybody is pretty good at that. When we are rebounding and everybody needs to check out, then we check out. When you put it all together in a game, it doesn't really happen that way, so you have to focus on one fundamental to the next. Then you're able to perform at a higher level because you are doing the fundamentals better. There are a lot of distractions when you go to state. Teams that are able to focus in and break things down and do the little things right, are more successful when they get there."

McEldowney concluded his varsity coaching experience with the 2003-2004 season and became an administrator. He knew it was time to step down after 11 years of head coaching experience, seven of those with the boys in Versailles.

"It seemed like the right time. We had this dream of getting to the state. We realized it, but we fell a little bit short. I put so much into that season that I was just tired. It had been a lot of stress on the family. I just felt it was time to go in a little bit different direction. I think you just kind of know. The grind got to be harder and harder. When I was offered the principal's job, I just had to leave it to somebody else.

"Dealing with the media was a chore, too. They were good people, but I just wanted to be with the kids after a victory or console them after a loss. Scouting and watching tape were a problem, as well. The times I was home, the girls would want to play and I was hammering it out on video. The other irritations I tried to turn into a positive somehow. If we couldn't get a gym and had to go somewhere else, that was good practice for going on the road and going through the tournament. Whatever we encountered, we tried to turn into a positive."

McEldowney calculated the rewards of coaching by the relationships he has with his former players rather than by the number of trophies in the case.

"I have kids come back and stop at the house. When Holly [McEldowney's wife] had a battle with cancer this past year the girls from Jackson Center came over to see how she was doing. The guys came home from college and went out of their way to stop over to see her. I taught at Jackson Center when I started coaching here, and the only time I spent with these guys was the time we had practice. You can't have a whole lot of bonding there. We always played Friday and Saturday, so Holly would fix big breakfasts at our house. Big breakfasts. The kids would come over and eat while we popped in a tape and watched who we were playing that night. I'd give them the scouting report and talk about the game the night before. That was our bonding time. They were there playing with my daughters, so when you take them into your home like that, and show them that you care about them, it takes care of a lot of problems that might arise. They know you do care about them. Definitely, Holly was as much a part of it as I was. I couldn't have done it without her. Kids don't always see things the way you do when they're playing, so when they come back afterwards and are appreciative of what you did and they now understand, that's pretty neat."

Some of McEldowney's players have gone on to join the coaching ranks.

"To be a good coach, you have to study the game. I always offer my library. If you want to be good at it, you need to know it inside and out. Fundamentals are the most important thing. The footwork gets boring, but if you can't do that, you can't run any type of offense, so stay basic and treat kids they way they want to be treated. Loyalty is huge in a coach. The head coach needs to be supported through thick or thin. You should look for diversity in your staff. Of our assistants, Kevin Ahrens and Doug Hughes were more post players, and my brother and I were more guard oriented so I think we had some diversity there. I can teach post, but not being a post player myself, I probably wasn't very good at it.

"It was tough having practice on Tuesday night from three to five-thirty then jumping in the car and going to Northeastern by myself and not getting home until eleven at night. Not seeing my family on those days was the worst."

Game days were usually good for McEldowney until he got to the gym and his stomach began to churn.

"On game day I was usually okay until I got there and saw the JV team warming up. I'd see the other team's players. The crowd would start filtering in. It was kind of like the flu. I'd get that sick feeling in my stomach that wouldn't go away until the game started. It was agony. I hated it. Sometimes it started at home or on the bus ride. From the time I got to the gym until the time the ball went up for the game, I was miserable. As soon as the ball went up, I was fine.

"I wasn't real big on giving lots of pre-game or post-game rah-rah talks. I might get them pumped up a little at the start, but it didn't last very long. I was big into giving them things to think about the night before the game. I read a lot of John Wooden's philosophy. One of the things we always used was that we couldn't control how the opponent was going to play. We could only control how we were going to play. We talked about not looking at the scoreboard. We were competing against ourselves. We were just going to play as well as we could. If we did that, that's all we could do and the score would take care of itself. That always put them at ease a little and got them to focus. You can't start getting caught up in looking at the scoreboard, whether you're up here or down there. Obviously, you have to look at the clock at the end of the quarter and know situations, but for the most part, you're just playing the game. More often than not, the more we did that, the more we came out on top.

"Mostly, the pre-game was player personnel and what we were going to run and how we were going to handle their pressure. Halftime was adjustments. A lot of times I would ask them at halftime what was going on out there. If you needed to calm them down, you calmed them down. We were used to winning, so if anyone gave them a challenge and they got a little flustered, I would use half-time to tell them, "Hey, come on. This is fun. You have to work a little bit. Let's go.' Post-game was a time to pat ourselves on the back and look at who we had next. They were to enjoy the win, but we had to get ready for the next game. After a loss, we'd pick out one or two things that were our downfall that we had to do better. We always tried to end on a positive."

The time a coach puts in can restrict time spent with family and friends, so McEldowney truly made his program his family.

"Your assistant coaches become your friends. My daughters were very young and I made them a part of the program. If they wanted to see me they came to the gym, so they spent a lot of time at practices. Holly served as a pretty nice buffer if the guys maybe were mad at me. The players took my kids in which made that a lot easier. My assistant coaches are what made it fun. I had my brother, Scott, by my side the whole time I was here. In fact, I can sit at home now and listen to the game on the radio and tell what play my brother [who succeeded McEldowney as head coach] is running. Gregg Niekamp was a teacher here. Since I wasn't here at the school at first, he was a good organizer. Kevin Ahrens was a volunteer assistant of mine as well. They were great guys, and I don't think we would have had the success we had without any one of them. For scouting, we just sat down and made a schedule. I wasn't much of a delegator. During the state year, I turned over the out-of-bounds plays to Doug Hughes, but I always had my fingers in it. Other than scouting, we all worked together, but I liked to have my hands in it. My best scout was my junior high coach Bob Stammen. He could get down their plays and he had a good feel for personnel, plus he had coached all our players. Doug Hughes helped me out our state year. He was pretty good at picking up tendencies. Having been a coach, he was a great asset.

"I always defined successful coaches by what they taught kids and what kids could take away from them. I wanted them to view me as a good dad, a good husband, and a good teacher. You have to be flexible and adaptable. You have to put up with things that happen. If you start to let your peeves bother you, you're going to get negative, and then you're going to struggle with that. If you can turn those things into positives, it goes a lot better for you. You have to be demanding. You have to have a vision and a goal. I used to read some of Zig Ziglar's motivational stuff and he said that you could have anything you want in life if you can get enough people to care about the same thing. That was always my thing, to get kids to care about the same goals."

McEldowney believes in a set of criteria that defines a successful team. Talent and skill top the list, but the quality of team chemistry is essential.

"A lot of people talk about team chemistry, but no one really knows what it is. The really good teams that I had got along on the floor. They were able to put aside little things that bothered them. Any coach will tell you that those little things can cause problems and just eat you up. Besides chemistry, you have to be a competitive person. I've had some competitive teams, and you don't always have that. Yeah, everybody says they want to win, but will they do what it takes to be competitive?"

McEldowney answers with the word, "pride" why this part of Ohio is a good place for outstanding basketball

"Kids come from good families. Education is important. Playing for your school is important. People go to the games and it's the focal point of their Friday and Saturday nights. You aren't only playing for yourself or the team; you're playing for the community. There are outstanding coaches in the MAC and right next door in Russia is Paul Bremigan. Kids see success and they want to experience it. It seems like every year we have somebody in the area going to state. I remember taking Gehle, Shappie, and all those guys [to Columbus in 2002] when Russia played Delphos St. John. We had played both St. John and Russia during the season that year and we beat Russia, so when I took them to Columbus, their eyes lit up thinking they could get there. The coach has to create that vision for them because then when they are out shooting baskets during the summer, they'll shoot a few more because they want to get there. We wanted to experience that.

"Year in and year out, our Russia game is always packed. We're so close and a lot of families maybe have a mom from Russia and a dad from Versailles which makes that our biggest rival. I think Paul and I hated that game. It meant more to everybody else. For us, it was just another game. Usually after a knock-down, drag-out Friday night league game which we'd put all our time and effort into, we'd have to come back and try to win that game on Saturday for the community. It keeps the townspeople happy if you win that one. We used to joke that it was a contract game. If you won, you'd get your contract renewed."

McEldowney has accomplished the extraordinary by winning regional championships with both the 2004 boys and the 1995 girls, who went on to secure a state championship. To win those championships, McEldowney started by looking at the previous year's championship game tape.

"I took a look at that tape and tried to figure out what they had that we didn't have and what they could do that we couldn't. In the case of our boys team, we saw Reading run a motion offense, and they were able to control the game and the tempo better than we could. We were running more set plays so we had to work on running more motion offense, and I think we were pretty successful. We were able to spread the floor and move. In the second half I let our players run and they were unable to guard Gehle because we were unpredictable. That was something we didn't have the previous year and we struggled a little bit more. Anytime you go with something that has that freedom, you have to have skilled athletes who make good decisions. The lower your skills and talents, the more structure you need.

"You get that lead of about four and a lot of people go into total delay and just wait to be fouled. My philosophy was always to take my best play and run it in that situation. If our best player could run that play successfully, the game was over. I can remember a dogfight at Fort Recovery. We were up two and we went to this play which usually went to our best player. In that case, he would be in a one-on-one situation and he would probably be fouled and we'd have a chance to score or when they denied him, which was what they did most times because he was our best player, he cut back door with the whole side cleared out. It was a wide open lay-up for us. We ran this twice and both times we had both the back-door lay-up, plus we got fouled. Then you just knew it was over, but if we missed it, we were still in a dogfight. This was all Harmon stuff.

"Nobody likes to be behind at the end of a game, but you look to drive and get fouled. You take a three if the opportunity presents itself, but you play right up to the end. You get to the four-minute mark and you kind of know, but in this day and age with the three-pointer, you can put up a lot of points. I'm not familiar with that situation enough because we never were in a position to get blitzed, so it was maybe two or three minutes, but I don't know."

McEldowney had off-season plans for his teams, too. His players had an opportunity in the summer to get into the gym and play some games.

"In the summer kids had an opportunity to play in a summer league on Tuesday and Thursday. We had open gyms on Monday and Wednesday so there were four nights kids could get in the gym. We had a team camp at Delphos for four days. We'd go up, play three games, and come back, so it was a twelve-game league. We did one or two shoot-outs and maybe get another six or seven games in there. It seems like our kids had the opportunity to play twenty or twenty-five games over the summer. I didn't do much conditioning in the off-season because our kids played football. It was a difficult task setting up scrimmages, because you never knew when you were going to get your full team. You didn't want to get a top-notch team and have to play with your freshmen and JV's. You'd try to get some three-ways with one pretty good team and one team that we could compete with. We usually saved one or two scrimmages for when we had everybody here. I ran a youth league in the fall for fifth and sixth grade and ran a camp for grades 4-9 during the summer. It was basically fundamentals and then we played a few games.

"Practices started with warm-ups, shots, and break-downs just working on form and fundamentals. Then we'd go into our full-court drills. I was never a big believer in just running lines, so we did full-court fast-break drills for maybe twenty to twenty-five minutes to start out just to get their hands on the ball. It could vary from three-man-weaves to ball handling drills to the Chicago fire drill which was a four-on-three situation to simulate the fast break. Then we'd do free throws and then go into our defense, working on stance and first-step. We worked every day on one-on-one competitive defense. Then we'd break down to off–the-ball, help-side, and rotation, just the basic defense work. Then we'd do some shooting and end up with team offense and special situations."

Taking the team on the road didn't bother McEldowney unless they were traveling to Delphos St. John.

"The Vatican at Delphos St. John was the worst place to play because it was so loud. They'd sit right on top of you and the fans were right next to you. You couldn't coach because you couldn't talk to your players unless you were right there in their faces. I respected their coach Brett Norris because he prepared as hard as anyone. He knew what you were going to run and knew your out-of-bounds plays and he could take it away. They were very difficult to play against."

The biggest changes in McEldowney's career involved the difference in officiating styles from one league to the other.

"We always had trouble playing non-league CCC teams and then playing MAC schools. The games are officiated totally differently the farther south you go. We always had trouble when we played our own league games or CCC teams and then we'd play MAC schools. It was so frustrating because we'd go to the MAC and couldn't run anything because we were afraid we'd get fouled. They'd come here and we'd shoot forty-one free throws and they'd have guys fouling out. It was just because of the different styles of officiating. Before we got in the league, MAC schools would come here with our CCC officials and they felt like they couldn't do anything but foul. Then, we'd go there and we'd feel like we got mugged. That's just the way they called the game. Then when we got in the MAC, we had those officials and got used to it and didn't have any problem. The officials' impact is supposed to be minimal. The ones I respected were the ones you didn't notice. They understood it's about the kids. They understand that coaches get fired up and don't mean what they say. The key is consistency."

The difference in coaching when ahead or behind in a game is aggressiveness.

"When you are behind in a game, it's hard to keep kids relaxed and they may have a tendency to shoot a little more quickly. When you're ahead you can be patient and a little more selective. Defensively you have to pass a little more when you're down and trap here and there.

"Tempo depends on who the better team is. If you had the superior team, you wanted to play up-tempo and attack most of the game. If the other team was better you wanted to shorten the game a little bit and be more patient so there weren't so many possessions. I always thought that the more possessions there were the more that favored the more athletic team.

"A good player is one who has skills, natural ability and an understanding of the game. We had lots of competitive team players. I think kids enjoyed playing for us. I'm not a control freak. I like to let kids go on their talents. Every year I looked at what we had coming back and who could score and how they could score best. We tried to tailor our offense around what we could do to take advantage of the strengths of our personnel. We never liked to give up the easy basket. At first I tried to coach like I did with the girls, just press, press, press. It didn't take me long to realize that these guys can handle the ball better than the girls. We became more of a position-defense team to make people shoot over the top of us.

"We tried to teach kids how to manage pressure by trying to put them in some game-like situations. If they miss free throws, they have to run, or we put them in disadvantaged situations. We've been blessed with some outstanding leaders. The teams we've had that have been really successful have had good leadership. A lot of that carried over from football. I let them select the captains. Then we let them compete in practice every day. They don't play much against the JV's because you don't get better that way. Instead, they may be competing for a slot or playing time.

"Harmon used to tell me you had to practice two weeks before they'll ever be able to do it in a game. Offensively, you start with footwork and square up to the basket then the follow through. Defensively you start with your stance, butt down and back straight, then you start with a step and then you add a drop-step, and then you move up to do two-on-two where you help. Then you rotate, going to a three-man progression, then a four-man, and then you add a post. Then you're helping on the post. We have a progression of drills from start to finish and that's what we do."

As the head coach, McEldowney is in charge of the total program, which means not only coaching kids, but also being involved with influences on his team or the game away from the basketball court.

"I've written some letters to college coaches when I've had a player they might want to look at. If we have players who ask me about a certain college team, I'll provide tapes if the college wants them.

"I want parents to be involved. They've earned their right to be involved to a certain degree. We've had great parents who support the team concept. Our fans were phenomenal that state year and we have a great student body. It was a whole school-wide and community-wide thing.

"I like working with media people but I wish we could talk after the kids leave. We won a regional semi-final game back in 2000, and I got hit up by two radio stations before I got off the floor. They'd been with us all year long, so I felt like I had to do that. Then I had to go into the press conference and by the time I was done, the kids were all showered and I never had an opportunity to talk to them. I said I would never do that again, so I had an assistant talk to the radio. I changed my practices after that."

McEldowney has some thoughts about ways the game could be improved. Free throws, the shot clock, and tournament seeding are worth his consideration.

"If there is a long rebound on a free throw, the person who has the inside spot is at a major disadvantage. They should back it up so the first person on the block has the advantage. If we had a shot clock, I could play against Bremigan's stall ball, but I really wouldn't like to see that, though. You can keep the game close, so I wouldn't want to see them go to the shot clock. Another thing is seeding. I like the way they seed every team all the way out. A seeded team might not like that, but it's probably fair that way.

"This is a great school in both academics and athletics. I've been fortunate to be a part of it. We have great kids. You can be the best coach in the world, but if you don't have talented kids who are willing to work hard and sacrifice for the team, it doesn't matter. I've been blessed everywhere I've been. I've seen better coaches than I am who haven't gotten the opportunities I have. I was fortunate at Jackson Center and I'm fortunate here at Versailles. I was in two great situations. It's about the journey and building relationships with kids. I don't think I would have felt any differently about those kids if we'd won that final game. It would have been nice, but it wouldn't have changed how I feel about those kids."

Chapter  Thirteen

MIKE LEE

MINSTER HIGH SCHOOL

2005 STATE SEMI-FINALS

"You are blessed if you have a point guard who understands the pacing of the game....That can make up for a lot of ills that you might have offensively."

C ompetition was something Mike Lee understood from an early age. He grew up on a farm with two brothers and one sister who assisted his father and uncle with milking about 90 head of cattle, and the competition to avoid the chore was fierce.

"There were things that had to be done, but there was always time when the work was finished at night for a little competition among the brothers and my dad. We had a hoop up in the haymow in the barn and one down on the stone driveway. When that security light would pop on at night, we'd compete. If we weren't at the house, we were at the park playing pickup games because there weren't the open gyms of this day and age. I grew up in Vanlue just outside Findlay and graduated in a class of forty-four which is still one of the largest to go through the school. I had knee problems growing up, and the doctors told me football was not an option, so that was the calling card for going the basketball route rather than football. When I left high school, I went to Heidelberg and played for awhile, and then had to decide if I wanted to play basketball or walk the rest of my life.

"When I landed my first teaching job at Continental, Don Huber was the head coach there. I had an interest in lower level coaching and they had a seventh grade opening. My classroom was adjacent to his room and he was a tremendous father-figure that

first year of teaching. I was coaching cross country and getting my
bus driver's license and spreading myself pretty thin. I spent my first
three years there and coached seventh and eighth grade. I got my
groundwork there and spent a lot of time at his practices. Back in
the '80s, most of the schools in Putnam County didn't have football,
so basketball [generated] a lot of interest. After those years, I knew
basketball was really something I wanted to pursue. I knew that they
had established coaches, so I thought that if an opportunity came on
board, I would look into it. Anna had a varsity and JV opening in
1983-1984. Mike Muehlfeld was hired as the head coach and I was
hired as his JV coach. Under Mike for eight years, I learned the ins
and outs of what to do and what not to do. When you are with a
person that long, there are a lot of positive things you can take away
from that experience. It was the perfect opportunity for me to begin
the move up the career ladder."

   As he moved from junior high to JV and eventually to varsity at
Minster in 1993 he gathered a set of core principles that guided his
coaching every season.

   "I'm very big on routine. Over a long period of time, there's a
right way of doing things and a wrong way of doing things and that's
where the word 'routine' comes into play. Once I get something
established that we're pretty comfortable with doing, my coaches
understand what's going on and my players understand what's going
on. I'm big on repetition. We'll zero in on certain things that kids
need to be doing over and over again. Some coaches would say that's

boring, but that allows us to accomplish the more important things. Kids know that we'll zero in until it's done in the right fashion.

"You have to be patient. Through time, I've learned to be more tolerant with kids in this day and age. Maybe earlier on in my career if something would have happened, I would have blown up or made a mountain out of a molehill. I think through time that there are some things you have to be more patient with, whether off the court or in practice.

"Another principle has to do with relationships. The coaches should feel just as valuable as the head coach. Not only relationships with the coaches, but relationships with the kids are important, too. There is a fine line, and I can't tell you how you get to that line, but the kids need to respect you as a coach. You have to delve into relationships with these kids on and off the floor. I can go back to my second, third, and fourth year of coaching, and I still stay in contact with many of those kids in some form or another. Those are the kinds of relationships you hope to get."

Lee found trusted resources to supplement what he was learning through his own experiences. That knowledge, coupled with his desire to eventually become a varsity coach, took him from junior high coaching at Continental and landed him his first JV position in Anna.

"There is so much more information out there than there used to be when I started coaching. You almost become a copycat and take bits and pieces from what you learn. I had a very good collegiate coach. I jumped to the junior high and I attended varsity practices, taking bits and pieces, there, too. I've pulled out and scraped the dust off of things that I'm still using fifteen years later from being at Anna with Mike Muehlfeld. I came to a hotbed of coaching in this area. I'm not afraid to admit that Dan Hegemier, Jerry Harmon, Jack Albers, and Fran Guilbault had the things that not only worked in their programs but also worked with all kids. I don't use a whole lot of the Internet. If it had been out there fifteen years ago, maybe I would have. I still go to coaching clinics every year, but I just don't write down and zero in on as much because I believe that, 'If it ain't broke, don't fix it.'

"In this part of the state, basketball is the livelihood of Friday and Saturday nights. When I came to Anna, basketball was the kingpin.

Rivalries developed with seven schools playing two conference games. It was tooth-and-nail. And then, after my years at Anna, I didn't know if I was ready to jump from Shelby County to the MAC. Fran Guilbault probably had five hundred career wins and Jack Albers was in the MAC, too. I remember wondering if I was able to go up against these great coaches. I can't think of anywhere else better to coach, though, because I have friends coaching in other places who have maybe seventy-five to one hundred people showing up at their games on weekends. Basketball just isn't that important. When I made the move from Continental to Shelby County and this area, it was a wake-up call that this was big-time stuff at the high school level."

Lee had several important games in his career that were demonstrative of his and his team's abilities. Many of those were tournament games, but his very first game as a head coach at Minster was unforgettable.

"We had a glitch in the schedule that first game. We were supposed to open with a non-league team, but that got switched and we opened against Jack Albers at Marion Local and it was a league game. That was my wake-up call, 'Mike, ready or not, here we go.' I had a good group of kids. Things just happened to fall our way that night. It was a dogfight back and forth and somehow we came out of Maria Stein 1-0 to start that particular season. I look back and think, 'Good Lord, things could have gone south in a hurry.' That year, we also had a big non-league win against Ft. Loramie right before Christmas. It's amazing what a couple of games can do to kids' confidence.

"Anther big game was the '96 sectional final at St. Marys against New Knoxville. We had gotten beat by them during the regular season and that place was phenomenal. We won in triple overtime. Then we won the district but ended up getting beat at the regionals. That particular team, with the strides they made during the season, was catapulted through the districts to the regionals because of that game.

"The regional semi-final in '98 against Jackson Center was a game we could have played ten times and gotten smoked nine out of ten. Scott [Elchert, Jackson Center coach] had done a great job. Just looking at that tape and watching how things evolved, I'm not sure we could have played any better. Jackson Center had an outstanding basketball team that I'm sure had a ticket to Columbus. They beat us by ten or twelve in the regular season, but sometimes the games come down to match-ups. When we knew we were going to be playing Jackson Center, we just felt really good about the match-ups of our kids with their kids. Naturally, we knew we had to have a lot of things go our way, too.

"The regional game in '05 was our fifth time to the regionals, and you learn that you just don't take these things for granted. We beat Cincinnati Lockland to get out of the regionals which was finally the relief that we were going to Columbus. We were down four or five at half-time, but the kids came out and played well the second half. That was a tremendous feeling for kids, the community, and everyone else. We had played all our regionals at different venues from UD Arena to the Columbus fairgrounds to Wright State University to Miami University and back again to UD Arena. You have to pinch yourself when you think that you've been to the regionals five out of fifteen years and say, 'Did that really happen?' It's having good coaches and good kids who buy into the system. It takes a lot of different pieces to get to that particular point."

"We had that regional final well in hand and it didn't come down to a last second shot, so probably the most exciting games were the triple-overtime game against New Knoxville in the '96 sectional final and the '98 regional game against Jackson Center. We were pretty good underdogs going into that Jackson Center game. I can go back to other games, too, where things just happened to go our way and think, 'That was pretty special.'"

On other occasions, things didn't go Minster's way but Lee was willing to learn, even in those disappointing situations.

"In my first year, when we'd beaten Marion Local in the first game to get off to a good start, we played at Ft Recovery in the second or third game of the season. They were favored to win the league, and that night they put a total waxing on us on our own floor. I'll never forget that their head coach, Jeff Roessner, came back to our locker room after that waxing when the kids were pretty down and I was trying to find words to gather the troops and get back to work. He knocked on the door and I wondered what he wanted. This was only my third or fourth game at the varsity level, and I thought he was there maybe because of something one of our kids might have done during the course of the game. He told the kids we were doing things right. He was complimentary in terms of all the intangibles and if they played hard they would see good things happen. As far as our total program, he told us we had nothing to be ashamed of. It was a big confidence-builder. After that, things started to really come together for that team and we had a very successful year that year. It was good to hear things from a different perspective because sometimes kids keep hearing the same things over and over only from me. It was special because he didn't have to do that.

"The team who played in the state semi-final game against Cleveland Lutheran East in '05 had a lot of adversity that year. A classmate took his own life during the week we were preparing for the St. Henry game which was going to be for first place in the league at the time. Basketball really became secondary. After the state semi-final game, I remember addressing the team in the locker room and as depressed as they were and as disappointed as the coaches were, I was thinking, 'We just got beat in a state semi-final game on a last second shot in double-overtime, but the lesson is that it was a game.' The kids had overcome so much more during the course of the season. You try to impress on kids that there are much bigger things in life.

"I'm not sure we would have done anything a whole lot differently in that game, but when you lose like we did, there are a whole lot of things that you look at. The first thing was something we had no control over. We were a sixty-seven percent free throw team over the course of the season and had shot free throws pretty well in that particular tournament. I'm still throwing out numbers that are in the back of my head years later, but we shot sixteen out of thirty-three in a state tournament game and lost by two points. It's very obvious that if we had done anything better from the free throw line, we would have been in the state final game. There are some stats that are worth forgetting, but unfortunately, that one stays with me and it will stay with me a very, very long time."

In Lee's memory, the balm for that wound is the sectional final game in 2000.

"We were playing Marion Local in Coldwater. They had an outstanding team. They had beaten us by fifteen or sixteen during the regular season and only had one loss. They were league champs. Again, we could have played this team nine out of ten times and gotten waxed, but we had some things go our way. We got into a position where we maximized every situation. We were patient when we needed to be patient. The kids responded after time-outs. I've been in games where nothing works, but that was a game we won by four points over a very good Marion Local team."

Even with talented athletes, there are parts of the game that are difficult to teach or difficult to overcome.

"For me, one of the difficult things is the whole, entire screening action on the floor. It's more prevalent than it used to be. There are all kinds of screens at every level. It is ball screens. It is off-the-ball screens. That was not a big part of the game ten to fifteen years ago.

"The older I get, the more experience I get, one of the things that stands in the way of success is the confidence levels that you can't coach. Confidence breeds confidence and we had that during that state tournament year. There's a carryover from week to week to week. When it happens you ride it as long as you can possibly ride it.

"It's time to hang up the tennies when [trying to teach the game] becomes work. I'm to the stage where I keep getting the question, 'How much longer?' [The answer is] as long as the community is okay with what Mike has done or will be doing. I still enjoy getting ready for camps. I still enjoy preparations for the year. I like mapping out a strategy going into the season. It's time to take a step back when it begins to become a burden and it weighs on you. It's when you don't enjoy going to practices and when you are apprehensive about coming back because it's a major workload."

Lee has learned to balance the irritations with the rewards that come with coaching the game as many years as he has.

"The irritations come when you feel you are doing what's best for the program and the week-to-week preparations and you get phone calls and emails questioning that. But if you didn't want those, why would you be in the position you're in? It's part of the game. I think when the irritations become a sore and it consumes your energy and your time, it's time to say that someone else should handle it. Every coach goes through these things and you just hope they are limited.

"Also, there are many more media outlets than there used to be. They want you to fax a roster to this radio station or send stats to another place. A station from out of town will call you on Wednesday or Thursday and want comments. Now, that's part of the job. I understand you have to do that. It's not a bad thing; it's just there are so many more media outlets. Then the phone calls and emails begin. When we went to state in '05, we were finishing our season in March and, I'm not exaggerating, but the next Tuesday or Wednesday, I got a phone call from a parent wanting to know when summer camp was going to be. You didn't have all this involvement fifteen or twenty years ago.

"Winning is important and every coach wants to win, but you are in the business for kids. We hope we instill what we think are quality characteristics these kids can take with them after they leave. It doesn't happen with every kid, but you try to make those connections. That's huge. The reward is what comes after the fact. Over time, you hope you've made some sort of a positive impact with kids."

"One of the things I would tell any young coach coming in is to be flexible. You need to have an understanding of what you want your program to be like, but you need flexibility built in so you don't have tunnel vision. It isn't, 'My way or the highway.' Kids come from many different social venues where values aren't what they used to be, and that's where flexibility comes in. I see young guys coming on board [needing to understand] time constraints and burn out. You also have to remember that in small communities basketball is not the only sport.

"One of the qualities you need to survive as a coach is organization. I don't see how you can survive without it. You also have to be willing to be flexible with all the things going in the lives of your players, but the most important personal skill is making a connection with kids. That would be number one.

"When you have a losing streak and you have weeks and seasons go by and your kids aren't making the strides you want them to make and it seems like you've tried everything, you second-guess yourself and ask if you're doing what you are supposed to be doing. That's tough."

Lee believes that his game-day schedule is probably a little different from what other coaches go through and how they plan those hours before the game begins.

"I like to be busy. Being a high school principal, my day on game-day Fridays, whether it is a big game or a middle-of-the-road game is just that. I like to think that our preparation has occurred Monday or Tuesday through Thursday and I'm hoping I'm staying busy. I've done all my homework ahead of time. Now, if school is dismissed and I don't have any student issues, and it's becoming that 3:30 or 4 p.m. hour, then Mike's in his routine mode, so don't anyone come in my office unannounced. You have to be personable and you have to do those types of things, but the time of day has come when certain things have to be done. The hour before getting on the bus is my routine. Don't upset my routine because that can throw me into a little bit of a loop I don't want to experience. I've been down that road a few times. In that routine, I make sure I've covered all my bases. I make sure we have all the materials we need, especially on an away trip. As the head coach, I can delegate most of this, and I do. My coaches know their responsibilities. Getting tapes and stat sheets, checking the video equipment to be sure it's functioning, and preparing the trainer's kit is what I'm responsible for. If Mike's responsible for it, if something is screwed up, it's Mike's fault. It's probably not the route to go, sometimes, but that's how I am.

"Most of the pre-game talk, then, is a review of Monday through Thursday. Here's what we're going to try to do. Here's what we're going to do to try to be successful. Since we're predominantly a man-to-man basketball team, we're going to review our match-ups once again and every now and then I'll throw in a question to a kid to be sure we have one last opportunity to be sure everybody is on the same page. In the three hundred-plus games I've had coaching, that can blow up in your face in the first five minutes of the first quarter because a kid can get in foul trouble or start doing things that are uncharacteristic of a sixteen-year-old kid.

"Predominantly what happens at halftime is we give kids a cooling off minute to do what they need to do. Then we address what we need to change or what we're doing well defensively. That comes from us, the coaches, walking off the floor and taking the first few minutes without the kids to determine and map out what we need to change or adjust. Then we flip the coin to offense and we talk about what we are doing well or what we need to do to be successful. A lot of times at halftime, you try to build up the confidence level of your kids.

"I go back to that regional final game against Cincinnati Lockland.

Halftime came at a great point because we were down five or six. The last two or three minutes of that second quarter, things started to get away from us. We were able to re-group, re-focus and adjust what we were going to do to start the third quarter, and then things just started to fall in place. Again, that doesn't work all the time. I've been in halftime situations where we're down five or six and within the first few minutes of that third quarter, we're down fifteen or sixteen.

"Post games can be happy and congratulatory, reviewing what we did well as a team, or they can be addressing why things didn't go so well. What I've done more in my last few years of coaching, as opposed to what I did earlier, is instead of Mike being the predominant speaker, I've let the captains take ownership. It's not all just coming from Coach Lee. I turn to my captains because that's why they are in this role. The kids need to hear it from the captains."

All the involvement in running a varsity program can mean less involvement socially. Lee discovered that it meant navigating social situations carefully to avoid criticism of possible favoritism.

"We really didn't have a social life. If we became friends with a couple in the community, and they had a young son, I was leery of getting close because I didn't want it to come back to haunt me later in second-guessing what I was doing with the team. I didn't want to put myself in those situations. It gets very, very tough."

The ingredients necessary to produce a successful team are varied in Lee's opinion. Being multi-dimensional creates the opportunity to attack and defend in unpredictable ways.

"To be successful around here, year in and year out, you have to be able to put guys out on the basketball floor who can score in a variety of ways. If you are one-dimensional, you are going to have trouble. I've had one-dimensional teams, and we've struggled. I've had one-dimensional teams and we've been successful, but I look at some of the teams when I could put three, four, or five guys out on the floor who could do a lot of things, and if you're flexible, you can be pretty successful.

"There are some intangibles that go into this. I've had some teams that worked harder than others. I've had teams that worked well together, and if you needed to get in touch with all of them on a Saturday or Sunday, you could call one of them, and the rest were right there with him. The kids understand the workings on the floor, but they are pretty darned good friends off the floor."

Lee finds that there is a combination of characteristics in this area that creates the excitement and the excellence that is basketball in western Ohio.

"When I first came into this particular area, we had the likes of coaches like Jack Albers, Bob Arnzen, and Fran Guilbault. Add the small communities and the great athletes. Our kids sometimes joke when they see a kid out and about somewhere and he's wearing a sectional champions T-shirt. It's wrong, but you don't take for granted getting to the regionals five times and the state once because when a following season doesn't go well, that's an eye-opener. These communities value athletics. Academics are the number one priority, but the kids all over the area have a good work ethic. It's not just Minster, but our kids are up at 5:30 to be at school to lift, then they're off to a job, and they're back for open gym in the evenings. Or better yet, they're playing in an Acme baseball league four or five nights a week. I'm convinced this doesn't happen anyplace else. My friends, who coach in other places, know that when you are talking MAC or Shelby County, you're talking very good no matter what sport it is. They are very aware it's just quality."

When two teams who have this dedication get together to compete, the rivalry can be intense.

"We're just a stone's throw from New Bremen, and when I first came here, we played New Bremen twice in the regular season. The first time we played them counted as a conference game. The very last regular season game was, by tradition, always against New Bremen and counted as a non-conference game. I absolutely hated that last game. We had been through eight or nine extremely tough league games, but from the school and community's viewpoint it was going to be a packed house. We'd already played New Bremen once and I was thinking, 'I don't need this.' From my perspective it's New Bremen, but you could ask the kids and they'd say Marion Local or St. Henry. I think that because of the proximity, you can throw the records out. These games are usually pretty sloppy because one team knows everything about the other. The kids run around together. They play together in the summer. There aren't many secrets. That's one regular season game that's easy to prepare for in one sense, but it's tough to prepare for in another. It's like you've been in their locker room and they've been in yours. The kids pretty much know what you're going to say ahead of time. What makes that even worse now is that when I first came to Minster, my assistant coach Mike Ernst was with me for eight years and he left to become Bremen's head coach. That game has become even tougher for me because Mike does an outstanding job."

Lee has won five district championships and one regional championship in fifteen years, so he has something to say from his experience about winning tournament trophies. He's a believer that, even with the most talented and prepared teams, the stars have to align and the ball has to bounce just right to get to the big games.

"Just like winning a district championship, to win a regional, you have to have a lot of intangibles go in your favor. You have to stay away from a major injury. Yes, you're playing with five, but if you have lean bench and some kid happens to go down, it can put a major hurt on whether or not you make a successful tournament run. You can call it Lady Luck, but the year we went to state, we were down thirteen heading into the fourth quarter in the sectional finals against New Knoxville and pushed that game to overtime to get out and get to the districts. We had waxed Dan's team in the regular season by twenty-five, and knowing the Dan Hegemier I know, I knew that his team was going to be totally different, and there we were down thirteen against them going into the fourth quarter. There were some things that began to go our way in the fourth quarter, and we were fortunate to get out of it and survive. We took that victory as a springboard and rode it into the districts. We thought that if we had been down by thirteen in the fourth quarter of that game, what an obstacle we overcame.

"We didn't really play outstanding district games. We were down, I think three, at half time against Ft. Recovery in the district final, and I'm sure at half time I brought up the fact that we had overcome adversity before and we had the opportunity to do it again. And when we won that district final, we knew we didn't have to face another MAC team or a Shelby County team because Russia, who was favored, lost in their district final. It was a perfect opportunity for us if we could continue to do the things that we had done thus far. We won by about twelve in the regional semi-final and then we beat Lockland in the final. But, again, we didn't have anyone go down in practice with an injury. We didn't have to nurse a sore knee.

"I'll never forget the bus ride and going to Columbus. The players had their headphones and everything else. It was almost like the weight of the world was gone. It was the culmination of all the practices and all of the things that you think you are doing to make your program successful. Yes, Mike had done his organization. I kept making sure I had this, this, this, this, and this, fifteen times before we got on the bus. From the regional finals, getting up on the ladder, and from that time frame, the preparation, and the practices, well, it was quite a feeling. That bus ride is one thing I'll never, ever forget. All these hours and all the time frames and all the time constraints and all of the banquets were all worth it. No, you can't get to the state tournament every year, so it was a feeling that is hard to come by.

"I never realized ahead of time the magnitude of the media interest in the game. The week before, I was getting calls from Newark or wherever, and their radio stations were doing the game. They didn't know where Minster was, so that was different from the *Sidney Daily News* and the *Celina Daily Standard*. After the game, it was extremely tough because of how the game ended. They did a good job of informing me that they were going to contact one or two of my players. I had an opportunity to talk to them so they weren't blindsided. It only takes one comment to put a bad light on things.

"You try to do the best job with the media in promoting your kids and I have no problem as long as they communicate what I've said. They are there for their job and I've never turned them down. Sometimes that can be difficult because there are maybe three guys outside waiting to get the first thing that comes out of your mouth, and sometimes the first thing is the thing I needed to say but shouldn't have, and they are standing there with a pad and pencil. I've had to say, then, that I don't want to see this in print and they've understood that."

Then there are the years when the best-laid plans go awry. Lee and his point guard both suffered bad breaks but in two different ways.

"My first year at Minster, Botkins beat us in the regional final. Our point guard had broken his foot earlier, and somehow we were able to offset his injury in the regional semi-final and beat Ansonia who had beaten us by twenty in the regular season. Botkins' team that year was a pressing team, and nothing against their coach Tony Rogers, but I would have loved to have seen that game if we'd had our guard. If you're going to win a regional championship, you have to have things go your way, but you have to stay away from a kid going down.

"It's a good feeling when you are winning. I do a lot of clock watching and have conversations with my coaches, making sure they keep an eye on the time to make sure the timer is flipping the clock on when we throw the ball in, and to be sure the guy doesn't go to sleep at the scorer's table. When you know the game is in hand, it's a great feeling to discuss how to get kids off the floor and get others on the floor and what kind of a mix we are going to have out there. You want the kids to get the necessary applause for the effort they put out there. Besides, you want to get your younger kids out there because that's their future. You want to make sure you do as much of that as you possibly can.

"I've been in many situations on the flip side when you look up and you're down ten or twelve points and there's a minute and a half left. You want to throw in one last ditch effort, but I have to look at that when we are having a tough league game on Friday and we're getting beat by twelve to fifteen points, there are two minutes left, these kids have expended every ounce of energy, and we have a tough non-league game on Saturday. There's a fine line there. Yeah, you'd like to go down using your best five, but there's a time when you need to clear the floor and get certain kids off the floor and at least give them an extra two, three, or four minute breather, knowing you're going to come back in less than twenty-four hours and go right back at it again. You know you've exhausted everything in your repertoire and it's just not working. That's when you take your hat off and say that we were beaten by a better ball club."

To get to those big decisions in games is to have prepared for those moments. That work is done in the off-season and, true to his self-analysis, Lee's year is planned and organized.

"When you've been in a situation as long as I have here, preparation is much easier than when you first land a job, you have a lot of different things thrown at you, and you aren't really sure about stepping on the toes of other people and other programs. You try to stay one step ahead of where you are going to be. For example, the dead period runs in the summer through about Labor Day, so we have to think about what we're going to do with kids who aren't in a fall sport from September to mid-October. Then what are we going to do with those kids coming out of golf and cross-country? We need to have some sort of conditioning. My conditioning schedule will be set in September, even though we won't start until the middle of October. I prioritize based on what's coming down the pike. The practices and games will be a major, major priority come November. The first two weeks of the school year, other coaches will be calling about scrimmages that we'll play in November. In setting up scrimmages, I need to communicate with our girls coach to be sure I don't step on her toes. I'm setting up media day and picture day, making sure all that works with her program. Over the course of the last fifteen years, it's become a bit of a joke with the kids that if you aren't in football, you have to run a timed mile and they have to make a set time. But kids are kids and they'll wait until a week, or even two days, before the actual run and not prepare ahead of time. I keep my practice plans from last year to this year, but I'll go back and tweak that a little bit here and there. I have a pretty good idea what we'll be doing the first four weeks of practice to get done what we need to do before that first game. Football playoffs can put a major crinkle in your planning. If your football team gets on a roll in tournament and they're two to four weeks into your basketball season, it would be tough. I'm amazed at how Keith Westrick [Marion Local coach] does it. He probably can't get a good feel for his team until January.

"Our practices change from the first two weeks to the middle of the year. As the season progresses, we'll cut back. If we're sixteen to eighteen games into the season, it'll be an hour and we'll be done. Yet, the first two weeks into basketball, we'll be there for two hours. In that session, we'll break things down into an extreme amount of teaching. You try to instill in kids that what you are doing in these drills will go from part to whole. Once we get into the season, we'll still be teaching, but not the extreme of the earlier weeks.

"Keeping a team fresh throughout the season comes from scaling things back. I know there are some very successful coaches who don't do that, but I've not had a two-hour practice in January, February, or March in my last ten years of coaching. You have to pick your times to give the kids a few days off at Christmas. I also try to pick some spots where we have a Friday/Saturday schedule and don't come back until the next Friday. Maybe then we'll give the kids two days of absolutely nothing. We try to put those in the schedule mid-to late-season because at that time of year illness is much more prevalent. There are situations when we will scale things back: an hour and a half on Tuesday, an hour and fifteen minutes on Wednesday, and an hour on Thursday, and that's our week. Probably others are doing that but not taking it to that extreme. If the kids looked gassed or are not clicking on all cylinders, maybe we need a clearing out of the mind for forty-eight hours. When we have the kids take that extra day, practices are much, much better, but that's sometimes a risk.

"I would like to think our kids are a little further ahead by the year 'round work, but sometimes it's like trying to keep up with the Joneses. I wonder what we are doing when these kids are up at 5:30 and then I'm getting on them for not pushing it on the floor at open gym that night, but you have to do the open gyms and all those things to keep up. On the flip side, we're in a society where it's non-stop. Our athletic council, comprised of all our head coaches, meets four times a year, and we want to implement a dead period when there is no contact with kids at all. There are some schools that have that, but we can't do anything in Ohio until the OHSAA [Ohio High School Athletic Association] makes it a priority. They have heard issues about this, but I have yet to see anything come down the pike from that particular office to address that concern. Sometimes you have to keep pressing the issue, but no one will act until it becomes a high priority."

Lee has grown to enjoy a quirk in his game schedule that doesn't include away games at Delphos and New Knoxville in the same year. He and his team find that those venues often spoil their plans for success.

"The Barn at New Knoxville and the Vatican at Delphos are the toughest places to play. I can't remember the last time we won at either one of those places. I'm thankful we don't have to go to both places in the same year. If we did, I'd have a major headache. Both places are so friendly for the home team. The fans are sitting right on the floor.

They do a great job of positioning their fans in certain sections of the gymnasium. In New Knoxville, you're only going to get X number of seats when you go there, and the same thing at Delphos. Not only are you going to get X number of seats, but it'll be in some corner where you'll have to scream pretty loud and hard to be heard."

Behind the scenes are the scouts who are important in beginning the process of drawing up a game plan. Many of those people are Lee's assistant coaches who understand what the Minster program needs from a scouting report.

"Mike Wiss was my freshman coach three or four years and whenever I want someone scouted thoroughly the way I would scout the team, he helps out. He's very detailed. If coaches [at other schools] are at a particular venue for a certain length of time, I don't scout as much as what I used to, because I pretty much know what we're going to get. I look at personnel and what they are going to do defensively and offensively, but I have a good idea what they are going to do. We'll try to see every team at least once, between my assistant coaches and me. We'll split up some nights and other times we'll go together. Mike Wiss was with me for eight years and now Kurt is on board. I'd like to think they would say that Mike allows them the opportunity for input. I not only allow it, I want it. I value their input. I listen and use a lot of what they communicate. You want the camaraderie to be able to bounce things off each other. It's good for kids to get the different perspectives at practice. I don't want Mike Lee clones. I don't have all the right answers. We communicate well and we aren't afraid to say what needs to be said at a particular time.

"On the bench during the game, we have a volunteer assistant, the freshman coach, and the JV coach. One assistant coach keeps track of fouls. I know our guy at the scorer's table keeps track of them in the scorebook, but I want to know right then and there. One of my assistants gives me suggestions about substitutes. He makes sure we're watching that kids don't go long stretches without a break. Everyone looks for [what's working and what isn't]. During the course of the game, I can't say we have definite responsibilities on the bench, though, other than keeping track of the fouls.

"If we see that we're behind in the second half and we're just grinding it out and struggling to put the ball in the hole, I take the word flexibility out. We'll zero in on a set play that either worked in the first half or we know we're going to get the shot we want. In other words, when I have five guys on the floor and I want this kid to get a shot in this particular situation, I become much more patterned. As opposed to when we're ahead, the kids are confident, and we're scoring from different spots on the floor, we don't want to change anything because it has worked for us.

"You are blessed if you have a point guard who understands the pacing of the game. It didn't take me long in the varsity coaching ranks to understand the value of your quarterback on the floor. That can make up for a lot of ills that you might have offensively."

Lee has been in basketball long enough to see some of the developments in the game.

"The three-point line was the one that opened up the middle of the floor to put a little more emphasis on the perimeter. One of the worst changes was that you could not enter the lane until the ball hit the rim on the free throw. You used to be able to go in on the release and you could work on positioning. That rule threw positioning out the door. As soon as the ball hit, it was pretty much man against man. There are a lot of things that go on in the free throw lane that don't get called because of that change."

He has also coached against some of the best coaches in Ohio and has the experience to identify those who gave him some of the greatest challenges he faced.

"Hegemier is at the top of the list. If you didn't have your ducks in row, you were going to be had. And I had been had by that man on many a night. He just does a tremendous job. You know what you're going to get, going in. Marion Local still runs Jack Albers' famous match-up zone, so you have to prepare totally differently against Marion Local than you do any other team. You have to prepare differently for a Hegemier team than you do for some of the other teams."

Lee has had many good players over the years to pit against the formidable opposition he faced on a regular basis. A good player, in Lee's estimation, should have a desire to be coached.

"Kids have to be coachable. I've had a lot of good players who had a mindset of how they wanted things to be done. We didn't have confrontations, but we did have some one-on-one sessions for me to say, 'It will be done in this fashion.' Kids have to be good listeners.

Again, we do a lot of teaching. Our practices are often repetitive, so the kids have this more than once. It's not like we're changing things right and left. I put a little more on my seniors than I do my sophomores and juniors. I give them ownership to develop the kid rather than the overall basketball player.

"When I first came to Minster we had big kids and that kind of matched the things I had learned under Mike Muehlfeld at Anna and from Dan Hegemier's teams. They ran a particular offense that I thought could be well-suited for Minster players and we still do it sixteen years later. It's more of a style that is going to get the shot that I want to get. We try to ingrain in our players that these are the spots on the floor that the offense is designed to get.

"If I go back to the '04 and '05 state team, we went totally away from that offense and opened up the floor, trying to break teams off the dribble. Mike didn't have as much rein which was very difficult for me because I was allowing kids to make decisions on the basketball court by themselves. That was tough for me, but looking back, as the year progressed, they got more comfortable with the style, and as they got more comfortable being successful with it, that's the team that got to Columbus. That's not the style I would choose. The final score of the semi-final game was 86-84. For us to score 84 and give up 86 would be like, 'You've got to be kidding me. A Minster team gave up that many points?' You knew what you were going to get with a lot of my other teams. If you were going to beat us, you would have to do this, this, this, and this. Many teams did that, but on the flip side, we were successful that particular year because we got the shots we wanted to get and we played good man-to-man defense for most of the night. That state team had a totally different make-up. We could put kids on the floor that could score and handle the ball. We didn't have a true post man that year. That was hard on yours truly. We had already been to the regionals four times and had fifteen or sixteen wins a season with things that had worked well for us, so why would we want to chuck it? It was a matter of what we could do and what the team make-up was. This team was up and down the floor much more and we could mix or match kids by playing eight or nine of them. We were pressing, and we aren't typically a pressing team. I remember the preseason and telling my assistants, 'I don't know if I can handle this. We're chucking up shots like there was a shot clock and we needed to get rid of it.' That was an experience."

Lee also had methods for teaching the intangibles. Learning basketball is one thing. Handling competition, taking leadership, and managing pressure are something else.

"You are blessed when you have kids who've been in pressure situations before and can handle it. You have kids who have been three-sport athletes, so in that pressure-packed game on Friday night, they've been the quarterback or the wide-receiver or the linebacker or the running back who has been in those situations, and that helps them handle pressure more. Some kids don't handle it as well and we end up shooting forty or fifty percent from the free throw line and someone says, 'Gee, Coach, I'll bet you don't shoot any free throws.' Then my answer is, 'You're right. We don't shoot any at all in practice.' There have been two nights in my career when we shot free throws poorly even though we won. The kids thought they were going to jump off the bus to head to the local eatery and I had to say, 'Hold the fort. We're going in to shoot free throws.' We flipped on the lights in the gym at eleven at night and they shot two hundred free throws before they could get out of there.

"I've had players whose talent level was average to below average, but because of the drive they had and their willingness to compete, they ended up being very, very good basketball players. I've also had kids who were talented in spots, but they were passive and turned into great kids but average players. I'd like to say there is a drill that builds that, but it comes from them and their willingness to compete at that particular level.

"Most of our work with kids is with defensive man-to-man. We use shell drills to get kids into position depending on where the ball is. That's the biggest thing defensively. They learn this early on and build on it as they move through the levels of the program. As we get into the regular season, we scale that back. In terms of player development, we do one-on-one or two-on-two or beating a kid off the dribble much more than we used to. We put emphasis on doing something off the dribble because how often do you see a kid anymore standing wide open with two or three seconds to shoot. Our drills are sequential and kids eventually see the connection."

Lee believes it is his responsibility to get the word out on a particular player who is interested in playing at the college level. That communication is done through phone calls and emails or word of mouth. It's a part of my job to get the word out. It just spreads from there.

"We haven't had that many go on to play in college, but the parents' perspective of where the kid's talent is might be different from the coach's perspective. We hope parents are supportive of the program, and in many families, we've had an older sibling go through the program, so they know what to expect. We've had strong parental support from people who encourage their kids through situations that aren't the best and remind them that coaches have their best interests at heart."

Lee believes that sometimes the people most likely to get the blame in basketball are the officials.

"They sometimes bear the brunt of a tough loss. You know how far you can go with some officials. You can talk to one guy and not get anywhere with another. You learn that over time. In tournament, you hope that these are people you know have been voted on and you're getting the best of the best. Sometimes that's difficult for them because they haven't worked with each other.

"I got T'd up once in my fifteen years. It happened to be at Russia. We were in a competitive back and forth game there and just out of the clear blue the official blew his whistle and motioned the coaches over. The fans were livid because they didn't know what was going on. He told us to settle down or we'd get a technical foul. The game resumed and Paul [Bremigan, Russia coach] jumped up off the bench. Nothing happened. Then about thirty seconds later, I jumped up and before I could say anything, I had a technical foul. We still laugh about that. It's the only one I've picked up in fifteen years."

In thinking of the future, Lee hopes high school games don't get a shot clock anytime soon and he'd like to change his northwest sectional tournament draw to a super-sectional much like the southwest region.

"Our biggest push in the Northwest is to get our district to look at a super-sectional. Most of us would like to see that changed, but we haven't done that. There's not much of a choice in looking at brackets.

When you go to the Southwest to Piqua, you have some options. Our tournament draw normally lasts five minutes. In a super-sectional, you bring in teams from other areas and conferences. When we go to our sectional, we are just revisiting our league schedule.

"I don't want a shot clock. It's hard enough to get the regular clock operators trained. Every district struggles with that because it will require one more person to be trained. My state team could have put up shots with a shot clock, but the other fourteen years, I would have been up the creek without a paddle. I hope the shot clock doesn't come to the high school level or that might be Mike's ticket to retirement."

Chapter  Fourteen

Matt Meyer

Anna High School

2008 State Semi-Finals

*"The best coaches are great teachers. They know how to teach.
They're the masters of the fundamentals. They communicate.
They balance courage and consideration."*

Matt Meyer came to the game of basketball early and often. His family didn't take vacations when he was young, opting instead to travel to various gyms in the area wherever his father, Tom, was playing basketball.

"It seemed that he was in a league every night of the week. We went wherever Dad was going. He played extremely hard. He was kind of nasty, too. I think he instilled the competitive side in me. We knew when he took his [false] teeth out, the kids had to leave the gym. It was something we weren't allowed to watch."

By the time Meyer reached high school, he had already been playing several years in the Jackson Center program, directed by head coach Jerry Harmon. Playing basketball for Coach Harmon was predictable but demanding. Those years harnessed a young boy's enthusiasm and refined the mental approach to the game. Harmon was able to motivate players and demand dedication to the fundamentals of basketball, elements that are the foundation of Meyer's coaching at Anna.

"We didn't do a ton of different things at Jackson Center when we played. It was pretty basic. We played solid defense and ran the flex. We didn't do a lot of set plays or a lot of X's and O's. What Jerry Harmon could do was teach you the fundamentals and work on them every day. He motivated you so that you wanted to play hard for him. He was fantastic at picking out the individual tendencies of the other team. 'What can you do to make yourself better than the other guy?'"

After high school, Meyer coached with Larry Leffel at Edison Community College in Piqua. Those years brought precision to his game.

"At X's and O's, nobody is better than Larry. Even today, it doesn't matter where you are, whether it's a napkin or the back of a flyer, he's constantly drawing up plays. He has a passion for the game like no one I've ever been around."

In 1994, Meyer accepted the head coaching position at Anna, staying until he decided five years later to focus on his young family and his education. He did, however, assist as Brian Leppelmeier coached the Anna Rockets through much of the period until Meyer returned to the helm in 2006. What Meyer learned from him was advanced organizational skills, even to the point of teasing Leppelmeier about the need for detail leading to "ironing his own undershirts."

Meyer credits these three individuals as having the most, direct influence on his coaching. He has, however, gained additional knowledge from books written about college and professional coaches Rick Pitino, Phil Jackson, and John Wooden, but says that being exposed to the coaches he's worked with and against has produced an even richer lode of expertise.

"Some of the stuff we use, we come up with, but the majority of stuff, we steal. We watch ESPN, or we scout, and if we think that something will work with our kids, we take it. We have a set philosophy, but if we see something we can use, we steal it. We might shape it, bend it, or twist it to fit our personnel, but I think that's what good coaches do. You don't reinvent the wheel."

Through these men and these observations, Meyer formed and tweaked his goals, resulting in the five principles of coaching that he believes are critical for success: fundamentals, conditioning, preparation, family, and Anna pride.

"One of the biggest mistakes young coaches make is that they try a hundred different things rather than looking at it as a marathon. 'I've just got to do the fundamentals every single day starting when they're young and just keep working.'"

It's a theme Meyer revisits day after day, thought after thought.

Every decision he makes is reflected somehow in the fundamentals of the game.

"We teach fundamentals, we're in condition, and we're ready. We preach to our kids that this isn't your home family but this is a family and we really try to treat it like that. I can't believe the amount of recruiting going on, especially in the bigger cities. We try to instill from day one that it's about Anna. In this area it's natural. You're from Anna, you play for Anna. You're from [Fort] Loramie, you play for Loramie. Let's say Marion [Local] had a 6'10" kid suddenly come to play at Anna, and we ended up winning state. It taints it a little bit."

Time away from head coaching ripened Meyer's approach to the game as well. His first stint was marked by emotional excitability and by placing more importance on game coaching. The second time around, he has put more effort into practice and preparation so at game time he's more relaxed.

"Being emotional is a sign of weakness to the kids. They feed off it. Now, I'm a stable factor. I don't throw water bottles or scream or shout anymore. The kids are comfortable. They know from Monday through Thursday what's expected and they enjoy themselves. I think there's a total difference between getting kids to perform out of fear as opposed to getting kids to perform because they are a part of something they feel a responsibility for – the outcome. The only time now that I truly get on a kid is because of lack of effort."

And Meyer has seen a range of effort and talent all over the state. He traveled throughout Ohio when he was coaching at Edison, and he watched games and players. He is convinced that coaching in western Ohio is the challenge he wants.

"You see the basketball in this area, southwest Ohio, and it's different. There are teams in our league and in the Midwest Athletic Conference that could be in just about any similar size league in the state and win it, yet they finish fourth, fifth, and sixth in the leagues here."

Winning league titles is impressive in western Ohio, particularly in the MAC and the Shelby County Athletic League, but Meyer's biggest career game was the 2008 state semi-final match-up between Anna and Ottawa-Glandorf.

"It's an absolute dream. I'm sure there have been some teams that made it there that weren't like a family, but we were. There was kind of a love between the coaches and kids that made it really, really special to experience it with them. In years previous, a lot of those kids had gone to the state tournament with us to be spectators, so you dream about making it there. When we first went to the hotel, we drove by the Schott [Schottenstein Center] and to turn around and see those guys looking out those windows, well, they were like kids going on their first vacation to the Grand Canyon. They were just staring at it. To go underneath and be escorted in and go through the treatment, it was just fantastic.

"Sectional, district, and regional all have security, but I never imagined the level of security at the Schott. You're almost like royalty. They assign you an ambassador that meets you at the door. They cater to you. They come get you at the time you want to go to the locker room. Nobody, I mean nobody, gets to that locker room without an approved ribbon. Even our superintendent didn't get down because he was carrying his son, who didn't have a ribbon. The TV cameras and the sideline reporter who kept coming up to me during the game were nothing compared to the room full of reporters after the game. You're up on a stage, just like you see at the NCAA. They've got your name on a placard and afterwards two players, Joel [Naseman] and Kreg [Elsass], were interviewed by a TV network. It was surreal. Paul Bremigan and Mike Lee, who had been there, kind of warned me to hold on because we wouldn't believe what we were going to experience. It was much beyond my expectations. The difficult side of that was they played their hearts out and things just didn't bounce our way. It almost sours it...but it doesn't. Almost..."

As important as that game has been to Meyer, the game that he recalls as being the most exciting game of his career was the regional final with Columbus Academy in that same run-up to the state tournament.

"I pride myself in keeping control of my team during victories – not celebrating. Don't show emotion. Don't rub it in the other team's face. Just wait until the locker room. But the way that game ended, the way we played so well as a team, we still needed individuals to step up. Kreg Elsass just dominated the fourth quarter and overtime. Then Derek Billing, as a sophomore, took it on his shoulders there at the end. I called a time out and a questionable play, at best, and he saw something open up. But then, to end the game on that defensive stop, needless to say, I didn't practice what I preached and lost it. It was just fantastic."

The thrill of a game like that doesn't come without some study. There are lessons to be learned along the way before a team threads its way through the bracket to Columbus. Meyer counts the regional game of 1996 against Southeastern as the best opportunity to learn.

"The whole year we had one sideline play that sufficed, and we either got something off of it, or we set up an offense. Late in the game against Southeastern we had a dead ball, sideline out, but we didn't execute well. We needed a quick hitter from the sideline and we didn't have it. That taught me to do more situational things in practice, to be more prepared for different situations: down two sideline out eight seconds, down four underneath eight seconds, down five full court six seconds. We do more situational work. All others, every win and every loss, the coaches immediately go into the coaches' office and are thinking about what we can do best. Whether it's a loss or a win we try to take lessons from it. The difficult part is we hardly ever enjoy a win. We're always trying to determine what we did not do well."

One game that Meyer cannot critique, cannot even watch on tape, is the 1997 regional final game against Springfield Catholic Central.

"We were up seven at half with a chance to go to state. I don't know what I would have done differently. To be real honest, I've never watched the tape. I put it in maybe two years ago and got a minute or two into it and had to turn it off. I just couldn't watch it. It was the second half from torment. Until this year, it's the one I continually replayed in my mind, but luckily there are some new memories beginning to block it out."

An old memory also crowds out the despair over the game that slipped away. It's from Meyer's first year as head coach in 1994-1995, and it's no surprise that it was against Fort Loramie. The atmosphere changes whenever Loramie is on the schedule. The players know it's one of the biggest games of the season, regardless of the records each team brings to the gym.

Meyer believes the game that year was when his team was best-prepared. It was the sectional finals against the number-one seed. Loramie had "drubbed us in the regular season a couple times. I was pretty predictable – always playing man. If we're going to go down, we're going to go down playing man. We ended up taking a bye, so we had a whole ten days to prepare. I remember I was home by myself, since my family had gone to Florida. We threw the kitchen sink at them. Every time they got the ball, we were in something different. Sometimes you can do that and it doesn't have much of an effect, but since we had so much time to prepare, they'd be coming down and we'd be in a triangle-and-two, and the next time we might be man, or a full-court man, or back to a one-three-one. We had different signals for each one. We weren't a very talented team, but we were smart. The kids really got in and out of things. We would switch in mid-possession. It came down to the very end. We had them. We had two or three turnovers, though, and at the end we just couldn't get over the hump. I don't believe in moral victories, but I believe that was a turning point in Anna basketball because we weren't picked to win many games – between five and ten – and we had won thirteen and had gone up against the best team in the county at that particular time. It kind of made a statement."

All that preparation couldn't have made the difference it did, however, if his players hadn't possessed what Meyer calls "basketball sense." It's that intuition for the game itself.

"You can take a kid and put him in the driveway and drill him and drill him and make him be the best fundamentals kid, or shooter, dribbler, and passer, but if he's never watched ESPN, gone to high school or college games, or been a student of the game and played a lot, he just doesn't have that basketball sense. He's the person you'll know when you see something developing and you're just assuming he's going to make that pass and he doesn't. You just can't teach that. Luckily, we have kids who like to play, so they understand and they have that sense.

"The other learned trait is situations – when to push it and when to pull it out, when to attack and when to be patient. We still struggle with that. I'm a firm believer in the kids developing that over time, so from time to time we'll take a shot and I'm sure there are a lot of people who are thinking 'Why did they take that?' But over the course of a game, those questionable shots more than make up for themselves with the kids being comfortable and being willing to step up and being willing to put themselves out there on the line."

In addition to the qualities that are difficult, if not impossible, to teach, the obstacles to success can be formidable. Meyer identifies the biggest roadblocks as losing, the long season, talent, and selflessness.

"Any time you lose, whether it's a few possessions in a row, or a game, or especially when you lose games in row, it's hard to motivate kids. It's hard to get them to believe in themselves when they're taking it on the chin.

"It's a long, unbelievably long, season. You look at other seasons and it's often six to eight weeks and you're done. We start conditioning in October and won't be done, hopefully, until March. You're talking five or six months. You combine a long season with losing, and it can get tough.

"Another obstacle is talent. You have to have talent. Don't get me wrong. I've had teams with lesser talent that have overachieved and pleased me, but you have to have talent.

"The last one is selflessness. Sometimes it's hard to get kids to totally commit to the team concept, to saying, 'I don't care if I only shoot five times. I don't care if I only play three minutes.' If you can overcome that, or maybe if you only have one or two kids who do, it spreads."

Not obstacles, necessarily, but annoying distractions can be irritating. Meyer's pet peeve is people yelling things from the crowd that aren't what he wants the kids to do.

"My philosophy is that we get the last shot of the first three quarters. Those are three possessions the other team doesn't get. There were times when we were losing and people didn't know what to yell. We were telling the kids, 'Patience, patience,' and the crowd was yelling, 'Shoot it, shoot it!' Or another peeve is when someone walks up to us and says, 'Don't you practice free throws?' Well you want to say, 'No, that's a good idea. Maybe we'll try that. In fact, we could even try to drop kick them.'"

Some of the rules give Meyer pause, too.

"Not letting anybody in until the ball hits during a free throw creates a situation where it's hard to react. I just don't like it. I liked it when it left the kid's hands. Kids checked out and had responsibilities. When you have to wait until it hits the rim, it puts everybody on edge. Also the three-point line is sometimes good and sometimes not. I think we're entering a time in basketball where we're reaping the benefits of it. We're recommitting to the strength of the two-pointer and the mid-range jumper, and, at the same time, we have kids who have developed the long-range threat.

"There's been talk of a shot clock. I would not like to see a shot clock. I've seen what's developed in the NBA and sometimes when you get to mid-court the only thing that's left is one-on-one."

But these irritations pale in comparison to the rewards of coaching. The relationships are as close to a family as is possible, and the majority of the players return to Anna. "If you play for me, you do what's expected, and you commit, basically you have an ally for life and not just me. It's the entire coaching staff. Immediately there is a transformation from that last game, whenever we lose, to the next day. It's a different relationship. That relationship between a coach and a player is as close to being a family as you can get."

In two separate tenures as head coach, Meyer has had opportunities to step back, assess what works, and offer his lessons to others. For new coaches, Meyer has some sage advice.

"Stick to the fundamentals early, don't try to do too much, and don't let it consume you. I sleep now. The first time around, it dictated who I was. It consumes my time, now, but it doesn't consume me."

What new coaches will come to understand about being a head coach is that "you're on the island. The buck stops here. But that's true of any leadership position. People don't realize that Monday through Friday is already sixty to sixty-five hours—when you consider teaching, practicing, and scouting. By the time you do scouting and your games in a three-game week and what you're doing on Sunday, whether it's 5-Star or something else, it's a seventy to eighty hour week. There were a lot of times when I would tuck my kids in on Sunday night and wouldn't see them awake until Wednesday or Thursday. In tournament, sometimes, there were games on Wednesday, so it definitely wouldn't be until Thursday. By the time you make your calls after the game, the fans have been gone an hour and half. I'm walking out the other end of the building to my car at eleven at night and I parked it there at six-thirty in the morning. I'm walking by myself through the halls. There are times when I think, 'Man, I'm up here a lot.' And other coaches understand that. Sometimes there's a perception in other communities that coaching is fun. They think we're compensated for our school day and after that, it's just fun. But it's work. It's tiring."

And then there's game day, the hours before the clock starts.

"I used to get all worked up. I ate the same thing. I had the exact same routine. If we were on a winning streak I wore the same clothes. In 1997 we had a fourteen-game winning streak and I wore the exact same outfit every single game. About game eleven or twelve, I got a hole in my pants because my keys hit against the desk. My mother-in-law shopped everywhere until she found the identical pants. My game-day preparation was all about superstition. My scouting reports were five to six pages long. We'd go over them. It was really intense. Now, I'm more relaxed. I make it more fun. I work out before, probably, every game. When the kids see me, I no longer have my five-page scouting report. In fact, we give them three keys to winning, as opposed to, 'study these five pages.' That would mean in a game, in a tight situation, if they didn't do something I said in the scouting report I would go berserko on them – like they're supposed to remember five pages in the heat of the game with the clock running and twelve hundred people in the stands. Now we give them three keys to victory. Then we shoot. We relax. At pre-game there's not a lot of rip-roaring and screaming and hollering. It's basically, 'Guys, you are prepared to do these three things.'

"I often have fifteen or sixteen pages on a team that I'm going to use and Coach [Paul] Hohlbein is going to use for game situations or match-ups or game adjustments, or if we already have match-ups we'll tell them some tendencies of the kids. The three things we'll tape up on the wall, maybe on Tuesday, all over the locker room. And then in the pre-game, we'll talk about those three things. And it's usually pretty simple things, depending on the team. When we played North College Hill, the first thing was no dribble penetration. If one guy kills us, that's fine, but the rest of them – we just can't let them dribble penetrate. The second thing was don't help off the shooters – stay on the shooters – and three was no offensive rebounds. They had one great player – Butler – when we saw him. They barely won, and he had forty-one. They had some good set shooters and the way they won was having him dribble penetrate. We knew we couldn't stop him. But what the other team would do was, when they played Purcell-Marion, the guy next to the ball – the defender who is one pass away – would help to the dribble. Not only did he have forty-one but he probably had eight assists on that kick-out pass. So we said don't help off the dribble. Stay on the shooters. If I'm one pass away, I don't care if he's beat or not, the second rotation is going to help defense and if he scores, he scores. We're not giving them away. We won by twelve or thirteen and he had thirty-eight."

Game preparation for the team is Monday through Thursday, but in the minutes before the game, the staff reinforces the three keys. The staff already educated and dedicated themselves before the season to the idea that a game is about process.

"We've talked about John Wooden, but it's so true. In these pre-games, if you get so worked up, and holler and holler and holler, the only thing you're going to do is get them into this frenzied state, and they can't perform at their maximum level. We remind them of the three keys and remind them to believe. I share a quote or two – I like quotes – to get them to believe in their hearts that they are prepared. We don't have to go out and do high fives and jumping jacks and scream and hoot and do the things some teams do that drive me nuts. We want our kids to be prepared and go out and play hard. Sometimes that emotionalism can be pretty weak. It's easy to hoot and holler in good times and pitch a fit in bad times. It takes more strength to be composed. Sometimes, if a team is too wound up, one turnover turns into three or four or five in the blink of an eye."

After the game, Meyer conducts an evaluation. It's a moment to learn from the experience. Teaching is as much a part of the game in the post-talk as it is in the days and hours before the game.

"We try to teach, win or lose, and we don't single out kids. I've been in locker rooms where kids have been berated and singled out. I've done it myself, and then I've looked at the tapes and realized it wasn't as bad as it seemed at that particular moment. So in the post-game we try to analyze what we did well as a team and what we didn't do well. If there were certain aspects we need to improve, we mention it without naming the kids. They know it. When we say we have to cut down turnovers, I don't have to name that particular kid. He knows."

In addition to the time in the gym and locker room, many coaching hours away from the team are required. It's the work that must be done, but nobody likes the time away from the family and friends to put in the long hours after practices and games.

"It's the extras: stats, meetings, inventory, parental issues, personnel issues, evaluations, towels, water bottles, scouting, gym scheduling, practice scheduling, and video. I'm lucky to have some assistants who do the drudge work. Coach Hohlbein does the towels and makes sure we have water bottles. I do the gym schedules. I think sometimes people think we practice and play games, but there is so much more."

Good coaches also bring a wealth of personal qualities to the game that Meyer reduces to one thought.

"The best coaches are great teachers. They know how to teach. They're the masters of the fundamentals. They communicate. They balance courage and consideration. That means being thick-skinned.

"Maybe there's a mom who thinks her son is being mistreated. I step back and remember that it's her job to protect her child, so I don't judge the parents, but my commitment is to the whole team, not just her son. You have to be thick-skinned when people yell things from the crowd. They paid their six dollars. They can yell whatever they want. Sometimes it's not good. Once in awhile you get bikes and hubcaps and for sale signs thrown on your property, and you have to be thick-skinned then, too.

"You have to be someone people want to follow. You have to have that balance, once again, of courage and consideration. I think the times of dictator coaches are over. Now, it's being a collaborative coach and leading people to the water."

Meyer has led several teams to the water. He's found that success happens with a combination of talent, hard work, and selflessness. During his high school years at Jackson Center, Meyer believes all those teams had that combination. After Jackson Center won a state championship in 1985, losing several talented seniors including Meyer's brother Tony, the group came back the next year to win a county championship. It was an accomplishment that couldn't have happened without talent, hard work, and selflessness. His senior year in 1987-1988 was the most difficult when he moved to point guard. One of the players was a move-in, and the chemistry wasn't the same as it had been in the years past.

"You can give Coach Mike Krzyzewski no talent and he's not going to win. The successful teams have a commitment to getting better. They have to work hard and they figure out that unselfishness. There are teams that are pretty good with their Kobe Bryants, scoring fifty-five or sixty points, but I think the great teams have that selflessness of five guys clicking together."

Meyer points to the intangibles to explain the success of teams in this part of Ohio. And he doesn't mean only the teams that make it to the state tournament. In any given year, the MAC and the SCAL have teams that earn state, regional, and local honors largely due to the qualities that don't make it onto the stat sheet – hard work and commitment.

"That's how these kids are raised. That's how their families are. What we're asking them to do, they've already done. I think if you go anywhere in Ohio, the most employable people are in this area. There is a difference. That's what we get on the basketball court. I call it 'old school.' The other part is that kids are dedicated to their school. They want to play for their school. They're not going to play at one school in junior high, another school as a freshman, and yet another school as a junior."

Because of that commitment to the school, western Ohio has some great rivalries. For Anna, going back several decades, the biggest rival is Botkins, but in more recent times, it has become Fort Loramie.

"Loramie and Anna have been the top teams in the county, overall, for many years. Jackson Center had quite a run of about ten or eleven years and Russia has had a heck of run recently, but Anna people who have been here for fifty or sixty years, still think the biggest rival is Botkins. I had a man come up to me and say, 'You can go two and eighteen. Just make sure the two are Botkins.' And I had no idea. When he said that, I thought, 'Yes, the backyard rivalry is right down 25-A.'"

So how does Meyer figure to beat these teams, get through the early brackets and win a regional championship? The same way any successful team is built – with talent, hard work, and commitment – but with one additional ingredient – luck.

"When a number of people I talk to found out we were in the regional finals, old buddies and acquaintances would call, asking if the team was any good. I'd be thinking, 'Well, yeah. They're in the regional finals.' So you have to have talent, selflessness, hard work, chemistry, and you have to have luck. No doubt that ball bounced our way at the end of that [regional final] game. One of their kids was wide open and we were lucky enough to get a hand on it. On the other side of the scorers' table, I can't even describe how bad that was to watch."

When times get bad during a season or a game, Meyer falls back on his conviction to teach kids with every possession, every experience.

"You can use an opportunity when you're down to teach kids to never quit. To keep playing to the bitter end, but at the same time we're not going to prolong the agony. If we're down fifteen, we're not going to foul ten times in the last minute because all you're doing is teaching your kids ignorance. There are times you know you have the game in hand or the game is in hand for the other team and I think those are very important times to teach kids it's an opportunity to get better. I thought this year we did that pretty well. There were times when we sat back as coaches and thought, 'Man, they're fun to watch,' and then five or ten possessions later, they're slacking. Even though you know the game is in hand, we preach that every possession is a chance to get better. We tell them not to pay attention to the scoreboard. Pay attention to getting better."

Getting better doesn't happen just in the time between October and March. Having a game plan means having a season plan which means having a program plan.

"My first year coaching, when we first started in May, I wanted to do everything under the sun. Open gyms three or four nights a week along with team camps. I've gone from the amount of time, to maximizing the time we have. I used to have three to three-and-a-half hour practices. Now we'll go two-and-a-half at the beginning of the season and we're down to an hour-and-a-half at the end. You can wear the kids down. After talking to Mike Lee and some other longtime coaches, I learned they give the kids a day off. Recently, we've been doing that. If we don't have a Tuesday game, we'll come in and light them up on Monday with an hour and forty-five minutes of running. We'll do some fundamental stuff, but we'll light them up. We'll lift and run. They're hurting. Tuesday, we'll give them off. They'll go and do what they want and get their legs back. Wednesday will be crisp and Thursday will be game prep. I'm telling you, the past two years our legs and our mental approach have made all the difference. I try to do everything we can not to burn the kids out mentally and physically, summer and winter. I think we do a pretty good job with that."

The easiest way to describe Meyer's practices is that not once in the entire year did the team ever scrimmage five on five.

"Our commitment is to fundamentals and being competitive, so in practice if we're not doing fundamentals, such as dribbling, passing, and rebounding, then we're doing competitive situation type things that teach that. Let's say we're doing chest-passing. Five over here and five over here and we'll do a drill that requires them to use that chest pass. We do everything fundamental and then competitiveness. If we're going to do a five-on-five, we're going to do a five-on-five-on-five cutthroat. It's nasty. They run our offense out of that. We try to create a situation that whatever they see in a game is nowhere near as bad as what they see in practice from a physical, competitive standpoint. We actually had the parents in for a practice this year when we were doing this, and I looked up and some of the moms... well. It was bad.

"The only time during a game that I complain about physical play is when it's the shooter. My philosophy is let the shooter shoot, so if he gets fouled, call it, but I don't get worked up on moving screens or fouls away from the ball. Be physical and play."

Sometimes the game is tough, not because it's physical or the competition is overwhelming, but because the atmosphere created by the home team in their own gym is a mental challenge. Each team has some sort of home-court advantage, and Meyer can easily name the places that capitalize on it. The first to come to mind is Russia.

"For the past ten or fifteen years, it's easily Russia. Number one, they were good. Number two, they blare music. Have you been there?

They blare it. Number three, they encourage kids to wear a yellow shirt. It's packed. You have to go through everybody just to get to your locker room. It's just a hard place to go play. This year [2007-2008] we won, but it's been a long time since we won there.

"Another one is Houston. Houston is a tough place to play. But the toughest of all is Fairlawn. I've had some great teams go in there and really struggle. There was a year there when we were very, very good and we won by sixteen or seventeen but only because David Hurley got hot. Otherwise it would have been a ball game. It's a small facility. The locker rooms are less than adequate. You're in there on top of each other. It's dingy. You walk out and you're right in the fans. There is no sideline. The wall is right at the end of the court. It's just not conducive to the style of basketball that's played today. In the old days when there was more standing around and people weren't as big and it wasn't as physical, it was okay.

"Marion Local is one of the toughest places to play. One half of the JV game the locker room will be 50 degrees. Then you go get dressed for the varsity game and it's 80. But they never treat you wrong at Marion Local. You walk in and they're smiling, 'Hey, how you doing? We're going to kick your ass.' They've got this aura to them. I'm sure St. Henry has the same thing, but they're not on our schedule. There's nothing you can say to describe it. This year we walked in and we handed it to them, but when you walk in the gym and three or four of the girls keeping stats are taller than your players, it's tough."

Gym conditions don't necessarily appear on a scouting report, but sending scouts off to the competitors' gyms is a big part of preparation. These are the people who sit high up in the stands or way off to the side and they're carrying clipboards or notebooks or steno pads. They arrive at the end of the JV game and sometimes leave well before the final buzzer, particularly if they've seen a team before or if they aren't too amazed at the action.

Meyer likes his scouting combination of Paul Hohlbein and Jim Osborne, his varsity assistant and freshman coaches, respectively.

"Hobie is the best at going in, watching a game, leaving and knowing that if we do a couple of things we can win. He doesn't need to do all the X's and O's. He's got a knack for knowing that this kid can do this, this kid can't do this, and this other team can't do that, so if we do these couple things, we can win. He looks at the whole picture.

The other side of that is Oz, who doesn't miss a beat. They are the two perfect guys to send together because I'm going to get the big picture accompanied by every little thing that leads up to that."

His assistant coaches help in many ways besides scouting.

"Almost everything, when it comes to running the program, Hobie and I do. And it's pretty equal. Basically, I want the other coaches coaching their teams and Hobie and I do the majority of the little things. And Hobie does a ton."

Over the years Meyer has seen hundreds of games himself and has watched the game change before his eyes. The biggest change, he notes, is the emphasis on dribble penetration.

"I am a pass and cut type coach, the Bobby Knight move, move, move, get ball reversal, don't waste your dribble. Dribble on your own time. Now the emphasis is dribble, penetrate, kick, dribble, penetrate, kick. It can be pretty intensive. The negative side is that it's from the And-1 stuff, lots of fancy ball handling, but they don't get anywhere. The transformation to the dribble penetration motion offense, dribble, kick and then cut has decreased, in some ways, kids' understanding of basketball – how to move without the ball, how to screen properly. We use it, but it's been a transformation for me. We might come down and do a patterned offense that has spacing and screening and movement without the ball so the team gets into that, and then we'll switch to the dribble penetration. So they're used to jumping into the passing lane or getting to the midline. Then all of a sudden you have to be an on-the-ball defender. If you use a mixture of both, it makes a difference. It's harder to prepare. Dribble penetration is not a bad thing. It's a change in philosophy over the years. You didn't see Jerry Harmon's team putting it on the ground very often. You saw those teams moving without the ball, setting screens, and shooting when they were open.

"Right now the biggest craze in basketball is dribble penetration motion offense. It's hard to guard. Ottawa-Glandorf did a ton of it, and they were a little bit successful. It's hard to guard players who put their heads down and dribble to the hoop."

Appreciating the game dynamics means respecting the coaches who have developed that versatility with their teams.

"If you're going into an evenly-matched game, you respect all the coaches in that situation. Scott Elchert [Jackson Center coach] and I going into an evenly-matched game – wow. I can't imagine respecting a person more. I can't imagine anyone getting more out of average talent than John Willoughby. When they're good and we're good, his thing is he is just fundamental. John doesn't try to do fifty different things. What they do, they've mastered, and the kids do very well. What makes basketball good in this area? You aren't going to run into bad coaches."

Meyer believes the majority of the officiating in this region is "pretty darned good," too.

"I used to think coaches could influence officials, but it's the duty of the coach to teach his players to adjust to how the officials are calling the game. If they're not calling a hand check, then hand check. If they're letting the moving screen go, then move. The officials here don't succumb to pressure or intimidation from coaches."

Then comes the time of the game when the first half is over, and the teams head to the locker rooms. If people aren't making their way to the concession stand, they are standing in the bleachers, wondering what's going on beyond the closed doors at half time.

"My assistant coaches in the last four minutes of the second quarter are to come up with three things I need to go over at half-time. The four of us coaches meet before I go into the locker room. Sometimes I change that, but for the most part they are dead on. It keeps me focused. Sometimes when your juices are flowing and it's the heat of the game, and there might have been a bad situation, you can waste half-time screaming and hollering and talking about something you can't change.

"Before every half time, each coach has an index card with their three ideas and they put them together. Then Hobie hands me the card with the three things on it. We review the three keys from the beginning of the game and they get an A, B, C, D, or F on each of them. Then I give them the three things the coaches came up with that we have to do better.

"The one thing we started to do this year that I thought was rather effective at Anna, was hanging a white board on the wall leading to our other gym, and we have our half-times there. Then we're in a gym, instead of a hot, sweaty locker room, so if there is something technical, we do it right there. The important thing about half time is what we developed over the years – the three keys and keep it simple. I've been in lots of half-time situations and you can walk out and think you've gotten nothing done. Kicking and hollering doesn't accomplish anything in the long run. That doesn't mean people don't do it from time to time, but overall the Bobby Knight style of fear is gone. If I can't do something in the locker room with the kid's dad in there then I won't do it. Not some moms, maybe, but dads."

When the team is behind in a game, Meyer doesn't change the way he coaches. There shouldn't be a difference between coaching when ahead and coaching when behind. Every single play is coached so that the kids can get better is Meyer's philosophy.

"There are some serious dangers when you start playing like you're winning and playing like you're losing. In the Wooden book, Wooden says that you get kids to play like they're going to get better, and when they start playing like they're ahead or they're behind – Ay-yi-yi. When we're ahead, the kids don't back off being fundamental. They don't back off what we ask them to do. They just change their philosophy. They go from attack, attack, attack, to making the clock run, out of respect for the other team. Same intensity, different philosophy. We had one person this year who wasn't great at this and there were times when the coaching staff wanted to take some time, since we were up eight points or so, and then the kid would stroke one. It's not an exact science. It's a sense they develop from about the fourth grade or so, when to back it out or when to keep attacking. It's interesting to watch younger kids who have that sense and others that haven't developed it."

Meyer credits his staff with being able to teach players all aspects of the game because each is a classroom teacher, and especially helpful to Meyer is that they are all teachers in his building. The staff assists with the off-season conditioning and training. This is a time for players to get better.

The off-season has changed at Anna from a lot of team camps to more individual skill development. The kids lift on Monday, Wednesday, and Friday. Open gyms are on Tuesday and Thursday. In the coming seasons Meyer plans to incorporate some individual skills after lifting. A couple of tournaments will be planned as well. Open gyms, though, are meant to be fun time and competition. They are meant to develop the qualities of a good player.

"The best players are fundamental, they have floor sense, and they go the extra degree or they have an extra gear others don't. Chad Platfoot in 1994-95 was far from athletically gifted, but he had gears that willed us to thirteen wins that year, no doubt. Kreg Elsass had gears that others don't. What he did at that Columbus Academy game in the regional final was amazing. I've had some very, very good players. I love the players who do everything perfectly fundamental. I was drilled when I was little on fundamentals. Coach Harmon was a fundamentals freak and that's how I am. Chad Platfoot matched that intensity. I've had a lot of guys like that. To be honest, Nathan Snyder is about as fundamental a kid as I've ever coached. That kid can do it all perfectly. If his body, his athleticism, ever catches up to his fundamental skills, holy moley, get out of the way. I've had a ton of players that match me in intensity, but Nate Barhorst always went hard to grind it out. He was Mr. Consistency."

Getting players to buy in to leadership, which is another element of the game, means creating ownership on their part. To some degree, either they have leadership or they don't and there is only so much a coach can do, Meyer believes, and if they don't have a competitive drive, they probably won't get it, but the majority of them do.

"You create competitive situations and they get to the point where they can't stand the heat. You have to put players under pressure in practice. You do a ton of fundamentals and then you put them in competitive situations. Jerry Harmon was the best at purposely not calling fouls or purposely calling violations in practice just to get in your mind. And I do the same. I purposely put kids in situations where they want to lose it, but they have to deal with it."

Additional player development comes through big impact workouts in practice. Meyer has several drills that create immediate and long-lasting results.

"In fifth grade, players learn Series One face-to-the-basket drills and Series Three back-to-the-basket drills. This gives players like Snyder a pretty good repertoire of moves they can fall back on. Something I neglected for a lot of years is one-on-one. We'll start three-quarter court and you've got to stop that guy from getting to the basket. We have a ton of different drills on a huge net that shoots the ball back to them. The one thing we started was individual workout stations."

Then, after years of work and development, the player looks to college and the discussions with the coach begin. Meyer, however, doesn't believe it's the coach's responsibility to get the kids in to play at the college level.

"My responsibility is to make them as good a player as their physical being will allow in hopes that Anna has a state championship. Whether or not the player plays at the college level isn't my concern. Now, if I get questionnaires from college coaches, I send them in. I connect coaches with the kids. I do anything they ask. I direct kids in positive directions as far as I know.

"I do those sorts of things, but it's not my responsibility. My responsibility is to Anna and finding a way to get a state championship. When the coach loses sight of that, it opens a Pandora's Box. 'You're doing this for that kid. I thought you were supposed to be caring about Anna.' Bottom line is that it is so tough for a kid to play college ball. The opportunities are so limited. If he's going to do it, it's going to have to be the involvement of the family. I'll counsel them, but it's going to have to be them doing it.

"The role of the parent is to be a parent, and that is to love your son, be there for you son, be a listening ear, and then stay the hell out of it. I listened to Don Donoher speak at one of the first Anna Education Foundation banquets and he made the statement that the biggest problem in high school athletics is the parents. I have not witnessed that in a long time because I have a group of parents who support their kids and support me and give me the freedom to do what we have to do to be successful. And that's why we're successful. I think they know we're not going to do anything to hurt their kids – at least not intentionally. So you don't get enough playing time? It's nothing personal. Parents help us get them to understand that it's better to be a part of it."

The other influences outside the game have been good in Meyer's estimation. He believes it's the duty of the fan to cheer for the team when they are doing well and support the team when they aren't. He's had nothing but positive relationships with the media and feels he's lucky that the boosters have been generous with the team.

"I'm lucky to have administrators who have been former head

coaches. My superintendent Andy Bixler and my athletic director Mike Muehlfeld know. They've been through it, and sure, sometimes, there can be some politics, but overall, in this area, the majority of coaches do what's best for kids and what's right."